AF736194

TRUTH, REALITY, AND THE PSYCHOANALYST

THE INTERNATIONAL PSYCHOANALYSIS LIBRARY

General Editor: Emma Piccioli

IPA Publications Committee

Emma Piccioli (Florence), Chair; Salman Akhtar (Philadelphia); Sergio Lewkowicz (Porto Alegre); Peter Wegner (Tübingen); Otto F. Kernberg (White Plains), Consultant; Piers Pendred (London), Ex-officio as Director General; Cesare Sacerdoti (London), Ex-officio as Publications Director

Violence or Dialogue? Psychoanalytic Insights on Terror and Terrorism
edited by Sverre Varvin & Vamık D. Volkan

Pluralism and Unity? Methods of Research in Psychoanalysis
edited by Marianne Leuzinger-Bohleber, Anna Ursula Dreher, & Jorge Canestri

TRUTH, REALITY, AND THE PSYCHOANALYST

Latin American Contributions to Psychoanalysis

Edited by

Sergio Lewkowicz & Silvia Flechner

Foreword by

Daniel H. Widlöcher & Cláudio Laks Eizirik

International Psychoanalytical Association

LONDON

ROUTLEDGE

Routledge
Taylor & Francis Group

LONDON AND NEW YORK

First published 2005 by The International Psychoanalytical Association

Published 2018 by Routledge
2 Park Square, Milton Park, Abingdon, Oxon OX14 4RN
605 Third Avenue, New York, NY 10017

Routledge is an imprint of the Taylor & Francis Group, an informa business

Copyright © 2005 by The International Psychoanalytical Association

The rights of the editors and contributors to be identified as the authors of this work have been asserted in accordance with §§ 77 and 78 of the Copyright Design and Patents Act 1988.

All rights reserved. No part of this book may be reprinted or reproduced or utilised in any form or by any electronic, mechanical, or other means, now known or hereafter invented, including photocopying and recording, or in any information storage or retrieval system, without permission in writing from the publishers.

Notice:
Product or corporate names may be trademarks or registered trademarks, and are used only for identification and explanation without intent to infringe.

British Library Cataloguing in Publication Data

A C.I.P. for this book is available from the British Library

Produced for the IPA by Communication Crafts

ISBN: 978-0-9523905-6-5 (hbk)

CONTENTS

THE INTERNATIONAL PSYCHOANALYSIS LIBRARY

IPA Publications Committee

The International Psychoanalysis Library, published under the aegis of the International Psychoanalytical Association, is the product of the editorial policy of the IPA Publications Committee: to serve the interests of the membership and increase the awareness of the relevance of the discipline in related professional and academic circles, and to do so through a continuity of publications so that the benefits of psychoanalytic research can be shared across a wide audience.

The focus of the Library is on the scientific developments of today throughout the IPA, with an emphasis within the discipline on clinical, technical, and theoretical advances; empirical, conceptual, and historical research projects; the outcome of investigations conducted by IPA committees and working parties; selected material arising from conferences and meetings; and investigations at the interface with social and cultural expressions.

Emma Piccioli
Chair, IPA Publications Committee

ACKNOWLEDGEMENTS

The project of this book was a suggestion from the IPA Publications Committee, the aim being to make known the similarities and differences between Latin American psychoanalysis and that which is practised elsewhere, seeking to highlight wherever possible what distinguishes the former. This project was based on the recognition of the importance of Latin American psychoanalytic ideas and the relatively limited knowledge of them in other areas of world psychoanalysis.

We would like to thank the following members of the International Psychoanalytical Association Publications Committee for inviting us to be the editors of this publication: Emma Piccioli (chairperson), Peter Wegner, and Salman Akhtar. We are also grateful for the tireless dedication and professional help of Cesare Sacerdoti and Rhosyn Tuta, as well as the availability of Klara King in the production of this book.

Our thanks also go to the authors and discussants for their cooperation, understanding, and collaboration with their tasks. Finally, but by no means least, our thanks must go to FEPAL and their President, Serapio Marcano, for their support in the production of the Spanish edition of the book, which is of utmost importance to Latin America.

We are extremely pleased and honoured with this work and were fully aware of the responsibility of having to choose the subjects and authors for the publication.

Our first task was to define the concepts that could be expanded in Latin American psychoanalysis. After some discussion between us and the suggestions we received from the committee, we chose eight concepts. With these eight concepts in hand and with the help of the secretary of FEPAL, we were able to find the authors who have published the most in the topics we had chosen. All the authors were selected in the same way—that is, by number and quality of publications, as well as taking into account the region and institutional balance.

We would like to point out that the chapter by Madeleine Baranger has been published in Spanish in the book, *El otro en la trama intersubjetiva,* edited by Leticia Glocer Fiorini (APA Editorial–Lugar Editorial, Buenos Aires, 2004), and we were given special permission for it to be translated into English and used in this IPA publication.

The concept of this edition—that of author and discussant—confirms, once again, that psychoanalysis is permanently enriched by this theoretical–clinical interchange, corroborating that the commentaries, the criticism, and the debate are fundamental for progress. The authors and discussants selected are some of the IPA analysts through whom we feel represented, recognizing in them, among other qualities, the depth to which they have developed the topics, based on their personal experiences, which today they write and comment about in this book.

Through the challenge that this book has meant, we have had the opportunity to encourage dialogue between psychoanalysts of the Southern Hemisphere with those of the Northern, aiming to promote confrontation and interchange between the different regions.

Starting from the common area of the discovery of the unconscious by Freud, we have formed an uninterrupted chain, with great contributions that have revealed the complexity and profundity of psychoanalytic thought. In this book we attempt to participate in this continuity through the individual accounts of analysts from distinct regions of the world, who have been nourished from different sources and diverse references—inside and outside psychoanalysis—and it is precisely this diversity that sustains the great part of the dialogue.

Sergio Lewkowicz and Silvia Flechner

PREFACE

When the Board of Directors of the Federación Psychoanalítica de America Latina (FEPAL) received from the Publications Committee of the IPA, via Sergio Lewkowicz and Silvia Flechner as editors, the proposal to realize a joint project between the IPA and FEPAL to publish this book, in English and Spanish, we were very enthusiastic. Despite the financial restrictions of our federation, we accepted the commitment to collaborate, given that the book would spread Latin American psychoanalytic ideas throughout the rest of the world and, particularly, throughout Latin America.

We know that linguistic limitations act as barriers to scientific communication, above all between Latin America and English speakers when, due to economic limitations, important works by Latin American authors cannot be translated into English. Exceptions to this are the classic work of Heinrich Racker on countertransference and, among others, the works of David Rosenfeld in 1988 and 1992, Horacio Etchegoyen in 1991, Stubrin in 1994, and Mariam Alizade in 1999 and that of Jorge Ahumada, published by Karnac, in 2001. Journals and papers by our authors are, in general, also not available in translation—and these are authors who have been the fount from which the great majority of Latin American psychoanalysts have drunk deeply. The same thing does not happen, however, to the texts and journals by authors from other latitudes, which have found, via publishing companies, sufficient support for their principal scientific productions to be translated into Spanish and Portuguese, thus enabling them to be known and studied by psychoanalysts from our region.

The primary motive behind our support for this project has been the conviction that the endeavour, initiated some years ago, to publish Latin American authors in both Spanish and English must be continued, improved, and made lasting over time. The first were those of the Pan-American Congresses of Psychoanalysis, where, via the proposals of outstanding authors from both regions of our continent, different ways of thinking about psychoanalysis in both North America and Latin America were gathered together.

Clinical meetings that have been held on various occasions between FEPAL, The European Psychoanalytical Federation, and the American Psychoanalytic Association, with members of working groups translating from English into Spanish and Spanish into English, have left us, along with many of the participants, not only with a fraternal closeness, but also with the welcome impression of working to find ourselves, in our similarities and differences, in a climate of consideration and respect between colleagues. It is regrettable that the materials and results of these various meetings have not been collected in publications and so have suffered a prolonged break in their continuity.

The *Libro Anual de Pscoanálisis,* which contains a selection of articles published in the *International Journal of Psychoanalysis* and the *International Review,* does not have a counterpart that might assemble a selection of the principal articles from Spanish and Portuguese publications. Translated into English, this could make known our particular psychoanalytic thinking, which, within a global conception of psychoanalysis, has its own specificity and identity, generated within a specific cultural sphere.

When in 1993 Moisés Lemlij, at that time the Director of Publications of FEPAL, gained the support of the President of FEPAL, Saúl Peña, and of both the President and President Elect of the IPA, Joseph Sandler and Horacio Etchegoyen, for the publication in English of *Psychoanalysis in Latin America,* he was taking a fundamental step in order to seek to establish a true scientific exchange with Europe and North America. In this way, linguistic barriers were crossed, and, also through him, other barriers were cleared. At the same time the publication of the book in Spanish also allowed the spread, among Spanish/Portuguese speakers, of a representative demonstration of the modes of clinical psychoanalytic thinking in each of the different Societies and Associations of our region.

Some years later, in 1996, Alejandro Tamez-Morales, then acting President of FEPAL, returned to the task of trying to break with the "punishment of the Tower of Babel", producing a new book, *Psychoanalysis in Latin America: Theory and Technique.* This, the equal of its predecessor, was published first in English and then in Spanish, its editor being Adelina Alcorta, Director of Publications of FEPAL. It received, once again, the valuable support of Horacio Etchegoyen, who was at that time serving as President of the IPA.

Eight long years have passed until this moment, when the above-mentioned proposal arrived with us, to see the light of day at the IPA International Congress in July 2005, in Rio de Janeiro, a city that counts itself among the pioneers of Latin American psychoanalysis and also has a particular relevance. The eight selected works, preceded by the history of psychoanalysis and its ideas in Latin America in the introductory chapter by Horacio Etchegoyen and Samuel Zysman, again have the special feature of assembling psychoanalytic theory, clinical psychoanalysis, and psychoanalytic method and also bring us something new: each of them is commented on by distinguished colleagues from other geographic regions represented by the IPA, which gives this publication a more global character, consistent with the objective of spreading widely our ideas.

As on previous occasions, we hope that the objective of disseminating our psychoanalytic theories, in which we have been engaged for a long time, will be widely attained and that it will achieve long-standing publishing success, so that the continuation and regularity of these publications can be maintained, thanks to the combined effort of the IPA and FEPAL.

Serapio Marcano
President, 2002–04, FEPAL

I have had the pleasure, in my position as Director of Publications, to belong to the Board of Directors of FEPAL 2002–04, presided over by Serapio Marcano. We have worked in a notable climate of harmony and democratic cordiality and published the *Revista Latinoamericana de Psicoanalisis, Vol. 6, 2004*, the publication of which coincided with the 25th Latin American Congress of Psychoanalysis: "Psychoanalysis in Latin America Today: Theory and Practice in Times of Crisis", held in Guadalajara, Mexico. Within its pages, it brought together the most important writings of psychoanalysts from FEPAL's component institutions.

Today we see our efforts to disseminate Latin American thinking remarkably completed with this book, for which we have been called upon by the IPA.

The reach of the diffusion of this knowledge has been notably extended, both by the possibility of it being read by English speakers in their own language and by the fruitful exchange created as a result of the articles of which it is composed having been commented on by important psychoanalysts from other latitudes.

We therefore joined this project with enthusiasm, the appearance of which at the IPA Congress in Rio de Janeiro in 2005 is a real event, as much for Spanish as for English readers, and one that will undoubtedly benefit psychoanalysis, which, as conceived by Freud, is open to thought and in constant evolution, serving the alleviation of the sufferings of the soul.

We hope that this book, supported by the IPA and FEPAL, will be the first of a series—one that will itself become a classic, the appearance of which will be awaited with anticipation at successive IPA Congresses.

Gloria Gitaroff
Director of Publications, 2002–04, FEPAL

EDITORS AND CONTRIBUTORS

Madeleine Baranger (Argentina) was born in France in 1920. She graduated in Classical Humanities and underwent her psychoanalytic training at the APA. She is now a member and training analyst of the APA. Between 1954 and 1965 she worked with Willy Baranger to form the Uruguayan Psychoanalytic Association in Montevideo. Her interests include the problem of training and institutional organization. She is particularly interested in metapsychology and the theory of cure.

Ricardo Bernardi (Uruguay) is a full member and training analyst of the Uruguayan Psychoanalytic Association. He is former Vice-President of the International Psychoanalytical Association and was Chair of the Scientific Programme Committee of the 43rd International Congress of Psychoanalysis (New Orleans, 2004). He is also former Director of the Department of Medical Psychology, School of Medicine, University of Uruguay.

Cesar Botella (France) is a psychiatrist and a full member and training analyst at the Paris Psychoanalytical Society. He currently holds the position of President of the UPEA (Unit of Psycho-Analysis for Children and Adolescents). He is an international lecturer, requested to participate in the Inter-regional Meeting in Montevideo (1999), and he served as a reporter at the Congress of French-Speaking Psychoanalysts (2001). He has participated as a panellist at two IPA Congresses (Barcelona 1997, Nice 2001) and was a speaker at the EPF Congress (Portugal 2005). He is the author of many papers and two books translated into English, Spanish, Italian, Russian, and Portuguese.

Jorge Canestri (Italy) is training and supervising analyst for both the Italian Psychoanalytical Association (AIPsi) and the Argentine Psychoanalytic Association and is Professor of Psychology of Mental Health at the Roma 3 University. He received the Mary S. Sigourney Award for 2004. He is Chair of the IPA's Ethics Committee, Chair of the Working Party on Theoretical Issues of the EPF, and a member of the Conceptual and Empirical Research Committee of the IPA. He is Editor of the Educational Section of the *International Journal of Psycho-Analysis* and is a member of its Editorial Board.

Cláudio Laks Eizirik (Brazil) is the incoming President of IPA. He is a psychiatrist, psychoanalyst, and PhD in Medicine. He is a Training and Supervising analyst at the Porto Alegre Psychoanalytical Society, of which he is a former President and Institute Director. He is an Adjunct Professor of the Department of Psychiatry at the Federal University of Rio Grande do Sul and the Chair and professor of the programmes of Psychoanalytic Psychotherapy and Supervision on Psychoanalytic Psychotherapy. Former positions in the University include Dean of the Medical School and Chair of the PhD Program of Psychiatry. He has been President of FEPAL and Vice President of the IPA, as well as member and Chair of the House of Delegates. With other colleagues, he has edited books on *The Human Life Cycle* and *Theory and Technique of Psychoanalytic Psychotherapy*. His papers and chapters in books deal mainly with psychoanalytic technique and the relation of psychoanalysis and culture.

H. Shmuel Erlich (Israel) is the Sigmund Freud Professor of Psychoanalysis at The Hebrew University of Jerusalem, where he also teaches in the Graduate Clinical Psychology Program. He is immediate past-President of the Israel Psychoanalytic Society and a training analyst and on the faculty of the Israel Psychoanalytic Institute. He serves as Representative (from Europe) on the IPA Board and is Chair of the Working Party on Interface Issues of the EPF. He has published on psychoanalytic and applied subjects, including adolescent development and treatment; psychoanalytic theory, especially

Sergio Lewkowicz (Brazil) is a psychiatry, training, and supervising analyst for the Porto Alegre Psychoanalytical Society and also Publications Director. He is Professor and Supervisor for Psychoanalytical Psychotherapy at the Psychiatry Department, Medical School of the Federal University of Rio Grande do Sul. He is also a former President of the Society of Psychiatry of Rio Grande do Sul and former Editor of the *Psychiatry Journal of Rio Grande do Sul*. His major area of interest is psychoanalytic technique.

Norberto C. Marucco (Argentina) is a member and Training Analyst of the APA, where he has served as Scientific Secretary (1997–2000). He was Scientific Secretary of the Executive Committee for the 25th Psychoanalytic Congress of Latin America and President of Pre-Congress Training at the 10th Latin American Congress. He also served as President of the first Latin American Editorial Committee of the IJPA/IRPA (1983–1988).

Antonio Muniz de Rezende (Brazil) is a member of the Brazilian Psychoanalytic Society of São Paulo and is currently Assistant Professor at the Durval Marcondes' Psychoanalysis Institute. He has degrees in theology and philosophy and was a professor of philosophy both at Trois Rivières' CEGEP and at the University of Québec, Canada. He previously held the position of Titular Professor of Campinas State University (UNICAMP), where he was the Director of the Education Faculty. He contributes to many specialist reviews dealing with psychoanalysis, philosophy, and theology. He is particularly interested in the work of Bion, which he has studied for many years.

Neville Symington (Australia) is a psychoanalyst working with his wife, Joan Symington, in Sydney, Australia. He trained at the Institute of Psychoanalysis in London and subsequently held a senior staff position in the Adult Department at the Tavistock Clinic. He is a clinical psychologist, but before coming to psychoanalysis he studied Philosophy and Theology for six years.

Alejandro Tamez-Morales (Mexico) is a psychologist, psychiatrist, training analyst, and child and adolescent psychoanalyst. He was Psychology coordinator of the committee on adoptions and adoptive parents at the Conchita Maternity Clinic of Monterrey (1993–2003). He was Instructor of Neurophysiology, School of Medicine, UANL (1975–1979) and Adjunct Professor of Psychology and Psychopathology of Adolescence, School of Psychology, UANL (1980–1987). He was also Adjunct Professor of Group, Couple, and Family Therapy at the School of Medicine, UANL (1984–1998). He is currently Institute Professor of ARPAC-IPA in private psychiatric and psychoanalytic practice.

Virginia Ungar (Argentina) is a full member and training analyst of the Buenos Aires Psychoanalytic Association. She has also teaching and supervising functions in the APdeBA and in Porto Alegre, Brazil. She is a child analyst and the current Latin American Co-Chair of COCAP.

Susana Vinocur-Fischbein (Argentina) is a training and supervising analyst of the Argentine Psychoanalytic Association. She is a Fellow of the Research Training Programme of the IPA and Secretary of the Publications Committee of the Argentine Psychoanalytic Association. She is a member of FEPAL and serves as the Substitute Chair of FEPAL's Publications Committee. She is a former member of the *Revista de Psicoanálisis* Editorial Board, Argentine Psychoanalytic Association, and past Responsible Editor of the *Journal of the Asociación Escuela Argentina de Psicoterapia para Graduados.*

Daniel H. Widlöcher (France) is outgoing President of the IPA, past professor of psychiatry at the University Pierre and Marie Curie, and Head of the Psychiatric Department at the Salpêtrière Hospital, where he is head of the centre for psychoanalytic and psychotherapy training. He was also director of a research unit in pharmacology and psychopathology in the National Institute of Medical Research. He trained in the French Psychoanalytical Society and was in private practice in psychoanalysis. He broke with Lacan in the early 1960s and founded, with Lavie and Laplanche, the French Psychoanalytical Association and Institute, in which he plays an active role as full member and training analyst.

Samuel Zysman (Argentina) is a child and adolescent analyst, as well as a training analyst and Professor of psychoanalytic technique at the Institute of the Buenos Aires Psychoanalytic Association, where he has served on the Governing Board. He also served as the co-treasurer of the 1991 IPA Congress held in Buenos Aires and as a member of the Finance Committee of the IPA. His latest written production deals with psychoanalytic perspectives on action; infantile sexual theories and cognitive development; and theories as objects in the mind.

FOREWORD

Daniel H. Widlöcher & Cláudio Laks Eizirik

Truth, Reality, and the Psychoanalyst: Latin American Contributions to Psychoanalysis, the third book published by the IPA's International Psychoanalysis Library, is an important achievement, in several respects: its title encompasses beautifully not only the content of the book, but also the main areas developed by psychoanalysis in Latin America; all the key ideas developed in the region are included in the book, as well as relevant historical events for psychoanalysis in each country; the authors of the chapters were selected from among the major analytic thinkers of Latin America; and the commentaries are presented by some of the leading contemporary names in the discipline.

The search for truth—an aim of psychoanalysis that Freud particularly stressed—is one of the main challenges in the social and cultural reality faced not only by the pioneers, but also by analysts in recent years, working under difficult conditions, under dictatorships, and in the midst of brutal social differences. The psychoanalyst is, as the title suggests, one of the main targets of analytic reflection in Latin America. The contributions of Racker to countertransference and the Barangers to the analytic field are eloquent witnesses to this.

In order to offer a balanced overview of the book without repeating its content or depriving the reader of the pleasure that each chapter and discussion will offer, we will only mention a word or two about each specific chapter and then try to convey a more general view of the rich material we have here and a certain reflection on the psychoanalytic development of ideas in this region.

The book begins with an accurate account of the development of the psychoanalytic movement and psychoanalytic ideas in the region, presented by Samuel Zysman and R. Horacio Etchegoyen, the latter himself an important participant in this history and the first Latin American to preside over the IPA. Beatriz de León and Ricardo Bernardi, who have been carefully studying the subject in recent years, report on countertransference and the vulnerability of the analyst, showing how the important ideas of Racker, the Barangers, and other authors have shaped the specific way this concept is seen and used clinically in Latin America.

Then we have the chance of reading the beautiful and cohesive chapter in which Madeleine Baranger tells us how she and the late Willy Baranger developed their concept of the analytic field, showing its origins and further developments. It is a rare opportunity of seeing the history of a deep and successful analytic idea told by one of its authors. This is immediately followed by Luis Kancyper's chapter on the confrontation between generations as a dynamic field. Kancyper, one of the most prolific and original Latin American authors from a more recent generation, illustrates the far-reaching possibility of the concept of the analytic field.

Susana Vinocur-Fischbein comes next, with a scholarly essay on a difficult and complex dialogue: psychoanalysis and linguistics. Drawing upon the creative proposals made by David Liberman and other more recent authors, this chapter is a stimulating *tour de force* that certainly will inspire further discussions on this fascinating dialogue. The experience of truth in clinical psychoanalysis is explored by Antonio Muniz de Rezende through a particular way of reading Bion that the author proposes from his vast psychoanalytic and philosophical knowledge. Starting from the original contributions made by Ignácio Matte Blanco and confronting them with those from other authors from the Río de la Plata, Juan Francisco Jordán-Moore offers an intriguing view of external reality/internal reality, challenging whether a real dichotomy truly exists.

Then we have the chapter by Norberto Marucco, one of the most creative Latin American authors, describing several of his own original contributions to the theme of current psychoanalytic practice, emphasizing psychic zones and the process of unconscientization. Alejandro Tamez-Morales, in his revision of Latin American contributions to dreams and the unconscious in clinical practice, does justice to the pioneering work of Ángel Garma on the subject and illustrates its current relevance. The final chapter shows the history and development of child and adolescent psychoanalysis in Latin America: Virginia Ungar, one of the most active analysts of this area in recent years, offers a clear and informative picture of this important trend, which is characteristic of this region.

Each paper is discussed by an author from another part of the world, and here we found briefer but equally stimulating and well-argued papers presented by Otto Kernberg, Antonino Ferro, Jorge Canestri, Neville Symington, James Grotstein, Cesar Botella, Shmuel Erlich, and Florence Guignard.

After reading these chapters and the discussion to each of them, a natural question emerges: is there a Latin American psychoanalysis? We do not think it possible to find a close unity in this mosaic of theoretical developments, practices, institutions, and different cultures in this region. By the same token, we speak not of a European psychoanalysis or a North American psychoanalysis, but of different expressions of the psychoanalytic corpus that can be identified in each region.

From what is presented in this book, as well as from other accounts on the development of psychoanalysis in Latin America and also from our own experience of close contact with its various countries, we would suggest that several common trends can be observed in Latin America. Among these, the first is a close exchange with the cultural milieu, which influences psychoanalysis and at the same time is influenced by it, the most remarkable example being Argentina and, in particular, Buenos Aires. The second is a growing theoretical pluralism, which allows and stimulates a dialogue among different theories, in sharp contrast with previous times when closer or very uniform theoretical systems used to dominate in each specific country or society. As a result, we can observe a more open atmosphere of theoretical, clinical, and institutional discussions, where the ability to listen to divergent views helps to face complexity, fragmentation, and uncertainty, the trademarks of today's culture, and a clear concern with protecting quality and rigour in analytic training, in spite of the existence of different training models in the region and of continuous economic and social constraints. It is possible to identify in many

Latin American societies—and here we are referring to our listening to successive clinical presentations—a particular way of addressing clinical material, one that is close and direct and searches to grasp the emotion present in the analytic field. And, last but not least, it is still possible to see a prevailing timidity in acknowledging the quality and depth of theoretical and clinical work produced here, which continues to lead to a certain paucity of papers and books written and translated into other languages. In this regard, *Truth, Reality, and the Psychoanalyst* is a remarkable achievement, and it will contribute to increasing international understanding of the main psychoanalytic developments in Latin America.

A recurrent theme in conferences, both national and regional, as well as in several publications, is the relationship between Latin American theoretical developments and those made in the most traditional centres of Europe and North America. These discussions suggest sometimes that what is produced here is just a repetition of the main analytic schools; others suggest or propose that what is needed is a specific regional production of knowledge. Behind the scenes, naturally, we can identify more global ideological conflicts on questions of power, dependence, domination, and so on. But perhaps this book, in the way it was designed and in what is finally accomplished, is an important contribution to the notion of interdependence, to acknowledging that we are at a stage of our discipline in which no clear boundaries can be established any longer.

The beauty of this moment lies in the fact that anyone who wishes to have at least a reasonable grasp of our main theoretical lines of development cannot ignore the main ideas produced in each region or country. Of course, as always, a synthesis of this situation was offered by Jorge Luis Borges, in a comment to his own work, after fifty years of writing:

> *La prosa convive com el verso; acaso para la imaginación ambas son iguales. Felizmente, no nos debemos a una sola tradición; podemos aspirar a todas.*
>
> [Prose lives with poetry; maybe for imagination both are the same. Happily we are not in debt to only one tradition; we can aspire to all.]

Another version of this conflict was offered by the Brazilian poet Carlos Drummond de Andrade, who said in a challenging tone, as a young writer:

> *Mundo mundo, vasto mundo, mais vasto é o meu coração.*
>
> [World, world, big world, my heart is bigger.]

Many years later, he corrected himself:

> *Não, meu coração não é maior que o mundo, é menor, muito menor, nele não cabem nem as minhas dores. . . . Por isso me dispo, me exponho cruamente nas livrarias. Preciso de todos.*
>
> [No, my heart is not bigger than the world. It is smaller, much smaller. In it, there is no place even for my pains. . . . That is why I divest myself, I expose myself in the bookstores. I need everybody.]

Because in international psychoanalysis we need everybody and the first step in our joint enterprise is to learn more about the Other—and since "The Uncanny" we know very well that this Other has much to do with ourselves—we congratulate the IPA Publications Committee and its chair, Emma Piccioli, and especially the editors of this remarkable book, Drs Sérgio Lewkowicz and Silvia Flechner, for their excellent work, which will certainly contribute to our better mutual understanding.

TRUTH, REALITY, AND THE PSYCHOANALYST

1

Psychoanalysis in Latin America: an approximation to the history and ideas

R. Horacio Etchegoyen & Samuel Zysman

In memory of Helena Besserman Vianna

The invitation to write an introduction to a volume intended to show to the psychoanalytic world the development of our science in Latin America we take both as an honour and a great responsibility.

Our continent, wide and varied in autochthonous cultures, diverse in the vastness of its geographical panoramas and abundant in natural riches, has also been, since the beginning of the twentieth century, the scene in which psychoanalysis has flourished.

It is precisely these abovementioned characteristics that contributed to give this development its peculiar traits, linked not only to the history and geography, but also to the great social, political, and economic changes that had their own trajectories in the different countries and regions. In tracing these, our task becomes a complicated one; it may even look difficult to grasp when it comes to finding a common path while at the same time pointing out the existing differences and particularities—a topic with which Andrade de Azevedo, Stucchi Vannucchi, and Hadaza Sandler have recently been occupied (2004).

We consider that there are two possible approaches: a historiographical one, with a chronological narration that follows the way step by step, and another, more theoretical approach, which shows the development and destiny of the ideas that came from Europe and the United States and led to the original contributions of Latin American analysts.

The task is no less if we take into account that we Latin American psychoanalysts are, generally, not well known in other countries, for reasons that also seem tempting to study. In any case, we find ourselves on a journey of a magnitude and a risk comparable to the expeditions that were made not only by conquerors but also by naturalists, researchers, and cartographers since the discovery of America.

As we knew that we had to write a chapter and not a book, we considered our approaches carefully and pondered on the boundaries we had to set ourselves. We decided to relate historical data, but with the purpose of following up ideas and relating them to social reality, just as we had tried to do in a previous paper (Etchegoyen & Zysman, 2004). In the latter, we made a clarification that we would like to reiterate here: there is a risk of omissions and biased judgements, and though we have tried to reduce these as much as possible for us, only the readers will be able to tell us how successful we have been.

Recently, efforts to let people know how much has been done and is being done in South America are comforting and seem decidedly to be growing in number. This publication is itself a testimony to the similar intentions that led to the creation, first, of the Consejo Coordinador de las Organizaciones Psicoanalíticas de América Latina (COPAL) and then of the Federación Psicoanalitíca de América Latina (FEPAL). Both institutions have fought against the tendency towards isolation in our societies, which contributed much to the lack of international knowledge of our scientific production.

We wish to point out the enormous turning point reached when Latin America was acknowledged as one of the three regions with full voting power in the representative organs of the IPA. In 1963, during Maxwell Gitelson's presidency, León Grinberg became part of the executive Council as Associate Secretary and was the first Latin American to occupy that position. In the following periods, with van der Leeuw and Rangell in the chair, Grinberg was vice-president of the IPA. His position was later taken over by other Latin Americans, such as Carlos Plata, David Zimmermann, Avelino González, Inga Villarreal, David Liberman, David Rosenfeld, Luis Feder, Moisés Lemlij (who was also treasurer of the IPA), Agustín Palacios, Carlos Mario Aslán, Ricardo Bernardi, Inaura Carneiro Leão, Max Hernández, and Galina Schneider.

During Wallerstein's and Weinshel's administration [1985–1989] it was decided to hold an International Congress in Latin America; so in 1991 the congress duly took place in Buenos Aires, where for the first time a Latin American president—R. Horacio Etchegoyen—was elected.[1] The new rotational system now includes the three areas, radically changing the previous one, where only Europeans and Americans had succeeded each other.

The rapid spread of psychoanalysis in Latin America was furthered with the first translation of Freud's work into Spanish in the 1920s, inspired by José Ortega y Gasset. (The translator, Luis López Ballesteros y de Torres, was actually complimented by Freud himself.)

Current developments in information technology allow us to expand our knowledge of psychoanalytic ideas around the world. We would like to use it to spread our region's contributions, which, we hope, will allow us, in turn, to be better known.

A bit of history

A far as we know, what was then the young psychoanalytic science made its first public appearance at a scientific meeting in Buenos Aires in July 1910, the year in which the centennial of the Mayo Revolution was celebrated; this revolution had installed the first autonomous Governing Board in Argentina, which cut all political links with the Spanish monarchy. In such special circumstances, the International American Congress of Medicine and Hygiene was held at the Faculty of Medicine in Buenos Aires, where Germán Greve Schlegel, a delegate of the Chilean government, presented "About Psychology and Psychotherapy of some States of Anxiety" and showed his wide knowledge of Freud's theories, upon which he based his speech to propose the treatment of these states (Greve Schlegel, 1910). Greve Schlegel [1869–1954] was born in Valparaíso, Chile, and, after graduating as a doctor and a pharmacist, he travelled to Germany, where he specialized in nervous and mental diseases. His memorable paper, the text of which can be consulted in the Proceedings of that Congress—kept in the library of the School of Medicine of the Buenos Aires University—was rescued by Ludovico Rosenthal, an Austrian émigré who came to Buenos Aires in 1938 after the *Anschluss* and later became a new translator of Freud's work into Spanish. When in 1945 he introduced Greve's work in the *Journal of Psychoanalysis* (*Revista de psicoanálisis*), Rosenthal mentioned the source that oriented his search: it was Freud's acknowledgement of Greve in his "History of the Psychoanalytical Movement" (1914d).

A closer reading of Greve Schlegel's work led us to consider it an authentic psychoanalytic paper, and very much above others of his time. Vezetti (1989) was right in designating him as compulsory reading in the history of Latin American psychoanalysis. This paper now appears as the first chapter of *Cuarenta años de psicoanálisis en Chile* [Forty years of psychoanalysis in Chile], compiled by Eleonora Casaula, Jaime Coloma, and Juan Francisco Jordán (1991).

Rosenthal also discovered a second precursor in Buenos Aires. On 5 December 1912, in *La Semana Medica* [The Medical Weekly], W. F. Waugh published a brief communication under the title "Application of Freudian theories", in which he applied psychoanalytic theories, about the case of a man who killed his wife out of jealousy.

At the same time Freud (1914d) mentions Honorio Delgado, whom he also remembers in "A Short Account of Psycho-Analysis" (1924f [1923]), where he includes the Peruvian Psychiatry Journal, edited by Delgado in Lima, among Spanish-language publications that dealt with psychoanalysis. This eminent Peruvian psychiatrist from the first half of the twentieth century was very close to Freud, with whom he carried out a very interesting epistolary dialogue (Rey de Castro, 1977, etc.). Later Delgado drifted away from Freud and broke with psychoanalysis—something that his nephew, Carlos Alberto Seguín, analysed by Flanders Dunbar in New York, never did. Seguín was a professor of psychiatry at the Universidad Nacional Mayor of San Marcos, the oldest in America, and director of the psychiatry ward in the Workers' Hospital, whence future pioneers in Peruvian psychoanalysis were to come. Seguín always maintained good relations with psychoanalysis; his work at the Workers' Hospital can be compared to that of Mauricio Goldenberg later in Argentina.

Chile has the privilege of having had the first graduate psychoanalyst in Latin America: Fernando Allende Navarro [1890–1981], who obtained full membership of the Swiss Society of Psychoanalysis and the Psychoanalytic Society of Paris. Once back in Chile, Allende

Navarro revalidated his medical degree and in 1926 presented his thesis, "El valor de la psicoanálisis en policlínica" [The value of psychoanalysis in policlinics], the first paper ever of an IPA psychoanalyst to be published in Spanish (Arrué, 1990; Whiting, 1980).

Among other outstanding intellectuals in Santiago, Allende Navarro analysed Ignacio Matte Blanco and the Colombian Arturo Lizarazo, one of the founders of psychoanalysis in Colombia. However, Navarro was unable to form a psychoanalytic group in Chile, even though he had Freud's full support; only one of his psychoanalysands was able to do so, years later.

Interest in psychoanalysis in Brazil began in the mid-1920s, at about the same time as Allende Navarro's work in Santiago. A young doctor from São Paulo, Durval Marcondes [1899–1981], began to study and practise on his own account. His thesis on symbolism in literature (1926) was inspired by psychoanalysis and came out as a small book, which Marcondes sent to Freud, who read it and commented on it enthusiastically.

In 1927 Marcondes founded the Brazilian Society of Psychoanalysis, the first of its kind in Latin America, and published the first—and only—issue of the *Revista Brasileira de Psicanálise,* a journal that reappeared only in 1967.

Convinced that psychoanalytic training had to follow the Eitingon model, Marcondes had his mind set on an IPA analyst moving to São Paulo, and this was finally made possible when, at the International Congress of Marienbad in 1936, Ernest Jones and Otto Fenichel authorized Adelheid Lucy Koch (Fenichel's analysand) to go there as a training analyst (Nosek, 1994).

Koch [1896–1980] had studied medicine in Berlin and entered the famous Eitingon Institute in 1929, graduating in 1935. This studious young analyst arrived in Brazil with her family in 1936, and she contacted Marcondes in the following year. Marcondes helped her to settle in and started analysis with her, as did Darcy de Mendonça Uchôa, Flavio Dias, and Virginia L. Bicudo (Yutaka Sagawa, 1994). Koch's tenacious work—which included the multiple tasks of a psychoanalytic training institute—had to overcome various obstacles and necessitated more time for everything. It was only in 1943 that the IPA acknowledged the Brazilian Study Group that became the Psychoanalytical Study Group of São Paulo in 1944, of which Koch and five of her analysands were members. In a modest way, they did not think it wise to appear as representing all of Brazil. Frank Philips,

Enrique Mendes, Lygia Alcántara de Amaral, and Isaias Mehlson soon joined the initial nucleus. At the 1951 International Congress of Amsterdam, the IPA acknowledged the Brazilian Psychoanalytic Society of São Paulo as a Component Society, being the first in Brazil and the third in Latin America.

Meanwhile, in Buenos Aires a psychoanalytic group was being started: to begin with, two IPA psychoanalysts—Ángel Garma, who arrived as an exile in 1938, and Céles Ernesto Cárcamo, an Argentine doctor who came back from Paris almost at the same time—found fertile ground there: Since the mid-1930s a group of "porteños" (inhabitants of the capital, a port city) had gathered in Buenos Aires to read Freud and to study his theories (Balán, 1991). José Ingenieros, Aníbal Ponce, Gregorio Bermann, and Jorge Thénon, distinguished doctors from the first half of the twentieth century, had already been busy with psychoanalysis.

In 1942, fleeing from Nazi persecution, Marie Langer joined the group formed by Garma, Cárcamo, Arnaldo Rascovsky, and Enrique Pichon Rivière. Along with Emilio Ferrari Hardoy, who later went to live in the United States, they formed the founding group of the Argentine Psychoanalytic Association (APA), and Jones, president of the IPA, formally acknowledged it as a Provisional Society in December 1942. This was the first IPA society in Latin America, and its role in the development of psychoanalysis proved, after years, to be outstanding. The APA was acknowledged as a Component Society at the 16th International Congress (Zurich, 1949)—the first after the Second World War—that also acknowledged the Chilean Psychoanalytic Association. It is worth while noting that on this same occasion some Argentines met for the first time with Melanie Klein and her group, thus beginning a lasting scientific relationship.

What Allende Navarro had been unable to carry out in Chile was done by his analysand, Ignacio Matte Blanco [1908–1995], who went to London in 1933 and was trained with the British Psychoanalytical Society, where he was re-analysed by Walter Schmideberg.

Once back in Chile, Matte Blanco began to meet with doctors interested in psychoanalysis. Towards 1944, some of them began analysis with him, and in this way the group that was recognized by the Zurich Congress was started. Its members were Allende Navarro, Matte Blanco—by that time already professor of psychiatry at the University—Arturo Prat Echaurren, Carlos Whiting, and a few others.

A little later they were joined by Erika Guzmán, Enrique Rosenblatt, Hernán Davanzo, Ximena Artaza, Otto Kernberg, Ruth Riesenberg, Ramón Ganzaraín, José Antonio Infante, and Bernardo Arensburg—all of them outstanding analysts, many of whom would later emigrate. Matte Blanco moved to Rome in 1966 with his wife, Luciana Bohn, also an analyst, and carried out an extraordinary theoretical research that characterized the functioning of the unconscious in terms of a symmetrical and asymmetrical logic that goes beyond Freudian metapsychology (Matte Blanco, 1975). This very relevant work is now studied around the world and has many followers in our region, such as Juan Francisco Jordán-Moore and Juan Pablo Jiménez in Chile and Jorge Luis Ahumada in Buenos Aires.

After the Zurich Congress psychoanalysis expanded quickly in Latin America, and new societies started to be founded. Many Latin American colleagues found the possibility of training in Buenos Aires to be an attractive one; a large number of them later went back to their place of origin to form part of or create local societies.

We can find such an example in the origins of psychoanalysis in Rio de Janeiro (as carefully studied by Marialzira Perestrello, 1987). Once the Second World War was over, two European analysts arrived in Rio and were joined by other colleagues trained in the APA, in São Paulo, and others from Rio who were analysands of these two initial analysts.

The first references to psychoanalysis in Rio de Janeiro can be traced to Antonio Austregésilo's writings at the beginning of the twentieth century, but it was only in the 1940s that the first students to contact the APA and APCh (the Argentine and Chilean societies) appeared in search of a systematic training. These pioneers were looking for an IPA analyst to move to Rio, but they ended up studying in Buenos Aires and in London.

By 1948 the Brazilian Psychoanalytic Institute was functioning in Rio; it was here that, through Ernest Jones's inconceivable advice, Mark Burke arrived in February and Werner Kemper in December. Burke was a Polish Jew who had studied in England, and Kemper had belonged to the infamous Goering Institute in Berlin, an "Aryan" psychotherapy institution that did not admit Jewish psychoanalysts into its ranks. Such a contradiction marked the existence of two groups in Rio, and this turned out to have quite painful consequences.

At the 1953 International Congress in London, Kemper's group was recognized as the study group sponsored by São Paulo Society; but this was not the case for Burke's group or the Argentine-trained group formed by Danilo Perestrello, Walderedo Ismael de Oliveira, Alcyon Baer Bahía, and Marialzira Perestrello.

Not long after the London Congress, Burke returned to England, leaving his group on standby. Meanwhile, at the Geneva International Congress, Kemper's group became the Sociedade Psicanalítica do Rio de Janeiro (SPRJ, Rio 1).

The group started by Burke, as well as others trained in Buenos Aires and London, were finally admitted as Study Group at the 1957 International Congress in Paris; at the following one—the 1959 Congress in Copenhagen—it obtained recognition as the Sociedade Brasileira de Psicanálise do Rio de Janeiro (SBPRJ, Rio 2).

Uruguay's case is definitely different. Its geographical—not to mention affective and cultural—proximity to Argentina led Willy and Madeleine Baranger to move from Buenos Aires to Montevideo in 1954, where for a decade they worked and taught, contributing to the creation of the Uruguayan Psychoanalytic Association (APU) and the *Revista Uruguaya de Psicoanálisis* (*Uruguayan Journal of Psychoanalysis*) which first appeared in 1956. Among other Uruguayans important in this process, we can mention Héctor Garbarino and his wife, Mercedes Freire, Luis and Vida Prego Silva, Marta Nieto, Laura Achard, now in Monterrey, Gilberto Koolhaas, the Peredas—Alberto and Myrta Casas—and the Mendilaharsus—Carlos and Sélika Acevedo—and, more recently, Ricardo Bernardi, his wife Beatriz de León, Fanny Schkolnik, Carmen Médici de Steiner, and the Viñars.

In the early 1940s, the founders of the Mexican Psychoanalytic Association—whose biographies were compiled by Dupont (1997)—formed a group that was interested in psychoanalysis; members of this group later went to Argentina or to the United States for training: Santiago Ramírez, José Luis González, José and Estela Remus, and Avelino González moved to Buenos Aires, while Ramón Parres, Alfredo Namnum, and Víctor Manuel Aíza went to the States. Luis Feder was Ramirez's first analysand when he went back to Buenos Aires in 1952. That same year Ramón Parres returned from New York, after training at the Psychoanalytic Clinic at Columbia University, where he was analysed by Paul Goolker.

The Study Group was recognized by the IPA at the Geneva Congress in 1955; two years later the Paris Congress recognized the

Mexican Psychoanalytic Association (APM), whose first president was Ramón Parres. Rafael Barajas, another pioneer, later moved to Monterrey, Mexico, to form the group that in 1993 became the Regiomontana Psychoanalytic Association.

One distinguishing feature of the APM is their wide theoretical scope. One group coming from Buenos Aires, mostly with a Kleinian orientation, joined with others trained in New York and Topeka with a solid knowledge of ego psychology. In 1962 Ramón Parres translated Hartmann's book, *Ego Psychology and the Problem of Adaptation*. At that time, Erich Fromm was living in Mexico; he later moved to the States, leaving behind some disciples.

Psychoanalysis in Porto Alegre, Brazil, started with Mario Martins, who had moved to Buenos Aires with his wife Zaira, who later introduced child psychoanalysis in Rio Grande do Sul. Martins was already a distinguished psychiatrist when in 1944 he was analysed by Garma and worked with Pichon Rivière. He was the first foreigner to seek training in Buenos Aires, and he had the help of the Francisco Muñoz Foundation, which did such a great deal to promote psychoanalysis. He returned to Porto Alegre in 1947 and shortly afterward began to analyse candidates.

The first Study Group from Porto Alegre, formed by the Martins, Paulo Guedes, Ernesto La Porta, and David Zimmermann, was recognized by the IPA at the 1961 Edinburgh Congress and became a Component Society at the 32nd Congress in Stockholm in 1963. Some of the other members were Cyro Martins, trained at the APA in the 1950s, who did a great job both as an analyst and as a writer, Luis Meneghini, Germano Vollmer, Romualdo Romanovsky, Roberto Pinto Ribeiro, and Sérgio Paulo Annes. In 1989 a new Study Group was started and later (1992) admitted as such by the IPA. In 1997 it was voted at the Barcelona Congress as the Component Sociedade Brasileira de Psicanálise de Porto Alegre; this is the society to which Renato and Ana Tachtenberg, Newton Aronis, Gley Costa, Leonardo Francischelli, and many others belong.

The history of psychoanalysis in Peru was told by Saúl Peña (1991). Peña remembers the hard work of Seguín and his own arrival in Lima in 1969, after having graduated from the British Psychoanalytical Association. Carlos Crisanto returned in 1973 and Max Hernández a year later; they were also members of the Independent Group of that society. These pioneers worked tirelessly until they

sinki in 1981. In 1979 Noel Altamirano arrived after training at the APA, as did Alberto Péndola Febres. Gustavo Delgado Aparicio, also a member of the London Independent Group, came to Lima in 1979 and was the inspirer and editor of the *Annual Book of Psychoanalysis,* a valuable instrument in spreading the main contributions of the *International Journal of Psycho-Analysis* in Latin America. Nowadays, the *Annual Book* is edited by Roberto Doria Medina. It is also published in Portuguese, under the direction of Elías Mallet da Rocha Barros, and in French under Florence Guignard.

The Peruvian Psychoanalytic Society grew noticeably with the arrival of Moisés Lemlij from London, Jaime Heresi from Venezuela, and Carlos Rodriguez Rabanal and Hilke Engelbrecht from Frankfurt—until it became a Provisional Society in Hamburg in 1985 and a Component Society in Montreal two years later.

Psychoanalysis in Venezuela began in the 1950s; in 1961 a Study Group was formed when Manuel Kizer returned from Argentina, Obaica arrived from France, and Antonio García, Fernando Acuña, and Marlene Silveira Araujo returned from Chile. Soon César Ottalagano, Julio Aray, Antonio Briceño Monzant, Guillermo Teruel, and others joined the initial group. The Study Group was recognized by the IPA in 1965, at the Copenhagen Congress, and became a Component Society in 1971, at the Vienna Congress.

The Psychoanalytic Society of Caracas, separate from the Venezuela group, was formed in 1989 and was accepted as a Study Group at the International Congress of Buenos Aires in 1991; it became a Component Society in 1995, at the San Francisco Congress.

The first mention of psychoanalysis in Colombia appears in Pío Socarrás's writings in the 1920s, but the initial group was formed when Arturo Lizarazo returned from Chile in 1949 and Socarrás from Paris in 1953. The Study Group was formed in 1956, and in 1961 the Edinburgh Congress recognized the Colombian Psychoanalytic Society.

Socarrás and Lizarazo went their separate ways shortly after that. The Colombian Society—lead by Socarrás and, later, by Carlos Plata, who returned from Buenos Aires—continued to be a member of the IPA, while Lizarazo formed the Colombian Psychoanalytic Association; many years later, with Mario González Velásquez as its president, it was recognized by the IPA as a Component Society at the New Orleans Congress in 2004. (For a history of psychoanalysis in Colombia, see, among others, Guillermo Sánchez Medina, 1990.)

As can be seen in this brief outline, the history of psychoanalysis in Latin America began with the diffusion of Freudian ideas by the enlightened minds of that time and continued, on the one hand, with the journeys made by Latin Americans who went to train overseas and, on the other, by Europeans fleeing from the Second World War. Both contributions were decisive when it came to moving from early informal groups to the formation of societies and training institutes—what Cesio (2000) calls "the Latin American psychoanalytic endeavour". At that time the IPA was, and continued to be for a long time, the only worldwide psychoanalytic association.

The 1930s were marked by the Diaspora of Viennese, Germans, and—generally speaking—Central Europeans fleeing from the persecution of Hitler. Many of them, as Riccardo Steiner (2000) relates, found refuge in London, New York, California, and Chicago. Others—a smaller number—chose South American countries. Among them there were some Jews who were fleeing for their lives, and others who were running because they had taken part in political activities. All of them contributed decisively to the development and institutionalization of psychoanalysis. On the other hand, the defeat and fall of the Third Reich led a character who had participated in the Nazi adventure to our lands.

The 1960s and 1970s were, for our region, tumultuous political and military dictatorial times. Nevertheless, in the midst of these grave difficulties, psychoanalysis continued to advance: an example of this is the incorporation of Lacan's thought.

Further proof of the expansion of Latin American psychoanalysis is the creation of new IPA societies in Brazil (Pelotas, Riberão Preto, Brasília, etc.), Argentina (Mendoza, Córdoba, Rosario), and, very recently, a psychoanalytic centre in Asunción in Paraguay.

In the mid-1970s a group of APA analysts adopted an attitude of social and political commitment in face of a turbulent Latin America. They criticized the Association's aloof attitude, which, they thought, only sided with the governments in power, and they fought for an integration of politics and psychoanalysis. Some even thought that psychoanalysis should be at the service of the social revolution. In this way, two rebel groups were formed in Buenos Aires: *Plataforma* and *Documento.* In their ranks such distinguished analysts as Marie Langer, Gilberte and Diego García Reynoso, Emilio Rodrigué, Santiago Dubcovsky, Rafael Paz, Hernán Kesselman, Fernando Ulloa, Armando Bauleo, Eduardo Pavlovsky—a great fighter and a brilliant writer—

and many more were to be found. They finally decided in 1971 to "leave the IPA and its Argentine subsidiary" to go their own way.

After this split in the Society, Willy and Madeleine Baranger and Jorge Mom proposed a momentous change in the APA's training system. Under the banner of scientific pluralism and coincidentally with the rise of Lacanian groups, the establishment of the APA was strongly criticized, the hegemony of Kleinian thought being one of the main causes. Replicating in some way the model of class struggle, the Association's structures were to be levelled. Candidates had to be called training colleagues, and the members could—if they wished—ask to be granted training status. Seminars were basically the responsibility of those who attended them. In all this, the Institute mostly had to remain apart. With such statements, the renovating group won the governing positions in the 1974 elections—which were extremely even—and implemented the changes that had been announced, thus raising opposition from another group of members. This is how, in 1975, the Athenaeum of Psychoanalysts came to be formed; it was recognized as the Psychoanalytic Association of Buenos Aires (APdeBA) in 1977 at the Jerusalem Congress, and it became a Component Society two years later, at the New York Congress, while David Liberman was its president.

In 1974 an enlightened Argentine scholar, Oscar Masotta [1930–1979], who had started reading Jacques Lacan following Pichon Rivière's advice, founded the Freudian School of Buenos Aires. Threatened by the murderous Triple A during Isabel Perón's government—even though his objectives were merely scientific, and not political—Masotta had to emigrate to Barcelona, where he continued teaching until his premature death (García, 1980). His influence has been notable in Argentina, Latin America, and Spain.

A crucial moment in the settling of Lacanian thought in Latin America was Lacan's visit to Caracas, to attend the first Encounter of the Freudian Field, organized by Jacques-Alain Miller, Diana Rabinovich—then in exile—and the Athenaeum of Caracas (Graciela Brodsky, personal communication). This meeting later produced one publication: *Cinco conferencias caraqueñas sobre Lacan* [Five Caracas Lectures on Lacan] (Jacques-Alain Miller, 1979).[2]

Meanwhile, in Buenos Aires, as a consequence of Masotta's exile, the School went to another Lacanian group, while Masotta and his followers founded the Freudian School of Argentina. There are currently numerous Lacanian groups in Latin America—too many to list here. Let us just mention the EOL (School of Lacanian Orientation) in Buenos Aires, which follows the inspiration of the World Association of Psychoanalysis, where Graciela Brodsky, Ricardo Nepomiachi, Juan Carlos Indart, and Germán L. García stand out. There is also Roberto Harari's Mayéutica, the Freudian Forum, which follows the teachings of Colette Soler, and the Lacanamerican meetings of Sergio Rousseaux and others. Guillermo Maci has made original contributions to the order of the real and to narcissism.

Lacan is currently one of the most widely read authors in Latin America, together with Winnicott, Klein, and Bion. The work of thinkers such as Hanna Segal, Betty Joseph, Donald Meltzer, André Green, Piera Aulagnier, Heinz Kohut, Otto Kernberg, Jean Laplanche, and some others is studied and debated in depth.

Even though at the beginning—perhaps because of a historical inertia—the Societies belonging to the IPA and the Lacanian groups kept a certain distance and were quite hostile at times, Lacan's work is currently studied everywhere. This change to dialogue was without doubt a difficult one, but it was also positive since it allowed partisan and personal positions to be gradually replaced by scientific debate—the only rational way of advancing any discipline. The dialogue between Etchegoyen and Miller contributed to this; this was sponsored by Juan Carlos Stagnaro and Dominique Wintrebert, editors of *Vértex*, in July 1996, and was later expanded on and discussed at length in other meetings.

Original contributions from Latin America

It is difficult to follow the path of all the ideas that came to us and those that were developed here. We have already mentioned the most widely read and studied writers within this broad spectrum of what is produced around the world. We consider Buenos Aires to have exerted a great scientific influence on all psychoanalytic thought in Latin America and that there was a major turning point in theoretical standings in the 1970s, encompassing deep-rooted scientific, cultural, and social problems that ought to be studied. Wender, Torres, and Vidal (1995) deal with this issue in their outline of the history of Argentine psychoanalysis.

Many Latin American and European colleagues believe that theo-

we share this standpoint, even though we know we are not impartial witnesses. Upon reviewing history, we find ourselves, in fact, firmly in Buenos Aires.

Ángel Garma [1904–1993], who studied medicine in Madrid, moved to Berlin, where he was analysed by Theodor Reik. His paper to qualify as an Associate member—"The Outer Reality and the Instincts in Schizophrenia", presented in Berlin in 1931—refutes Freud's thesis (1924e) and maintains that it is the rejection of instinctual drives that really separates the subject from the external world, because the drives, the self, and reality all form a whole. This paper helped Latin American psychoanalysts to take an interest in psychosis, with Enrique Pichon Rivière as its major exponent. Garma (1970b) also developed an original approach to dreams, conceived as a product of traumatic situations masked by the satisfaction of wishes. His idea of illness in the coordinates of a sadistic superego and the masochistic ego impregnates the psychopathology of his time.

Arnaldo Rascovsky's [1907–1995] work on prenatal psychology, gathered in *El psiquismo fetal* [Foetal psyche] (1960), enters unexplored territory. Rascovsky maintains that some sort of psychic life exists before birth, and it is bidimensional—where the ego, as a double of the id, processes fantasies that are phylogenetically stored there. This is what Rascovsky calls the manic position, preceding the paranoid-schizoid position, since the id desires are admitted without obstacles by the ego. These papers preceded Esther Bick's, Meltzer's, Bion's, and Sandra Piontelli's post-Kleinian investigations.

In the last years of his life, Rascovsky emphasized the filicidal tendencies as the counterpart of the classical Freudian parricide.

Cesio's contributions (e.g. 1956) on lethargy find support not only in Rascovsky's foetal psyche, but also in Freud, Klein, and Racker. Lethargy reproduces a state of death and desolation in the transference and countertransference that leads to a negative therapeutic reaction.

Early psychic development is a topic that was frequently explored by the pioneers starting from Melanie Klein's theory of positions but introducing a previous state. Rascovsky's foetal psyche, in fact, precedes the paranoid-schizoid position, which only appears after birth; the same happens with Bleger's idea of a "glischrocaric" position (based on the assumption of an early undifferentiated nucleus) and with the concept of the basic illness introduced by Pichon Rivière.

Enrique Pichon Rivière [1907–1977]—an outstanding, universally accepted master—was born in Geneva and raised in Goya, a provincial town in Argentina, where the local Guaraní culture had left an indubitable mark. He studied medicine in Buenos Aires, married Arminda Aberastury in 1936, and was analysed by Garma. Following his experience in the Hospicio de las Mercedes in Buenos Aires, Pichon Rivière developed an original dynamic psychiatry. As Vezetti points out (1996), at first Pichon Rivière took epilepsy as the axis in psychiatry, but later, following in the steps of Wilhelm Griesinger, he considered melancholy as the basic illness from which neurosis and psychosis, as well as the other psychosomatic states, evolve. The concept of "the basic illness" implies that mourning and loss of object are the basis both of development and of illness.

The new approach to psychiatry that Pichon offers consists in promoting a dialectic spiral in the face of conflict, where a genetic continuity is established over the basis of successive synthesis, which resolves contradictions and makes a new learning of reality possible. Arbiser (2004) points out that the natural evolution of Pichonian thought is towards the internal group and the operative group, configured in the conceptual referential and operative schemata (ECRO), where the dialectic unity between theory and praxis is established.

Resnik's studies on frozen time in psychosis follow the same path, along with Jorge García Badaracco's on the maddening object, David Rosenfeld's on severe pathologies, and Liendo's work on mental functioning.

José Bleger [1922–1972] made some contributions to technique with his well-known study of the analytic setting, and also to psychopathology. He had an original understanding of early development and took Klein's ideas about positions and those on autism and symbiosis from Margaret Mahler. Bleger (1967) described a "glischrocaric" position, based on the existence of an agglutinated nucleus, which precedes the paranoid-schizoid position. Its manifestation is the fusion—different from the confusion—that projective identification brings about.

Marie Langer made some contributions to psychosomatic medicine, psychoanalytic technique, group psychology, and women's psychology. Her work *Maternidad y sexo* [Maternity and sex], published in 1951, is still valid. In her memoirs (Langer, del Palacio, & Guinsberg, 1983), Langer broadens what she had said in 1951 from a

Marxist and rather feminist perspective, in accordance with her membership in *Plataforma*.

Céles Ernesto Cárcamo [1903–1990], analysed by Paul Schiff, brought from Paris the stamp of Anna Freud and the ego psychologists. He dealt with myths, female sterility (in collaboration with Langer), and the actual neuroses (Cárcamo, 1992). Democratic to the bone, Cárcamo helped Schiff in the opprobrious years of the Vichy regime. His work on the Feathered Serpent opened the area of applied psychoanalysis in Latin America.

Myths were always of particular interest to Latin American psychoanalysts, as well as those in Greece and other countries of the old continent: we have already quoted Cárcamo, and we can also mention Luis Feder, Nassim Yampey, Susana Dupetit, Antonio Santamaría, Saúl Peña, Gela Rosenthal, and many more. Contributions from Mexico and Peru are outstanding, but there are psychoanalysts interested in the topic throughout the whole continent.

Among the most original Latin American studies on history and anthropology we have to remember those of the Mexican Santiago Ramírez (1959), the Peruvian Max Hernández's (1992), and the nucleus group gathered at SIDEA (Seminario Interdisciplinario de Estudios Andinos), where Moisés Lemlij and María Rostworowski participated, among others (Lemlij, 1991), together with the anthropologist Luis Millones. Hernández's beautiful and well-documented book *Memoria del bien perdido* [Memory of the lost good] (1992) follows the biographical and cultural itinerary of the Inca Garcilaso de la Vega, who acquires Hispanic culture but finally rescues his Inca roots.

Heinrich Racker [1910–1961] arrived in Argentina in 1939, having abandoned his career in Vienna; he made huge efforts to become a psychoanalyst, his career being as short as it was brilliant. In 1948 he presented his paper "La neurosis de contratransferencia" [The neurosis of countertransference], which made a big impression. Racker devoted himself to the study of technique, and he concentrated mainly on transference, countertransference, and interpretation. Already in his early work he realized that the analyst works with the same mechanisms as does the analysand (and it could not be any other way); but he went beyond this in pointing out that countertransference is not only an obstacle, but also a *tool*. Paula Heimann had reached that same conclusion, and so this huge discovery can be attributed to them both; we must, however, acknowledge that Racker had studied it in greater depth and made it more complete with his concepts of concordant and complementary countertransference and countertransferential occurrences and positions. His work *Estudios sobre técnica psicoanalítica* [Studies on psychoanalytic technique] (1960) is one of the few books from our region that is studied all around the world. Grinberg's contributions on projective counteridentification and Etchegoyen's on the forms of transference and the reconstruction of early mental states follow the same path.

Grinberg's contributions were not restricted to those previously mentioned. He studied mourning and introduced a distinction between persecutory and depressive guilt feelings (Grinberg, 1964). The peculiar mourning associated with migration and exile was the subject of a book written in collaboration with Rebeca Grinberg (1984). Alongside Langer and Rodrigué, Grinberg helped to lay the foundations for group psychotherapy in Latin America.

The theory of the psychoanalytic field (*Teoría del campo psicoanalítico*) and the concept of *bastion* were introduced by Willy and Madeleine Baranger (1969b), basing themselves on Kurt Lewin and Merleau-Ponty as well as on the concepts of introjective and projective identification. The analytic relation, seen as being constructed simultaneously by analyst and patient, is something that is widespread and accepted today. It should be taken as an antecedent of the theories that sustain the concept of *links* as being different from that of object relations. These theories are used with couples and families, an area in which the work of Berenstein and Puget (1997) is taken very much into account.

One of the most outstanding disciples of Pichon Rivière was David Liberman [1920–1983], who developed a transcendental work of great methodological rigour, with contributions from the theory of communication, linguistics, and semiotics. His classification of communicational styles as an empirical and methodological base from a psychopathological and technical perspective is very well known.

The stylistic complementarity between the patient's material and the analyst's interpretation opens a space for the conception of analytic dialogue as a *communicative interaction* (Liberman, 1970–72). In recent years David Maldavsky has introduced the David Liberman algorithm (ADL) to study his work.

One of Liberman's sources for his work was Luisa G. de Álvarez de Toledo's enlightening paper on the analysis of associating, interpreting, and words ["El análisis del 'asociar', del 'interpretar' y de las 'palabras'"], published in 1954, long before Austin's (1957) and Searle's (1969) philosophical books on language and speech acts.

In the years before his premature death, Liberman dedicated himself to psychosomatics and studied the states of over-adaptation. Garma, Rascovsky, Cárcamo, Langer, and Pichon Rivière also studied these issues in depth, and more recently Chiozza, Maladesky, D'Alvia, and others have dealt with them.

The original developments in the analysis of children were of great importance and spread in Latin America, and among the pioneers in this area we have to include Arminda Aberastury (1962) and Betty Garma (1992). There were also some original contributions in psychopathology, technique—especially diagnosis through play sessions—and the theory of early development. Aberastury advanced the hypothesis of a previous genital phase during the first year, and she also produced an important paper on teething, language, and walking in relation to the depressive position.

Emilio Rodrigué made some important contributions to the study of autism, and Alberto Campo made his in the field of the psychopathology of psychopathic states—the object of some serious studies in the 1960s, with important contributions by Joel Zac.

All this work, on which we can only briefly comment here, has kept its theoretical vigour and is currently complemented by contributions from our region that are too abundant to summarize. A new edition of the Encounter on Bion's ideas has just taken place in São Paulo, where the turnout was impressive. Grinberg initiated the study of Bion's work in Latin America, and this was continued by Darío Sor and Elizabeth Tabak de Bianchedi. There are similar meetings on Winnicott, Klein, Piera Aulagnier, and others, and the work produced in Río de la Plata, Uruguay, on the intersections between psychoanalysis, linguistics, epistemology, ethology, and other disciplines is very well known.

The epistemologist Gregorio Klimovsky (2004) exerts a great influence on many Río de la Plata analysts: he has worked both as a teacher of ideas and as a firm advocate of psychoanalysis as a science. Liberman, Zac, and Etchegoyen acknowledge themselves as being his disciples, along with Eduardo Issaharoff, Bruno Winograd, Antonio Barrutia, Susana Dupetit, César Merea, Daniel Biebel, and Samuel Zysman, who has devoted himself lately to the study of the psychoanalytic perspectives on action and to theories as contents of the mind (2004).

Ahumada's investigation (1999) has followed a unique path, preferring counterinduction to the deductive–hypothetical method favoured by Klimovsky.

At this point we must end our necessarily brief overview, asking the many brilliant colleagues whose achievements could not be included here to forgive us; had there been more space, they would surely have had explicit acknowledgements.

Psychoanalysis in extreme conditions

The history of psychoanalysis in Latin America must necessarily include a chapter on the practice of our profession under the dictatorships that we have endured. Just as there are psychoanalysts dedicated to the study of the consequences of the Shoah, so Latin Americans have begun to consider their work in the extreme conditions imposed by these dictatorial governments. We must ask ourselves about the effects of fear on ourselves and start the painful task of differentiating the human desire to protect oneself from indifference and complicity.

We felt that Helena Besserman Vianna's example had to be highlighted, because it dignifies the human condition and affirms the links between psychoanalytic technique, theory, and ethics. Helena tirelessly pointed out the risk we run when, in order to defend psychoanalysis, we may find ourselves consenting to, if not actually supporting, totalitarian regimes.

In the twentieth century, the majority of Latin American countries lived under some kind of dictatorship that did not respect the confidentiality of the dialogue between the analyst and the patient and severely endangered personal security.

All these regimes shared the common trait of imposing a unitary thought that was not easy to oppose. From suffering discrimination in selection for public or university faculty positions to the extremes of exile and death, psychoanalysts found themselves in a cruel ethical dilemma when it came to analysing people who were engaged in the political battle and others who might have arbitrarily become involved in what was happening. The exercise of our profession was hindered under regimes that did not tolerate neutrality or independence.

Further complications appeared when patients who were already in embattled positions asked for assistance. In this way, the limits of the psychoanalytic method had to undergo very difficult tests. We can mention, for example, the conflictual decisions that one analyst had to make when he advised a patient—whose son had been kidnapped and murdered by the Videla dictatorship (Argentina)—to urgently leave the country, or another analyst who, seeing his own life endangered, had to take the same decision without being able to communicate it beforehand to his patients for fear for his personal safety.

At the 1979 IPA Congress in New York, in the midst of the military dictatorship, the attending Argentines found themselves confronted with an ethical dilemma when Abraham Brill presented the draft of a declaration denouncing torture and the disappearances in Argentina. In different ways the Argentines, preoccupied with the safety of their families in Buenos Aires, decided not to support this statement; in the end, this was replaced with a more abstract declaration on the incompatibility of psychoanalysis and dictatorial regimes.

At the same time in Montevideo, Marcelo Viñar, who was later to become president of FEPAL, was kidnapped and tortured for keeping professional confidentiality; together with his wife, Maren Ulriksen, he later had to go into exile for many years. This experience was later published as *Fracturas de memoria* [Fractures of memory] (Viñar & Viñar, 1993), giving not only a retrospective look at the leaden years leading up to it in Uruguay, but also a deep psychoanalytic reflection on memory and future, on the function of remembrance and forgetting.

There were persecuted psychoanalysts, some disappeared, and many had to go into exile. Cláudio Campos—who was later president of Rio 1 and who belonged to the Grupo Pro-Ética (the pro-ethic group, now known as Rio 4)—was tortured in Rio de Janeiro in the Army Battalion in which Amílcar Lobo—about whom more below—worked.

This painful overview shows the difficulties under which the analysts had to think and act in extreme circumstances, as was pointed out by Janine Puget, Elizabeth Tabak de Bianchedi, Julia Braun, Marcelo Bianchedi, María Luisa Pelento, and others (Puget et al., 1991). We have to remember to this end the similarly difficult positions in which Freud, Jones, and other pioneers found themselves when confronted with the Nazi phenomenon, when they had to put up with the Goering Institute taking charge of the psychoanalytic societies of Berlin and Vienna (Steiner, 2000).

A tragic example of the confluence of Nazi perversion and the Latin American dictatorships is that of Rio de Janeiro. The two Rio de Janeiro societies, whose stories we have already summarized, found themselves in grave difficulties when it was proved that the abovementioned Lobo—a military doctor who was a candidate for Rio 1—had participated in the torture sessions.

At this point we arrive at a painful phase in Latin American and international psychoanalysis. The brave battle that Helena Besserman Vianna engaged in can be understood by saying that her report on the involvement of this candidate in the torture teams of the military dictatorship had, necessarily, to be anonymous. She sent notice of this to Marie Langer in Buenos Aires, who later reproduced the note in the book entitled *Cuestionamos* (1987). Her own life and that of her loved ones depended on anonymity. This circumstance, however, was taken as an offence by Leaõ Cabernite, president of Rio 1 as well as Lobo's training analyst. It would have been reasonable to expect that in these circumstances the first preoccupation of an analyst would have been to investigate the veracity of the report, not the identity of the person who had dared to send it under such difficult conditions. That, however, was not the road chosen by Cabernite, who hired the services of a government graphologist to uncover the writer and even alleged that it was all a plot against Rio 1 by Rio 2 (the society to which Besserman Vianna belonged). The life and professional practice of this colleague were in grave danger for several years; she bore this with dignity while being at the same time calumniated in order to protect the candidate under scrutiny.

At this point it is worth pointing out some circumstances deserving attention. As described in the historical section, Kemper had arrived in Rio de Janeiro on the recommendation of Ernest Jones, who knew that he was coming from Berlin, where he had been a member of the Goering Institute. Kemper had been Cabernite's training analyst, and it was Cabernite who considered it his duty to defend the torturer rather than the person who had denounced him.

For years the IPA wrongly processed the incoming information on this situation, giving credit to Cabernite and consequently protecting Lobo, while those who fought for the truth kept being ignored and left in danger. The delay in comprehending this opprobrious drama went on for such a long time that the clarification of all the facts and reparatory measures were not carried out until a Latin American took the position of President of the IPA [1993–1997].

The complete story can be read in Besserman Vianna's *Não conte a ninguém* [Don't tell anybody] (1994), first published in Rio de Janeiro and subsequently translated into both French (in 1997) and Spanish (in 1998). The example of her tireless efforts constitutes in itself sufficient explanation for our dedicating this chapter to her, even though many other persecuted colleagues, including the Viñars, Cláudio Campos, Valentín Barenblit, and others, also deserve our homage.

Notes

This chapter has been translated by Mercedes Remedi, Uruguay.

1. At the congress of Rio de Janeiro (2005), Latin Americans Cláudio Laks Eizirik and Mónica Armesto are taking office as President and Secretary, respectively, of the IPA.

2. Manuel Kizer, who had previously embraced these teachings, left the Venezuelan Association in 1983, in accordance with Lacan's position towards the IPA.

2

Countertransference and vulnerability of the analyst

Beatriz de León & Ricardo Bernardi

The concept of countertransference

The study of countertransference has had a leading role in understanding the analyst's participation in the analytic process. Countertransference relates to the way the analyst listens and interprets and also to his/her attitude and analytic ideals—mainly those of neutrality and abstinence. It is a notion that is necessarily associated with transference, with phenomena of change or lack of change during analysis, and with different conceptions of the evolution and aim of analysis. In this chapter we wish to include another dimension, linked now directly to the person–analyst. From this perspective, the study of countertransference may be useful in understanding the functioning of the analyst in the session, as well as the situations in which he/she becomes particularly vulnerable and the possible need to seek help for him/herself.

The notion of countertransference is a concept that is very close to everyday experience, around which multiple controversies have developed both in the technical and in the theoretical field. In fact, we can see that the characteristics, the importance, and the role of this notion vary widely according to the theoretical frame in which it is set. This introduces modifications in the concept.

Changes in the concept of the countertransference in over a century of the development of psychoanalysis allow two meanings of the word to be distinguished:

a. In a restricted sense, countertransference means "an unconscious way of participating of the analyst in the transferential–countertransferential process, whose effects on the treatment need to be elucidated so that the analytic work may proceed adequately" (de León & Bernardi, 2000, p. 14).

   From this point of view the notion of countertransference is predominantly equated to that of resistential obstacles the source of which must be sought in the analyst's unconscious conflict and which require a certain insight on the analyst's part (be it through analysis, self-analysis, or supervision) so that he/she can elaborate them and regain the freedom confronting his/her task.

b. In a broad sense, countertransference may be understood as *"the analyst's conscious and unconscious disposition towards the patient in the moment or period of treatment"* (de León & Bernardi, 2000, p. 14). In this sense countertransference encompasses the whole mental functioning of the analyst during the session. The concept tends to include not only the analyst's unconscious response to the patient's transference, but also a wider range of the analyst's preconscious–conscious functioning. Characteristics and circumstances of the analyst's personal and professional life, technical and theoretical orientations, relationship with mentors and colleagues and with the analytic institution must be included, since they may influence the analyst's attitude towards the patient. Countertransference is, *stricto sensu,* a reaction to the patient rooted in these conscious and unconscious features of the analyst, which must, therefore, be included when we refer to the countertransferential phenomenon as a whole. In a broad sense, we include everything that counts for the analyst's contribution to the therapeutic process—both his/her disposition to analytic work and his/her specific response to working with the patient. We have included, then, in the notion of countertransference unconscious, preconscious, and conscious aspects of the analyst's mental functions. In this respect we are in agreement with Louise de Urtubey (1994), and we distance ourselves from Laplanche and Pontalis's definition, which delimits countertransference as the whole of the analyst's unconscious reactions to the individual

> analysand—especially to the analysand's own transference (1973, p. 92). Accepting a broad sense of the word, we approach Kernberg's position (1987) of transference as a "global" phenomenon including *"in addition to the analyst's unconscious reactions to the patient or to the transference (in other words, the analyst's transferences),* (a) *the analyst's realistic reaction to the reality of the patient's life,* (b) *the analyst's realistic reaction to his own life as it may become affected by the patient, and* (c) *the analyst's realistic reaction to the transference"* (Kernberg, 1987, p. 214). But we also include the analyst's general disposition to analytic work, approaching in this respect Green's (1975) and Winnicott's (1960a) viewpoints.

This way of understanding countertransference questions the image of the analyst as a faithful mirror whose objectivity is not affected by what it reflects; it presents, rather, an analyst who potentially may be influenced by varied things that may happen in his/her life, training and working conditions. We will return to some of these points later on.

Both the broad sense and the restricted one are worth while, though we could argue about the convenience of using the same word for both. In any case, we believe that this double meaning clarifies the continuity of the phenomenon and at the same time allows us to discriminate between its different levels and its relative risks. The expansion of the concept of countertransference blurs its borders, including phenomena that may be described from other perspectives as well, such as the analyst's disposition towards self-analysis and reflexive ability to understand what goes on in his/her mind as well as in that of the patient. The expansion of the concept also implies the risk of favouring narcissistic aspects of the analyst in his/her practice, which may lead to being too concerned with the self and losing sight of the need to regain an objective look on the patient and on the work in order to pursue the fundamental aim of analysis: that of listening to and transforming the patient. On the other hand, the restricted vision of countertransference may impede the analyst, fostering a pseudo-objective, stiff attitude that would make the latter leave aside his/her own emotions and relate to the patient from a false psychoanalytic self, if we may use Winnicott's concept. Not including emotional reactions in the here-and-now could compromise the possibility of analysis, especially in patients with serious personality disorders (Kernberg, 1965) or with severe deficits in their ability to symbolize (Green, 1975). A recent controversy between Daniel Widlöcher and Jacques-Alain Miller was published in the *Revista de Psicoanálisis* (Widlöcher & Miller, 2003; see also Bernardi, 2004). In this argument, Jacques-Alain Miller, defending the Lacanian perspective, shows that such a perspective rejects the notion of countertransference, this rejection being grounded in the search for objectivity on the part of the analyst, who must follow the patient's discourse from a radically different position, which excludes any consideration of the analyst's own emotions. From our point of view, Miller's position is based on a very narrow notion of objectivity, leading to the impoverishment of the field of analytic observation and taking away from the analyst a useful tool for understanding the patient and assessing and correcting his/her own work. We believe that objectivity in psychoanalysis, though problematic, cannot take place without reflection on the part of the analyst about the contribution of the two participants in the analytic process. In this sense, the study of countertransference becomes unavoidable.

We believe, then, that it is useful to keep both the broad and the restricted meanings of countertransference, differentiating between the various levels of the phenomenon and its role in the analytic work. The restricted notion of countertransference as an obstacle aims at describing specific or disruptive moments in the process of analysis, while the broad notion makes reference to the continuum of the transferential–countertransferential phenomenon. As in a figure–background game, both aspects of countertransference interact dialectically. At times, upon examination, what might, at first sight, have appeared a countertransferential obstacle becomes, when integrated into the therapeutic process, the main drive of analysis. At other times, countertransferential settings that seem to foster the patient's free association and that seem to be independent from the patient's transference may, in fact, turn to be an impediment that paralyses the process and insolates patient from analyst, who only convene in the defence of shared attitudes of resistance.

Dilemmas of countertransference

Freud introduced the term "countertransference" in his 1910 work "The future Prospects of Psycho-analytic Therapy", and he refers to it again in 1912 in "Recommendations to Physicians Practising Psychoanalysis" and in 1915, in "Observations on Transference-love". Freud's main concern was to point out the dangers implied for the analyst in an inadequate response to the transferential regression of the patient. The analyst could react "to transference love" with his/her own neurotic and conscious aspects, which could become "blind spots" (1912e, p. 116) that make the task more difficult. The countertransference was seen, thus, as unconscious resistance on the part of the analyst, which interfered with his/her attitude of evenly suspended attention. To solve this, Freud (1912e) prescribes self-analysis of analysts as essential, which will allow him/her to dominate countertransference and establish an adequate distance from the work, preventing the patient from being subjected to the analyst's own emotional needs. In other words, the analyst needs to be free before countertransference in order to discover and respect the patient's truth: "Psycho-analytical treatment is founded in truthfulness. In this fact lies a great part of its educative effect and its ethical value" (Freud, 1915a, p. 164).

Freud's thoughts on the subject of countertransference influenced subsequent arguments, making it subordinate to transference, which diminished interest in the phenomenon. Even though at the beginning of the century we find some comments on the topic by writers such as Ferenczi (1919) and Helene Deutsch (1926), it was not until the second half of the twentieth century that a new turn in the concept of countertransference took place: from being considered an obstacle and a weakness in the Freudian perspective, it became a key tool for understanding the patient. Undoubtedly the spread of the Kleinian theoretical frame influenced these transformations, which, as Etchegoyen (1986) says, represented a change of paradigm in psychoanalysis. Thinkers such as Racker (1948) in Buenos Aires and Heimann (1950) in London,[1] influenced by Melanie Klein's ideas and by object-relation theory, made a great impact on the development of analytic technique.

Heimann described countertransference initially as the whole affective response of the analyst towards the patient. This emotional response became the main tool to search the unconscious:

> Our basic assumption is that the analyst's unconscious understands that of his patient. This rapport on the deep level comes to the surface in the form of feelings which the analyst notices in response to his patient, in his "countertransference". This is the

> most dynamic way in which his patient's voice reaches him. [Heimann, 1950, p. 82]

From this perspective, it is the analyst's emotions, rather than just the verbal associations of the patient, that allow anxieties and the deepest unconscious fantasies to be inferred. However, Heimann considered that this material, which appears in the analyst, should not be reintroduced as such in the therapeutic relationship. Maintaining a distance from those who recommend disclosing the countertransference, she pointed out that countertransference has to be dealt with by the analyst without abandoning a position of neutrality and abstinence. But unlike Freud, who thought that the source of countertransference was in the analyst, Heimann (1950) considers that it arises from the patient: "From the point of view I am stressing, the analyst's countertransference is not only part and parcel of the analytic relationship, but it is the patient's creation, it is a part of the patient's personality" (p. 83). Later, Heimann changed her mind about the idea that countertransference is entirely a creation of the patient (Thomä & Kächele, 1985, p. 103). Along the same lines, Hanna Segal, sharing Melanie Klein's concern that countertransference becomes an excuse to hide the analyst's confusion or difficulties with understanding, pointed out that countertransference is a good servant but a bad master (Hunter, 1944, p. 54).

The ideas introduced by Heimann were fruitful, though, in developing the Kleinian perspective that the analyst, through the mechanisms of projection, introjection, and projective identification, holds unconscious fantasies that repeat, in the transferential–countertransferential situation, primitive object relations. Consequently, the analyst will experience either the patient's projected feelings, or those resulting from his own defensive struggle against these feelings (Hinshelwood, 1989).

The concept of countertransference in Río de la Plata

The pioneer works by H. Racker in the Argentine Psychoanalytic Association in 1948 were the point of departure of the reflection on countertransference in Río de la Plata (Uruguay). Racker relied both on classic Freudian concepts and on Melanie Klein's ideas, which had, by that time (1948), started to prevail in this area. He conceived the analytic relation from a bipersonal point of view. Through various clinical vignettes, he showed that countertransference is an unconsciously co-determined phenomenon from patient and analyst and that it plays an ever-present role in the process of analysis. "Transference and countertransference are totally united, fostering each other and creating the interpersonal relationship of the analytic situation" (Racker, 1958, p. 95).

Racker's vision seems more subtle than Heimann's, as he distinguishes between two forms and characteristics of countertransference: "*Concordant countertransference*", which contributes to the development of the analytic process, is the expression of positive countertransference sublimated and is the basis of empathy and of the analyst's processes of understanding his/her function as an analyst, which allows him/her to be an "analyst interpreter" (Racker, 1953, p. 234). The phenomenon of resonance and attunement that characterize it are made possible by the mechanisms of projection and introjection, which lead the analyst's ego to identify concordantly with different objects, impulses, and defences of the analysand.

In "*complementary countertransference*", on the other hand, primitive infantile aspects transferred to the analyst are manifested, including the patient's neurotic aspects. Racker takes up the idea of complementary identification expressed by Helene Deutsch (1926), and he points out that in it, certain identifications are at stake, in which the analyst takes the position of an object of the internal world of the analysand, identifying with it and reacting with the corresponding feelings (Racker, 1953). These infantile objects are, for Racker, the figures of the genital Oedipus and its heir—the classical moral superego, as well as the early Oedipus described by Melanie Klein, with its primitive defence mechanisms.

The bipersonal point of view was enlarged upon and deepened in the notions of dynamic field and of bastion by Madeleine and Willy Baranger (1961–62; Baranger, Baranger, & Mom, 1982). For the Barangers the unconscious dynamics of the analytic field are determined by the activation of a shared unconscious phantasy, which is generated by the interplay of the mechanisms of projective identification in patient and analyst. This phantasy cannot be understood as just the sum of what goes on in the patient and/or in the analyst, but as something new created "by both". When in these unconscious fantasies transferential and countertransferential aspects come to be intertwined and they become fixed and make transformations in the analytic field, a defensive bastion that may paralyse the analysis is erected (Baranger, Baranger, & Mom, 1982). This happens silently, and it implies unconscious "complicities" and conditionings, repetitive of the infantile history.

Racker's perspective, as well that of Willy and Madeleine Baranger, marked the thought of their time. According to Winograd (1999), the intersubjective exchange, the emphasis on the link between analyst and patient and on the contribution of the analyst to the analytic field, is one of the most original contributions of Río de la Plata psychoanalysis. However, this conception of the analyst as someone more implicated in the field makes the latter more vulnerable, in that not only must attention be paid to the construction of a specific type of interaction with each patient, but the analyst's ways of participating may also distort the construction and dynamics of such interaction.

We can see how throughout history the notion of countertransference gave rise to successive questions—How can we avoid its becoming and an obstacle? . . . How can we make it into an instrument? . . . To what extent is it determined by the patient or by the analyst?—with these, in turn, based on two major questions: Is analysis essentially an individual process of the patient, or does it take place within a relational or intersubjective process with the analyst? And, if this is so, to what extent does our ideal model of analysis reflect what happens in real analysis, in which vulnerability and fluctuations of the analyst are inevitable?

For us, undoubtedly, analysis is for the patient's mind; but so as to make this possible, analyst and patient must establish a strong and complex interaction in which the analyst must be alert so as to calibrate his/her own analytic instrument.

Countertransference as an alert for the analyst

What we frequently call countertransference refers mostly to conscious–preconscious emphatic feelings that have an instrumental character and are related to the professional role. But at other times we find unconscious reactions that have a disruptive character and may cause sensations of alarm (signal anxiety) in the analyst, with a concomitant defensive movement of rejection or denial. Accepting the existence of feelings of love, aggression, masochism, rivalry, and so on, towards the patient questions our professional role and exposes us to the paradox of finding the third narcissistic wound pointed out by Freud—that is, that man is not the master, as he wishes, of what goes on in his mind, in ourselves, and precisely when we are working as analysts. This is why even though countertransference, appropriately used, may become one of the most enabling factors in the process of analysis, its use is neither easy nor simple. This painful distance between real experience and personal or professional ideals may kindle anew the loss of the analyst's boundless infantile ideals, as pointed out by Racker (1953).

It may also lead to an illusion of clairvoyance, making us believe that countertransference is an infallible radar while losing sight of the fact that the unconscious itself is not a reliable instrument of knowledge. The phenomena of reciprocal identification, described by Racker, imply moments of unconscious indiscriminateness between patient and analyst, during which we may be inhabited by various objects of the internal world of the analysand, enacting sadistic or masochistic impulses in which the analyst's aspects and those of the patient are intertwined, with unconscious objects, impulses, and roles of the latter intermixed with the those of the analyst. Along the same lines of thought, Sandler (1976) pointed out that the patient may put pressure on the analyst so that he may respond by acting out certain roles. Sandler believed that it is useful for the process of analysis and the understanding of the patient to consider some aspects of the analyst's enactment "as a compromise between his own tendencies or propensities and the role-relationship which the patient is unconsciously seeking to establish. . . . It seems that a complicated system of unconscious cues, both given and received, is involved" (Sandler, 1976, p. 47).

Interest in the notion of enactment has recently spread in Anglo-Saxon thinking (Jacobs, 1986; McLaughlin, 1991; Renik, 1993). McLaughlin defines enactment as those "regressive (defensive) interactions between the pair experienced by either as a consequence of the behavior of the other" (1991, p. 595). Progressively, countertransferential enactment was considered as one inevitable characteristic of the process of analysis and as a potential factor of change to the extent that it is understood (Panel, 1992).

It is important to underline how close this perspective is to that developed by Río de la Plata psychoanalysts during the 1950s and 1960s (de León 2000). Cassorla (2004) has pointed out the relationship between the notion of enactment and of bastion according to Willy and Madeleine Baranger, since both imply acting a phantasy shared by analyst and patient. These phenomena show patterns of unconscious relation, enacted in the analytic interaction that become fostering factors of the process as they are interpreted: "The resort of the analytic process seems to be constituted by the production of resistance and bastions and their subsequent interpretative dissolution creating insight" (Baranger, Baranger, & Mom, 1982, p. 541).

There is also a tendency to recognize that it is only at a later point in time that we may see these experiences in perspective—that is, when we go back over what happened during the session, helped by reflection from self-analysis, personal analysis, or supervision. López (1988), talks about a "suspended attention on countertransference", the meaning of which we can only have access to retrospectively. Similarly, Louise de Urtubey (1994) refers to "working on countertransference". If we remain alert to its manifest components and the questioning it causes, we can retrospectively get to see some of its unconscious dynamics.

We believe that the moments of entanglement between the patient's experiences and those of the analyst (de León, 1993), when they are "mutually affected" (Paz, 1994) and during which transference–countertransference links are produced as well as enactments on the part of the analyst, are the basis of the process of analysis. These moments, in which the analytic asymmetry disappears for a while, shock the analyst into reflecting on the scope of his/her participation.

During the eighth month of analysis, a patient—"Laura"—had a transferential dream (de León, 2004) that exemplifies what we mean. Laura is a young patient who has sorrowfully complained about a lack of communication with her parents, during childhood as well as now. This complaint pertains mostly to her father, who is unable to express his feelings towards those close to him, and to the family's problems with communication at various difficult moments of the family history. The dream appears after a long period in which Laura's negative feelings towards the analyst had been interpreted—

such as complaints about certain aspects of the analytic relationship, which seemed cold and overly formal, separation, and anxiety about facing advances in analysis that exposed her to feared changes.

> "I dreamt *I was in my childhood home, at the desk where I used to do my homework, crouching. This armchair was there, and you came in, ordinarily dressed, in bedroom slippers, much less foreign than in the other dream* [in a previous dream the analyst had appeared talking as if distant]. *You were sitting, but with your back towards me. I started to say something, but it was you who started talking in the same tone that I was using—you talked a lot. I left the door ajar and I saw my mother going by in the hallway. You talked and talked, very familiarly. You started calling me 'tú'* [familiar pronoun in Spanish]. *I sat in my little bed. You did too, and you told me, holding my hand: 'It is you I love.' I was scared of the situation: I was a little girl, but anyway there was something erotic; I laughed.*"

The intense and direct expression of affection shocks Laura as well as the analyst. The dream fulfils, in the analytic scene, the infantile desire to accomplish better communication and a bond with the analyst, who represents the maternal figure in its oedipal connotations. The intensity of the expression of love in the dream calls the analyst's attention and takes her to review and reflect on her different ways of participation in the "manifest" work with the patient and on its unconscious implications. At this point it becomes clear to her that the dream has partially collected, as the day's residues, some of her ways of intervening and interpreting during that period of analysis. It is true that the analyst has spoken "a lot" trying to interpret, from the beginning of the treatment, Laura's ambivalence towards the analysis and her strong superego resistance, which made the analyst fear that she may quit the treatment. She is a patient with great interior potential, but one who has been stopped in her mental growth because she is very demanding and intolerant with others as well as with herself and because of her great feeling of loneliness. Transferential interpretations have been frequent, seeking to verbalize various anxieties of the patient towards analysis and the analyst. Regression in the analysis has equated "talking a lot" with the loving bodily approach visualized in the dream. On the one hand the dream expresses a recognition of the analyst's efforts, but it goes beyond this by proposing to share a fantasy of cure by love. The analyst thinks that, in some way, she has accepted her invitation, enacting her ways of intervention and interpretation of the patient's demand for closeness without being conscious of this.

But at the same time this enactment has allowed the analysis to advance, even though the "talking a lot" of the analyst constitutes, to a certain extent, the acting out of a complementary role that intends to compensate for primary traumatic deficiencies and experiences of lack of communication and silence. The countertransferential enactment has, then, a double face: it expresses phenomena of unconscious repetition and manipulation, but at the same time it offers a way for the transformation of infantile pathological experiences. The transferential dream also shows the working through of the patient. Examining the countertransference allows the analyst not to reject the complementary role but to restate it from a wider understanding of what has been taking place in the field, and it warns the patient and the analyst of the possibility of sliding towards a dangerous circle of mutual seduction. Coming back to the analytic role implies giving up the fantasy of cure by love, but doing it in a way that is tolerable for the patient as it is the analyst who absorbs the first shock of making these affects conscious and at the same time giving them up.

In this example the emotions that the analyst must face seem to be the usual ones found in any analysis, and they should not imply a special effort. However, the analyst cannot stop listening to the patient from her own story, which implies putting at stake her neurotic aspects and the way in which she faced—with greater or less success—the experiences of silence and lack of communication in her own life. The way in which she has internalized her experiences in analysis and her theoretical background also appear in this analysis, shaping her professional identity and uncertainties about her role. Taking a closer look, it can be seen that, as with the decay of materials, this daily work exposes the analyst to micro-impacts, fissures, and lines of decay that may be hard to perceive, in an area in which we believed we were invulnerable. This limit between talking and doing, between nothing happening and too much taking place, puts the mind of the analyst into a situation of great sensitivity bordering on the traumatic experiences. The examination of the countertransference may, then, warn the analyst about these situations, preventing more serious outcomes.

Countertransference, trauma, and vulnerability of the analyst

The analyst may become especially vulnerable in response to both internal and external factors. The analytic literature has pointed out the incidence of severe enactments by analysts and their traumatic effects on patients.

The sexual acting out of the analyst may be released as countertransferential reactions in response to repeated and intense transferential impact from a patient with a severe pathology. Seriously disturbed patients, such as borderlines (Kernberg, 1965), with predominantly primitive defensive mechanisms, especially massive projective identifications and intense destructive impulses associated to a sense of fragility, expose the analyst to the development of intense countertransferential reactions, narcissistic suffering, and masochistic reactions, as well as to traumatic marks of failure as analyst.

The notion of "projective counteridentification" proposed by León Grinberg (1956) is useful for understanding the analyst's response to the patient's projective identifications (Klein, 1946). When the projections are massive, the analyst's reaction is to a great extent independent of his/her own conflicts, and it corresponds predominantly or exclusively to the intensity and quality of the projective identification of the analysand (Grinberg, 1963, p. 117; see also Etchegoyen, 1986). While in Racker's complementary countertransference the countertransferential response was to a great extent related to the analyst's conflicts, in projective counteridentification the analyst is forced to passively play the role the patient assigns, independently on his/her own conflicts. Etchegoyen (1986) tells us that making this difference is not always easy, since "we cannot ignore the possibility, if he has allowed himself to be dominated by the projective impact, it is due to the countertransference neurosis. In other words, the analyst's passivity can turn out to be an 'active' way of not understanding or of preferring to be invaded" (Etchegoyen, 1986, p. 285).

The notion of projective counteridentification accounts for an unquestionable clinical fact: many patients tend to provoke the same reactions in different analysts. More recent studies seek to pinpoint the kinds of countertransferential reactions generated by different pathologies and note at the same time the various risks, for the analyst, of getting involved. To this end, Cabanne and Suárez (2000) have attempted to characterize countertransference in schizophrenia, borderline pathology, and bipolar disorder.

Often unrealistic expectations on the part of analysts—be it because of an incorrect diagnosis or because of other factors—feed feelings of omnipotence that make them lose sight of their possibilities and limits, and expose them to intense countertransferential reactions.

Gabbard (2003) shows the way a patient, "Jenny"—with a serious personality disorder and with a history of previous suicide attempts, who, as a child, had had an incestuous relationship with her father—comes to manipulate her analyst with the fantasy that responding to her need for sexual contact was the only way to save her from suicide. The analyst gives in to the patient's demand, and the acting out of the complementary roles has the characteristics of a *folie à deux* (Segal, 1957)—that is, a shared transference–countertransference psychosis. Gabbard points to the vulnerable areas of the analyst caused by multiple losses he had suffered at that moment of his life (the death of a sister and of a friend, and his separation). His patient's suicide threat exposed him to the possibility of one more loss, now as an analyst, which strengthened the fantasy of cure by love as a way of forestalling feelings of guilt or failure. In this case, the analyst could not allow himself the examination of countertransference. Perhaps the first sign that countertransference can give us is the impossibility to reflect about it, or the impossibility that it sets in motion in us a better disposition for self-analysis, warning us about something that is not well in us as analysts.

But it is necessary to state that there is no invulnerable analyst, as shown by situations like that related by Nanni Moretti in the film *La stanza del figlio*, which shows the dramatic impossibility for an analyst to face contact with his patients during the mourning period for the death of his son. Probably one analyst keeps strong whereas another fails, but certainly nobody is invulnerable to everything, and the examination of the countertransference may be useful if it alerts the analyst to the way he/she is being affected by the various problems in life, be they problems of love, death, health, pregnancy, family, money, and so forth. Situations that make us vulnerable show us the distance to the ideal, for our technique has been described for an analyst who is not affected by these problems. But this is an ideal image rather than a real situation. Testimonies that show the development of clinical work when the analyst is affected by these situations are worth studying.

Evelyne Albrecht Schwaber (1998) has related the impact exerted by an illness she had on a patient, "Mrs B.", who had suffered an emotional distance from her mother during childhood. The patient started to perceive changes in the attitude of the analyst, who was not emotionally available as she had been before, leading to an important regression in her analysis. The reflection of the analyst about her experiences allowed her to understand the effects on the patient of her emotional self-involvement. The patient, who because of the analysis was experiencing a moment of affective and sexual growth, felt rejected by her analyst, repeating the traumatic experience of loneliness that she had felt during her childhood. In this case, the disclosure of the analyst's situation allowed real aspects of the interaction to be discerned, in order to be free to search in the patient's unconscious psychic reality. Even though the topic of the disclosure by the analyst has acquired some relevance lately, Heimann (1959), had already confessed to a patient that she had not heard her because of the commotion that a colleague's death had caused her. The patient had thought that she was guilty because the analyst had not heard her at various points in the session, accusing herself of not being clear enough. The analyst made it clear to the patient that the lack of understanding during the session had not depended on the patient but on the fact that she was moved by the death of a colleague. In these situations the analyst's disclosure intends to recognize the realistic perceptions of the patient without attributing to them an unconscious meaning. In these cases, the disclosure paradoxically facilitates the position of neutrality by preventing the analyst from defensively attributing to the patient his/her own aspects. It is convenient not to oppose, *a priori*, disclosure and neutrality but to assess when, how, and why one or the other attitude is taken. Works by Dewald (1982) and Colson (1995), among others, have shown that losses, sickness, or the death of family members promote in the analyst a state of narcissistic vulnerability that influences countertransference. Colson explores the conditions in which it is possible to continue working with the patient and when it is necessary to diminish or discontinue the work of the analyst. Porras (1991) describes how the sudden death of a patient can also represent a traumatic situation for the analyst because it can interact with other mourning processes, and the way this strong experience can influence other analyses will depend on the way the analyst is able to work through this mourning.

The attitude of the analyst towards the patient may, in turn, be influenced by shared situations in the social context (Puget & Wender, 1982). So, at times of social violence or serious economic crisis, we must take into account the influence on the analyst's countertransference of his/her own traumatic experiences when the clinical material relates to these experiences. With patients who were tortured during dictatorships, the analyst must be careful not to deal with the social events defensively, as if they were phantasies, not to be paralysed by horror, and to prevent the patient from feeling isolated in the therapeutic process and excluded from the possibility of regaining his human condition and social insertion (Viñar, Viñar Ulriksen, & Bleger, 1989).

At other times the stressing events affecting the analyst are less visible, or they spring from the session itself, out of conscious and unconscious factors that reach the analyst through various channels of communication—verbal and nonverbal—with the patient. Even though the analyst does not deal with death in the same way as other health related professionals do, he/she is exposed to destructive impulses and to the feelings of loss that come up in the session, as well as to experiences of failure and crisis of ideals. An accumulation of inadequately processed micro-traumas may create conditions favourable for the development of a "burnout" syndrome in the analyst. This syndrome was first described in the case of health-assistance teams that faced very demanding situations, associated with frequent frustrations and leading to wearing out or "burning out" of expectations and ideals connected with the work. Cooper (1986) was probably the first to describe the "burnout" syndrome in relation to psychoanalysis, pointing out that the analytic work implies multiple paradoxes that place the analyst into narcissistically vulnerable situations. The analyst praises the patient for working on relationships, but he/she works in isolation. Deeply involved in the patient's life, the analyst has no contact with its reality outside the session. Once the analysis has finished, often there is no feedback about the outcome of a task in which he/she had been deeply involved for a long time. As Cooper points out: "The masochistic defenses to which analysts are prone appear as discouragement, boredom, and loss of interest in the psychoanalytic process. Self-reproaches are translated into projected aggression against the analytic work" (Cooper, 1986, p. 593). Over the last 25 years, this syndrome has been systematically studied in various professions in which care-taking of people is involved (cf. Prag, 2003), the main dimensions of such disorder being emotional exhaustion, loss of empathy, and a decreased feeling of personal accomplishment. There is no denying that these reactions do take place occasionally among analysts, but the problem starts when these symptoms appear steadily and progressively and pervade the professional and personal life of the analyst. We do not know of studies reporting the extent of this phenomenon among psychoanalysts, but we probably all know of cases of colleagues growing more and more dissatisfied with their practice as analysts, along with a deterioration in their personal lives. This topic deserves a more systematic study, since one of the common mistakes when faced with these cases is considering them exclusively in relation to individual vulnerability factors and not in relation to professional stress.

Psychoanalysis has paid much attention to individual resilience factors that allow these traumatic situations to be confronted. Let us remember the emphasis Bion (1952) placed on the mental function that he called alpha-function, which allows emotions that would otherwise be impossible to assimilate and would disturb the development of thought to be metabolized. There is also much interest in symbolization phenomena (Green, 1975) and mentalization (Fonagy, Gergely, Jurist, & Target, 2002) and its protective role in adult life as well as in child development. Together with factors related to individual resilience, attention must also be paid to social support as a protective factor in the burnout syndrome. This support comes from personal life (family and friends) as well as from relationships with colleagues. Psychoanalytic associations probably offer their members a useful sense of belonging and a strong shared ideology. But they might do so at the expense of fostering over-idealization or a restricted examination of real problems of professional life and mutual trust. Mechanisms of idealization lead to an avoidance of taking difficulties and negative phenomena into account, which, in turn, creates a paranoid atmosphere and clear deficiencies in training in many associations (Garza Guerrero, 2002; Kernberg, 1986). The analyst needs a space to share his/her experiences and to listen to those of other colleagues, masters, followers, and opponents. Probably the isolation in which the analyst works increases the need to have psychoanalytic institutions that hold their narcissistic and object needs, as well as their ambivalence towards their work. They should also be able to feel that they, in turn, can help their colleagues with their needs. As analysts' ability to examine the countertransference is a good indicator of their availability for the patient, some characteristics of psychoanalytic societies can show us their ability to be of help to their members—and perhaps one of the most important of these characteristics being the extent to which it allows the free circulation of alternative ideas and the debate between them in a respectful, critical, and creative atmosphere (Bernardi, 2002).

Countertransference and self-analysis

Countertransference is a privileged instrument that alerts the analyst about his/her functioning, professional as well as personal, via two kinds of indicators: countertransferential attitudes and the analyst's ability to examine them during or after the session.

Countertransferential reactions, even if they do not constitute the burnout symptoms mentioned above, may contain indicators to alert the analyst. We often encounter difficulties in working in a flexible and, at the same time, limited way with the movements of concordant and complementary identifications. When concordant identification is very restricted, we find an inadequate empathy with the patient, and we must examine whether his/her conflicts are not involved. When, on the contrary, concordant identification tends to be excessive and is maintained for a long time, it probably shows a need for mutual seduction that may stem from dual or specular phenomena underneath.

In a similar way, the absence as well as an excess of complementary identification phenomena could be warning us about difficulties of the analyst. If the analyst does not to a certain extent play a role as an object of the internal world of the patient, and if this is not expressed in enactments with the patient, very probably the analyst is finding very little motivation in the work or may be paralysed by personal conflict and defences. Very probably, too, in this case the analysis will result in very few changes in the patient. But, on the other hand, if the analyst cannot cease playing certain roles, if the enactments are fixed and become bastions, then projective identifications of the patient have probably got into the analyst, or the analyst may be projecting his/her own conflicts in the analysis.

From this perspective, what really matters is not just the ways of countertransference at a given moment, but especially what the analyst does with it. An indicator of this is whether the analyst can take a second look (W. Baranger, 1979) on it in order to modify his/her attitude. We referred above to the examination of countertransference, and now we would like to relate it to the analyst's disposition for self-analysis. In accordance with the terms used by Baranger and Baranger (1961–62) to refer to the disposition to be analysed, we define disposition towards self-analysis "as a suspended attention attitude oriented towards the inner world of the analyst, where there is a suspension of judgment and a possibility to expose our own convictions and ways of thinking and feeling to a questioning spirit which stimulates free association while allowing them to be noticed. This is only a first step towards self-analysis; yet, it is an important one, since it determines the size of the internal areas to which we gain an access" (Bernardi & de León, 1993, p. 31).

This second look of openness to self-analysis does not necessarily take place during the session, and it does not mean that the analyst has to perform a self-analysis, as Freud did. The important thing is that the pleasure of discovering something new about oneself should prevail over the pain of finding our own limits and conflicts. These limits and conflicts may sometimes point to the need of re-analysis. It is the task of the analytic institution to foster a reflexive and critical attitude towards the analyst's convictions and ideals, which are then put at stake in the dialogue with colleagues and the experience with the patient.

Notes

This chapter has been translated by Professor Andrés Larrinaga.

1. In 1949, Paula Heimann read her work "On Counter-Transference" at the XVI Congress of the International Psychoanalytical Association in Zurich; it was published in 1950 in the *International Journal of Psycho-Analysis.* A year earlier, in 1948, Heinrich Racker had presented to the Argentine Psychoanalytic Association his work "La neurosis de contratransferencia", which was published in 1953 in the *International Journal of Psycho-Analysis.* In general, it is accepted that these works were produced independently of each other.

Commentary

Otto Kernberg

De León and Bernardi's paper is an excellent, updated synthesis of the concept and clinical usefulness of countertransference, and the contemporary, global definition of the concept in contrast to the restricted, classical one. They present an objective and thoughtful summary of the arguments on both sides of the definition of the concept and—rightly, I believe—come out on the side of the contemporary, global concept. At the same time, they also convincingly caution us about the risk of over-extending this concept, such as including with the countertransference the analyst's general disposition toward self-analysis and the reflective ability to understand what goes on in his/her mind as well as in that of the patient. De León and Bernardi also caution us against the problem of expanding the utilization of countertransference to the extent of favouring narcissistic aspects of the analyst.

In what follows, I shall expand on some of their observations and point to areas of potential disagreements and complementarity of our views. To begin, regarding Freud's introduction of the term "countertransference", it needs to be added that, in Freud's stress on the need to "overcome the countertransference", he was reacting to his awareness of the frequency of boundary violations by his early male disciples, leading to their sexual involvements with female patients. The counterphobic attitude towards this concept, lasting from the 1910s to the 1950s, reflects, I believe, the hidden concern over those past boundary violations within the psychoanalytic community. It was only in the 1950s that the significant contributions quoted by de León and Bernardi opened the field of countertransference to what turned out to be a rich contribution to psychoanalytic theory and technique.

The authors rightly stress Paula Heimann's (1950) contribution, a landmark in this new development, pointing to the emergence of the patient's projected material as part of the countertransference reaction of the psychoanalyst and to the analysis of the countertransference as a significant contribution to clarifying transference developments. With respect to De León and Bernardi's stress on the contributions of the Argentinean school, particularly by Racker (1953) and Madeleine and Willy Baranger (1961–1962, and Baranger et al., 1982), I believe that it is fair to say that Racker's clarification of concordant and complementary identification in the countertransference is the most important, practical clinical application of the new understanding of countertransference as a composite structure, contributed to by aspects of both the patients' and the analysts' conscious and unconscious contributions.

Here, there are several issues that deserve further attention. To begin with, the concept of the "bi-personal analytic field" now needs to be put into the context of the contemporary stress on a "two-persons psychology", in opposition to the assumed "one-person psychology" of Freud. It needs to be stressed that, in all the contributions that pointed to the bi-personal analytic field in the 1950s and in what followed in the elaboration of these contributions, the assumption was that, in making the analysis of countertransference part of his technical task, the analyst was split between one part of him/her that, under the effect of countertransference, contributed to the transference/countertransference bind of the analytic situation, while another part of him/her—an "excluded third party"—would analyse this total situation as an aspect of the analyst's interpretive clarification and resolution of the transference. In other words, as I have stressed in earlier work (Kernberg, 2004b), the analytic situation requires a "three-person psychology". This has also been stressed within French psychoanalysis as the symbolic triangulation of the oedipal stage and is an essential precondition for the analytic utilization of the countertransference in contrast to its acting out. I believe that this is in accordance with de León and Bernardi's own views.

Another issue relates to the concept of "projective counteridentification" proposed by León Grinberg (1956): namely, the analyst's "getting stuck" in an unconscious identification with the patient's projective identification—being unable, therefore, to carry out that internal division between the emotional enactment in the countertransference and the secondary self-reflection that is part of the analytic task. This situation relates to one aspect of countertransference that deserves further exploration: namely, the difference between acute countertransferences that vary from moment to moment in the analytic situation and chronic countertransferences that distort the experience of the patient in the analyst's mind over an extended period of time. The latter represent a chronic "blind spot", of which the analyst may gradually become aware, without, at first, being able to resolve it. It is particularly with patients presenting severe character pathology and borderline conditions where such developments of chronic countertransference reaction are frequent and, as I pointed out in earlier work (Kernberg, 2004a), require self-exploration by the psychoanalyst outside the sessions or consultation. I believe this situation needs to be differentiated from momentary projective counteridentification and potential partial acting out of the countertransference under conditions of severe, regressive acting out of the transference in the sessions: here projective counteridentification is a transitory phenomenon that can be analysed and resolved in the course of the same session or in a few sessions.

Regarding the Barangers' concept of "bastion"—blind spots contributed to by unconscious collusion between patient and analyst that may constitute a particular difficult area to resolve analytically—de León and Bernardi refer to the risk of the analyst's over-identifying with problems of traumatized patients: for example, victims of political persecution and torture. One related problem is the patient and the analyst overlapping in socially or culturally determined bias or prejudice that may restrict the analytic work. For example, if a female patient rationalizes her masochistic abandonment of her professional aspirations by means of a socially prevalent assumption regarding the exclusive role of a woman "in her home" and her analyst is strongly identified with a paternalistic ideology consonant with that rationalization, a "bastion" may emerge that may significantly hamper the psychoanalytic work.

Or else, to the contrary, if a country is sharply divided between opposite political camps and the analyst's work becomes threatened by helping either persons of a persecuted minority or opposition or conversely, persons with a politically dominant, totally opposite view to that of the analyst whom he/she may, in turn, experience as threatening, bastions may evolve that erode technical neutrality. In this connection, the position of technical neutrality, an essential aspect of the analyst's emotional attitude (that is the counterpart to abstinence) may be more dependent on cultural norms jointly adhered to by patient and analyst than what we are usually aware of. The changing views within the psychoanalytic community—on homosexuality, for example—illustrate how socially prevalent beliefs may influence assumedly scientific thinking and attitudes toward patients.

De León and Bernardi refer to Joseph Sandler's (1976) concept of "role responsiveness" of the analyst to indicate how certain projections by the patient may resonate with particular dispositions in the psychoanalyst and become part of countertransference responses. I believe it may be helpful to keep in mind that, with patients presenting with severe psychopathology and the corresponding severe regression in the transference—particularly intense, primitive aggression directed at the analyst over an extended period of time—the analyst's habitual defences against aggression, both external and intrapsychic, may become activated, so that the latter may appear as having "reactivated" his/her most conflictual characterological traits in the treatment of a particularly patient. Such developments are also part of chronic countertransference reactions and require careful, and sometimes painful, self-analysis by the analyst outside the sessions with that patient, or, of course, consultation. In this connection, I do not believe that anybody is free from such developments, and from the need to consult with a trusted colleague in the course of the treatment of very sick patients.

One major, controversial issue is the extent to which the analyst should communicate the countertransference under certain conditions. Here my viewpoint is that the countertransference should not be communicated as such but tolerated internally by the analyst and utilized only as part of transference interpretations. De León and Bernardi mention a case from a colleague, in which the patient felt abandoned by her analyst who, at that time, was suffering from a serious illness. Eventually, she told the patient about her illness, recognizing that in the process she might have withdrawn from the patient, which led to an intensification and a change in the transference.

I believe that if a partial acting out of the countertransference occurs, in the sense that there is an actual behaviour by the psychoanalyst that implies that he/she has abandoned the position of technique neutrality—that is, of a concerned objectivity toward the patient—and the patient is aware of that inappropriate or changed behaviour of the analyst, the analyst should acknowledge that observation and not deny it. However, I do not believe that the analyst should go any further in detailing the nature of his/her problems but should simply acknowledge that he/she has been concerned with personal issues, may temporarily not have fully done justice to the patient's needs, and is aware of the responsibility of either being able to resolve these internal issues to an extent that would not influence the relationship with the patient or, should that not be possible, to interrupt, for this session or for the time necessary, the treatment of the patient. I believe that such an honest statement is truthful yet protects the patient from being overloaded with the analyst's problem and preserves the possibility of a full analysis of the transference.

I am fully aware that there may be extremely difficult life situations on the analyst's part that may interfere with his/her work, but, insofar as our work uses our own psychic responsivity to our patients, we owe it to them to treat them only when our psychoanalytic instrument permits us to do so. Again, absolute honesty about behaviour that, indeed, reflects something coming from the analyst rather than representing a distortion on the part of the patient is of the essence.

This brings me to the important reference by the authors to Cooper's (1986) contribution, pointing to masochistic defences of the analyst that may lead to "burn-out" symptoms—a development to which, as the authors state, has not been paid sufficient attention and that is an indication of the analyst's search for help on the part of colleagues. De León and Bernardi's points in this regard are very well taken. I wonder, however, whether addressing this supportive function for the analyst to the "psychoanalytic institution" is the most useful: I believe that, under such circumstances, consultation with trusted colleagues or peer group supervision may provide the most powerful assistance to an analyst in trouble.

To conclude, de León and Bernardi's contribution is a most welcome overview of the state of the art regarding countertransference assessment, utilization, and risks, enriching, in the process, the field of psychoanalytic technique.

3

Field theory

Madeleine Baranger

We first began to speak of the analytic situation as a field over four decades ago, after several years of observations, commentaries, and elaborations (M & W. Baranger, 1961–62). Over the years, this conception has been modified and has acquired greater precision, not only by means of our systematic observations but also through the contributions of various writers who have enriched our thinking.

I will not go into the initial conception, expressed in later works, at this time. Equally, there would be little sense in discussing directly today's provisional position with regard to our "field theory".

I have chosen to write a history of the birth and development of this concept and to point out the different stages and the mutual and foreign influences that have led to the present concept, which is always open to possible modifications and further development.

Field theory emerged for us when we realized that the conception of psychoanalysis and the psychoanalytic process that was being practised and taught had grown away from and had diversified markedly since its beginnings with Freud and his first disciples. Ideas used commonly as if acquired and forming part of our thinking implied,

---

First published in Spanish in: L. Glocer Fiorini (Ed.), *El Otro em la Trama Intersubjetive* (Buenos Aires: APA Editorial–Lugar Editorial, 2004).

when we thought about them more closely, a conception of psychoanalysis—the treatment, objectives, and process—that was quite far from and at times contradictory to Freud's initial teaching. The "classical" or "orthodox" concepts were not enough to explain what we understood and were doing. It was not only a personal difficulty; I think that no analyst could be satisfied with the technical works of 1911–15 [1914]. For the most part, the advice and instructions that they gave are still valid, but the practice itself began to expand them and make them more complex, so that they became almost unrecognizable and, in the case of some, obsolete.

André Green (1995b) said that the changes we see now had taken place much earlier: the date he set was Winnicott's article on regression in 1954. Changes are always detected long after they have occurred or begun. These changes had begun with Freud himself and kept on occurring, as is foreseeable and necessary in any scientific discipline, because of the corresponding demands of practice and theoretical development.

At the beginning, the analytic situation was described as the observation of a patient by a therapist or a neutral eye. But Freud soon discovered the obstacle of the transference: it emerged as a resistance opposed to the observation. On further consideration it emerged as constituting the analytic situation: the transference and its interpretation are characteristics that differentiate psychoanalysis from the other psychotherapies. Subjects diagnosed as or assumed to be incapable of transference—the "non-neurotics": psychotics or narcissistic neurotics—were not considered analysable, since they were unable to develop a "transference neurosis". Pathologies were seen as repetitions of traumata and childhood experiences that had not been overcome at that time. Their actualization in the analytic situation was indispensable for acting on them, because "it is impossible to destroy anyone *in absentia* or *in effigie*" (Freud, 1912b). They are new editions, copies of drive emotions, and fantasies that have become conscious during the analytic process, but whose particular characteristic is that they substitute a person from former life for the person of the doctor. The transference is linked to prototypes or childhood "imagos" that come up again in the present moment of the treatment.

The "transference neurosis" is an intensification of the transference in which the patient's major conflicts hinge on the personality of the analyst, with a simultaneous decrease in neurotic manifestations outside the treatment (symptomatic relief). It is a regressive process, the ultimate explanation for which is found in the "repetition compulsion", but which, in the present tense of the cure, allows conflicts to be interpreted "live" and to become memories, the infantile relation with the analyst thus returning to the past and ending neurotic suffering.

Transference, considered an obstacle when first discovered, became a special tool for the treatment, the analyst's otherness as an object becoming important beyond the therapist's authority or power of suggestion.

The conceptions of Melanie Klein and the theory of object relations proceeded to give it even more importance, as it considered these as total situations, repeated in the analysis, that transferred emotions and defences as well as object relations from the past to the present. Assuming that the source of the transference lies in the earliest stages of development that have formed the "deepest" levels of the unconscious, they recommend a technique by which the unconscious elements of the transference are deduced from the totality of the patient's material. The patient's accounts of daily life reveal, when we explore their unconscious contents, anxieties awakened in the transference situation that are handled with the same methods that were used in the past. Each detail of the transference is interpreted in terms of object relations and each reference to external objects as splitting and "acting out" of the analytic relation in the here-and-now.

In reaction to this conception and its excesses, which extend the transference to the whole relationship with the analyst, the current tendency is to differentiate and separate what corresponds in the transference to "real" persons—what we can consider as based on the contract, the so-called therapeutic alliance or the "basic" or "primary" transference—from the vicissitudes of the transference relation itself, the origin of which is in the past. A differential criterion that is often used is whether what the patient expresses is appropriate to the analytic situation and the analyst's person.

The important point in all these conceptions is that the analyst needs to use the transference—a natural and normal phenomenon of psychic life that emerges in the analysis as resistance—as a source of discovery.

The history of the countertransference has taken an analogous course. Freud himself soon recognized that certain errors or difficulties in understanding the material and its therapeutic handling were due to inaccessible aspects of the therapist's unconscious, and that he could only understand and accept the existence of affect or representations of it in the patient when he had previously recognized it in himself. It is precisely this observation that led him to recommend the personal experience of psychoanalysis before trying to analyse another person. The history of the concept of countertransference was no more than this: unconscious aspects of the analyst's childhood neurosis that impede an understanding of the patient.

But when he mentions it in 1910, at the Congress in Nuremberg, the prefix *counter* is aimed at reactions, mostly unconscious, revived by the patient's influence on the therapist. "We have become aware of the 'counter-transference', which arises in him as a result of the patient's influence on his unconscious feelings" (Freud, 1910d, p. 144). The countertransference is a remnant of the analyst's insufficiently analysed conflicts—something rather shameful and unconfessed, usually kept quiet, even in theoretical discussions.

The concept was reviewed and developed, on a parallel and nearly at the same time, by Racker in Argentina and by Paula Heimann, a disciple and follower of Melanie Klein at that time. Both announced its use for the understanding of the analysand's psychic processes, though with differences in theory and technical management.

The recognition of countertransference was more strongly resisted than that of the transference, and it was not as widely accepted. For some, countertransference is still a bad word.

In spite of this, analysis is considered a bipersonal situation (Rickman calls it "bipersonal psychology"), the debate centring on the precedence of transference or countertransference; the aim is always the greatest possible objectivity in understanding the patient, and the recommendation is to further deepen the analyst's analysis, in order to prevent or eliminate possible "blind spots" (a metaphoric term proposed by Laforgue and questioned by Freud).

The analytic situation now hinges on two centres: the patient and the analyst. The patient is no longer the exclusive and privileged object of observation. The totality of the situation is seen as the interplay of transference and countertransference. The analyst is considered a full member of the relationship. It is no longer a question of one person facing him/herself, through the analyst, but of two complementary and interacting people. Transference–countertransference neurosis (or psychosis) is seen as an artificial product of analytic technique, indispensable for the development and resolution of the treatment: it is now banal to admit the existence and efficacy of the countertransference (Pontalis, 1977).

Jorge Canestri (1994) characterizes today's psychoanalysis as "change" in the perspective that progressively converted the analyst's approach to the patient's life events and pathology into an analysis of situation, relation, and analytic process. The complex configuration resulting from the joint work of analyst and analysand—conceived in various ways depending on the psychoanalytic theory applied—finally created a new object of study. If a science can be defined by the limits of the subject it is studying, then it is true that the psychoanalysis of the second half of the last century can be conceptualized principally (if not entirely) as the science that deals with this new and unique figure of intersubjectivity.

Our question was whether this new approach in psychoanalysis, explicitly recognized by and underlying many clinical commentaries, is in line with previous knowledge, or whether it is a deviation, ultimately due to foreign influences, that finally disfigured the essence of what was considered psychoanalysis.

Our response was field theory.

The notion of field was not foreign to Freud's thinking as he described the analytic situation as a "battlefield" or a "chessboard".

De-centring the approach

We decided to take the analytic situation—precisely as it is occurring in the session and also throughout the process—as the starting point for our observation. Our guiding principle or methodological proposal was to begin with a study of clinical work and, from it, to deduce the factors that configured it, instead of constructing its comprehension as the sum and combination of the contributions of its two members.

For us, this concept was directed towards the theory of the cure. We did not intend to apply it, in these terms, to psychopathology or to metapsychology. It is true that the observation of what we consider the field allows us to add precision and definition to the knowledge of psychopathology. In this sense, the "field theory" seems to correspond fairly well to metapsychology as Widlöcher (1996) defines it: "a theory of psychoanalytic discovery which explains the mental work that ensures this discovery in analytic experience, as a model intended to represent the processes that develop in the course of a treatment".

But our initial intention was to contribute a different way of understanding the analytic situation that would lead to new progress and technical resources.

Origin of the concept

If we wish to trace how the concept progressively came to the fore of our thinking, we need to begin by quoting the influence on our training of Racker and Paula Heimann. We were accustomed, in theory and especially in supervisions, to warnings about the countertransference and its different effects on the patient and the analytic process.

We were also struck by some clinical observations, particularly in connection with children and psychotics: we saw that, in a family group, certain roles were distributed in a relatively fixed way and that, when an ill member was treated and managed to improve, another member of the family frequently stepped into the role of the sick, crazy, or stupid member. Analysts who treated children told of experiences that could be considered the opposite: as the symptoms or inhibitions of a child in treatment improved, one of the parents, more often the mother, who had perhaps presented serious limitations, changed her way of being, including even surprising physical changes. At that time, we described these situations as circulation of affects and roles.

We could only evoke Gestalt psychology and the developments by Merleau-Ponty, in *The Structure of Behavior* (1942), of the concept of Gestalt. Actually, in the case of each more-or-less lasting relationship in which the roles are distributed and become chronic or are interchanged in the context of a stable background—whether in a couple, a family, or a professional or institutional group—we are justified in speaking of a field situation. None of this is very new or deserves to be shown as anything but a coherent application of Gestalt concepts.

Other factors

Later, two factors intervened, leading us to take another step towards understanding the analytic situation more systematically as a field.

The first was a clinical factor, something that we had been questioning for some time in treatments, which we viewed as a peculiar resistance. It was manifested as a crystallized structure paralysing the treatment—a continuous, fluid, and multiform resistance that often seemed impossible to overcome. We attributed it to the patient's narcissistic defences that were fighting to avoid at all costs having to deal with a more or less important sector of the internal world—probably an unconscious refuge for powerful fantasies of omnipotence.

The experience of supervision with many colleagues taught us that, when the process got stuck, the supervisor's eye often detected the source of the stoppage: not only the patient's resistance, but also the analyst's counter-resistance, the two resistances communicating with each other and operating together. The analysts themselves, if they stopped to think and pay attention to their countertransference feelings and thoughts, with a "second look", often realized that the arrest of the process was due to involuntary complicity or collusion between the two members of the relation, who were working to keep the sector the patient did not want to discover either silent, separate, or split off.

We called this artificial neo-formation, a sub-product of analytic technique, a "bastion", using the metaphor of the advance defence that impedes approach to the more important, main part of a fortress. We later considered that a "bastion" underlies all serious resistances that endanger the treatment.

Another factor, a theoretical–clinical one, was our study of Bion's papers on small groups and our psychoanalytic group work, guided by his ideas: the recognition and comprehension of the "basic assumptions" that organize the life and work of a group.

Bion (1961) recalls Freud's observation that "individual and group psychology cannot be absolutely differentiated because the psychology of the individual is itself a function of the individual's relationship to another person or object" (pp. 130–131). Consequently, the analytic situation does not show us a psychology of the individual but a psychology of the couple; he concludes that

> the importance of the actual group is similar to the importance of analyst and analysed. [Bion, 1961, p. 132]
>
> . . . a group is more than the sum of its members. The explanation of certain phenomena must be sought in the matrix of the group and not in the individuals that go to make up the group. Time-keeping is no function of any part, in isolation, of the mechanism of a clock, yet time-keeping is a function of the clock and of the various parts of the clock when held in combination with each other.
>
> There is no more need to be confused by the impression that a group is more than the sum of its members than it would be to be confused by the idea that a clock is more than a collection of the parts that are necessary to make a clock. [pp. 132–133]

This is a version of the classical metaphor of the Gestalt as revised by Merleau-Ponty, that a melody is more than the sum of the notes that compose it.

> In a group the adult resorts, in what may be a massive regression, to mechanisms described by Melanie Klein as typical of the earliest phases of mental life. . . . [T]he regression involves the individual in a loss of his "individual distinctiveness" (Freud, 1921, p. 9), indistinguishable from depersonalization. [Bion, 1961, pp. 141–142]
>
> . . . no true therapy can be successful unless these psychotic patterns are made evident.
>
> Work-group's activity is obstructed, diverted, and on occasion assisted, by certain other mental activities that have in common the attribute of powerful emotional drives. These activities, at first sight chaotic, are given a certain cohesion if it is assumed that they spring from basic assumptions common to all the group. [p. 146]
>
> In group treatment many interpretations, and amongst them the most important, have to be made on the strength of the analyst's own emotional reactions . . . these reactions are dependent on the fact that the analyst in the group is at the receiving end of what Melanie Klein has called projective identification. . . . [p. 149]
>
> Freud's theories of the group derive from his study of the transference. Since the pair relationship of psycho-analysis can be regarded as a part of the larger group situation, the transference relationship could be expected . . . to be colored by the characteristics associated with the pairing group. . . . we should expect

> to find sexual elements prominent in the material there presented, and the suspicions and hostilities of psycho-analysis as a sexual activity in that part of the group which is in fact excluded from the analysis. [pp. 166–167]

I have chosen these passages to show how easily we can apply these descriptions of group dynamics to the analytic relation, following Bion's suggestion. It was not hard for us to make this step, since we were quite familiar with the Kleinian concepts that Bion used deliberately to explain group mechanisms.

Two Kleinian concepts

The first and, for our purposes, perhaps the more important concept is what Bion refers to as the "basic assumptions" organizing each moment of group behaviour. We consider that it refers to the Kleinian conception of "unconscious phantasy", as described in greater detail by Susan Isaacs in her article: "Nature and Function of Phantasy" (1952). Isaacs extends the concept of unconscious phantasy and considers that

> Phantasies are the primary content of unconscious psychic processes . . .
>
> [They] are experienced in sensations; later, they take the form of plastic images and scenic representations. . . .
>
> [They] are primarily about bodies, and represent instinctual aims, [libidinal and destructive], towards objects. . . .
>
> Phantasies have both psychic and bodily effects, e.g. in conversion symptoms, bodily qualities, character and personality, neurotic symptoms, inhibitions, and sublimations . . . early in the course of development, they are also rapidly elaborated as defenses, both against satisfaction of the wish and the contents of anxiety.
>
> Through external experience, phantasies become elaborated and capable of expression, but they do not depend upon such experience for their existence . . .
>
> Phantasies are not dependent upon words, although they may under certain conditions be capable of expression in words . . .
>
> Unconscious phantasies form the operative link between *instincts* and *mechanisms*. . . .
>
> Unconscious phantasies exert a continuous influence throughout life, both in normal and neurotic people, the differ-

> ences lying in the specific character of the dominant phantasies, the desire or anxiety associated with them and their interplay with each other and with external reality. [Isaacs, 1952, p. 112]

I think that these "unconscious fantasies" of the individual psyche are forerunners of the "basic assumptions" detected by Bion as schemes that organize group behaviour.

The other Kleinian concept to which Bion attributes special importance for group functioning is that of "projective identification", described by Melanie Klein in 1946 as a mechanism of the early psyche corresponding to the paranoid-schizoid and depressive positions. Bion describes this mode of projection as being aimed basically at the leader (therapist) in the group situation and at the analyst in the analytic situation.

The Kleinian concept renews the theory of the countertransference and naturally becomes a part of field theory as a mechanism of mutual patient–analyst influence.

Bion states that his

> experience in the counter-transference appears to me to have quite a distinct quality that should enable the analyst to differentiate the occasion when he is the object of a projective identification from the occasion when he is not. The analyst feels he is being manipulated so as to be playing a part, no matter how difficult to recognize, in somebody else's fantasy—or he would do it were it not for what in recollection I can only call a momentary loss of insight, a sense of experiencing strong feelings and at the same time a belief that their existence is quite adequately justified by the objective situation without recourse to recondite explanation of their causation. [1961, p. 149]

This is a striking description of the need for what we call the "second look", by the analyst personally or by a colleague consulted, in order to recognize the situation of the field as such.

Field theory

Speaking of the analytic situation and relation as a field simply amounted to giving another name to an increasingly recognized shift in the conception of the treatment—a development that we can summarize as going from the uni-personal to the intersubjective (A. Gibeault, 2001).

The analytic situation has a spatial and temporal structure that shapes an initial configuration: the setting, part of which is a contract to define the roles of both participants and the behaviour expected of each; free association for the patient and listening with evenly suspended and benevolent attention on part of the analyst; a limitation of *agir* [acting out], both for the patient, in and outside the session, and for the analyst, who must not intervene in reality (neutrality and "rule of abstinence").

The situation is organized to encourage the patient's neurotic regression and a partial regression, more controlled, in the analyst, that will allow him/her to share the analysand's unconscious experiences in his/her mental apparatus.

The discovery of the transference and later of the countertransference led to a clearer understanding of a bipersonal situation: analyst and analysand form a couple that participates in and contributes to a single dynamic process in which various situations constantly cover each other and occur in succession. It is a dual or multiple field, the basic ambiguity of which allows it to be inhabited by several possible couples in different types of relations that are experienced as being current.

Many analysts now describe this new vision of the treatment:

- According to Viderman (1970), the analyst is the second organizer of the analytic field, and the analytic situation is constructed as a creation of both persons.
- Pontalis (1977) describes in the countertransference movements triggered in the analyst in response to what is signified by the patient: discrete physical movements that echo a drive motion put into play in the analyst by what she/he has just heard, as if relayed for the analysand, who is often unable to perceive the drive motion; this is not produced only by the patient: the analyst's own history and ideology necessarily participate in the process.
- Guillaumin (1996) speaks of a migration of the analysand's internal objects in the direction of the analyst and, in return, a migration of the analyst's fantasies in the analysand's self representation.
- Luciana Nissim Momigliano and Andreina Robutti (1992) comment on field theory, saying that the analytic situation is an incubator of affects and thoughts that are not fully developed; it is mental functioning that comes from a part of the mind of one individual

and ends up in the mind of another, or in another part of the same mind from which it has come—a circulation of thoughts and affects.

- Minerbo says that the analyst listens to something that is different from what is said to him: the unconscious is not behind it, but elsewhere (1993). He quotes Hermann, saying that de-centring is the essential operation of the analytic method—also in divergent schools—and this de-centring determines the transference field that makes fantasies interpretable outside everything that the patient says (1992).
- Beatriz de León, also on field theory, says:

> in the analytic process a common base between patient and analyst is gradually created, making the movement between listening and interpretation possible . . . it is formed by the emergence of interactive dynamic nuclei when a close-knit interplay of images, affects and words is produced between patient and analyst, facilitated by regression . . . they emerge at special moments when the experiences of patient and analyst imbricate . . . these knottings support the dynamics of every analytic process and give each analysis its singular character . . . these interactive dynamic knots are true neo-formations, usually generated unexpectedly by the analytic situation . . . they condense conscious, preconscious and unconscious aspects of the interrelation between patient and analyst; the geometry of the analytic field . . . greater permeability to communication from unconscious to unconscious, where the flow of the analytic process evidences the primary process. . . .
>
> . . . made into images, the analyst's imaginarization, a representability produced by regression (as in dreams), they produce intense physical, gestural and affective representations—a phenomenon of active, mutual, regressive circulation in the analyst, something like what happens in the artist: a multi-mode functioning, comparable to the "capacity for rêverie", with which to metabolize and work through experiences in the session. . . . The patient's transformation is only made possible when it is mediated by a transformation occurring in the analyst's mind. [B. de L. Bernardi, 1993]

I quoted quite a bit of Beatriz de León's commentary because it provides a more detailed and beautifully expressed description than ours and translates our thinking with great precision.

Many analysts observe these facts; the divergences arise because of the way they conceptualize them and understand their mechanisms. Since I cannot mention them all, I will briefly quote from "interaction theory".

- Evelyne Albrecht Schwaber criticizes the term as foreign to psychoanalysis, since it suggests an external or social, rather than a psychic, field. . . . Although it can be used to evoke an "experienced" interaction, it always concerns the patient's psychic reality, with all its conscious and unconscious, conflictive and defensive expressions. That the phenomena it describes are central for our understanding of the psychic process and intrinsic to its results can be considered a truism: we always participate in what we observe and this observation is an integral part of the observation. It is the paradox that we can only understand what we observe from our own perspective, which is our specific mind model. [1995]

The interactionists are primarily concerned with discussing whether the analyst's objectivity is possible in the psychoanalytic clinical encounter, in spite of the analyst's irreducible subjectivity, as in the following comments:

- Real objectivity is assuming that subjectivity is an absolute condition (Renik, 1998).
- Interaction can only be elucidated by defining with precision the distortion and the point of view from which we are speaking (Albrecht Schwaber, 1995).

Sometimes, elements of reality are used:

- The situation is an encounter between two subjectivities, but there is a certain degree of objectivity in the analyst's subjectivity (Gabbard, 1997).
- The analyst's voice is a blessed voice that speaks partly the words of the patient's internal objects and partly his or her own subjectivity. The meaning is both constructed and discovered, and the need for the different object is outlined (Hanly, 1995).
- The analyst's perspective as an external object (partly) allows him or her to obtain information from this perspective (Dunn, 1995).
- The mere presence of analyst and analysand in the room creates an inter-subjective situation (Stolorow & Atwood, 1992).

These quotes go no further than to underscore the value of the encounter and the transference–countertransference dialogue, pointing out, in passing, the danger of a collusion with defences of all kinds, even complacency:

- There are examples of participation in a subtle analytic dance that could lead to an apparent success, which is actually pseudo-analysis (Albrecht Schwaber, 1997).

But they also try to identify a factor to differentiate the functioning of the analytic situation from a simple exchange between two people by emphasizing the structure of the relation.

Development of our thought

At first, somewhat tied to Kleinian thinking and the concept of the analyst's projective and introjective identification as empathy, we interpreted the field as being the result of intersecting projective and introjective identifications between patient and analyst; we even added the—borrowed—concept of projective counteridentification, which easily slides again to the centre of the situation, the starting point of the process, and the patient's "guilt": if the analyst fails, does not understand, or makes a mistake, it is because of the projective identification that the patient has forced inside her/him, in conjunction with the analyst's own characteristics, because the dominant fantasies of the analyst's world are not foreign to the shaping of her/his referential scheme or activity as an analyst.

It was when we reviewed Bion's studies on small groups that we modified and added precision to our thinking in a direction different from transference–countertransference interaction. Comparing what we understand about the analytic couple with what Bion described as mechanisms functioning in the group, we were reminded that "The explanation of certain phenomena must be sought in the matrix of the group and not in the individuals that go to make up the group" (Bion, 1961, p. 132) and that the analytic situation does not correspond to a psychology of the individual but a metapsychology of the couple. We then understood that the field is much more than interaction and intersubjective relation; we cannot explain its effects only by communication from unconscious to unconscious (mentioned by Freud) and the resonance produced in the analyst's mind by the patient's communications.

Translating what is described as the group's "basic assumption" to the individual analytic situation, we spoke of the "basic unconscious phantasy" that emerges in the analytic situation, created by the same field situation, which is the structure of the relation and which, in turn, continuously contributes to structuring it. This phantasy is not a sum or combination of the individual fantasies of the two members of the analytic couple, but an original set of fantasies created by the field situation itself. It emerges in the process of the analytic situation and has no existence outside the field situation, although it is rooted in the unconscious of the members, including important sectors of the history and personality of the participants, who take different imaginary, stereotyped roles in it, which vary with the moment.

Through these fantasies and their transformations, when understood and interpreted, the dynamics of the process are produced; from it, we can deduce characteristics of the two members, active and acting from the unconscious, that determine their psychic functioning and vicissitudes: "From intersubjectivity to intrasubjectivity, from the '*hic et nunc*' to the past and the future, from this apparently atemporal precipitate to the temporality of resignification" (Kancyper, this volume). This summarizes the dynamics of the field as Luis Kancyper understands it. Here, we are putting the accent on the notion of structure and its relation to a "basic unconscious phantasy", instead of searching for external factors.

Pontalis (1965) states that "the phantasy is a structuring and acting reality" and points out "the frequent collusion between phantasies" (pp. 252–253).

Minerbo (1993) assumes that the analytic dialogue itself gradually creates a new, previously nonexistent structure, constructed as a phantasy of the couple. Quoting Hermann (1992), Minerbo recalls that what is observable is the field, but what is not observable, which produces the field, is the subjacent couple phantasy, considered as the unconscious of the relation. He adds a commentary on clinical material in which the two members are actually "danced around by the field".

Beatriz de León thinks that the regressive situation of analysis produces this phantasy as a new structure—a basic unconscious fantasy of the couple,

> a mutual regressive circularity with a multi-mode functioning that is made possible by the substrate shared by patient and analyst . . . an actual, unconscious phantasy, acting at that moment, valid for both, in which both participate; it is not their production, but belongs to the field structure itself, which exists in function of the relation and the analytic process . . . something structured constantly, which supports and organizes the relation and the process. [B. de L. Bernardi, 2000, p. 32]

I have included these somewhat repetitive comments precisely to underscore what I consider differentiates field theory from other perspectives in terms of interaction and even of intersubjectivity.

In speaking of the field in the analytic situation, we mean that it is a structure, according to the conceptions of the phenomenology of Merleau-Ponty, constituted in the analytic relation, subtended by a "basic unconscious phantasy" in which analyst and analysand participate. It is a description of the observable and a hypothesis concerning the non-observable, as Hermann (1992) points out. What we do not describe is the source of the power to produce effects of mobilization and transformations in the analytic relation, beyond the contributions of its two members.

Perhaps others will help us to deepen our theory and hypotheses.

André Green: tertiarity and the setting

This is not an attempt to relate field theory to André Green's metapsychological contributions, which are constantly evolving and deepening. There would also be no point in trying to summarize our points of agreement and difference.

Already in 1974, in the paper he read at the Congress in London, "The Analyst, Symbolization and Absence in the Analytic Setting", Green made two exciting proposals: that the object of psychoanalysis is the construction of the analytic object and is the function of the analytic setting and its relations with mental functioning through the effects of symbolization that develop therein (Green, 1975). I consider that these proposals provide us with a clue that will help us to answer the question formulated above.

I think that "structure" corresponds to what Green speaks of setting, on condition that we explain—as Green does—that the setting includes a contract attributing functions (asymmetric) to analyst and patient, and that, at the same time, given the limitations and demands, the mental functioning of each of them is in effect. I view this structure, which stands above the two members and also envelops them, as the "third" that Green considers necessary for any relation to acquire the mobility that can lead to symbolization. Green attributes this function of the third, first, to the "analytic object, formed by the meeting of the doubles of each member of the situation", then to the potential transitional space created between the two, and, finally, to the setting itself, which enunciates the rules and their result.

The setting encourages movement towards symbolization, since containment or limits imposed on satisfaction necessitate the use of a substitute route, namely working through, which in its course of successive metaphoric and metonymic substitutions can lead to verbalization. This course is determined by the analytic situation and its demand to verbalize, which vectorizes it.

But the symbolization is already in the conscious and unconscious meaning of the functions assigned to the two members and to the relation between these respective functions that imitate, as they evolve, the different possible couple situations, metaphorically actualized by analytic regression, which encompasses the whole field of human behaviour.

From the start the analytic situation is organized as a symbolic and mythic metaphor. The power of the field considered as a structure is precisely its construction as a symbol; this is its symbolic weight, expressed at each moment by what we call the "basic unconscious phantasy". This is the way I understand Hermann's idea: that the analytic space is characterized by the fact of transforming all words into myths. Analytic clinical work can be viewed as offering the analysand a mythic–poetic circuit. The conventional history that he believes is his own reveals its mythical roots there (Hermann, 1992).

Other contributions

Field theory, whether or not it is called by this name, forms part of the thinking of many analysts today. I will mention a few who, though from different theoretical origins, have developed it along the same lines. These contributions are characterized by the mutation of perspective involved when focusing on the clinical situation as the fundamental fact and shifting the centre of study of psychopathology from the patient to the consideration of the analytic relation and the process, in order to reveal the phenomena constituting it and to encourage or impede the attainment of the aim of psychoanalysis.

Thomas Ogden

Perhaps Ogden should be quoted first, because he has a particular way of relating and integrating field theory to the role of projective identification as Bion sees it, and to the importance of the analytic object as a "third" as emphasized by Green, in agreement with Peirce.

Ogden (1994b) discusses the idea that in an analysis, apart from the analyst and the analysand, a "third subject of the analysis" functions: he calls this "the intersubjective analytic third" or simply the "analytic third".

Created by projective identification out of intrapsychic and interpersonal processes experienced asymmetrically, the subject of the projective identification contributes to structure the analytic relation, subjecting its members to this mutually engendered intersubjective third.

The "analytic third" is almost entirely an unconscious phenomenon.

Through reverie (Bion)—his/her ordinary thoughts, sentiments, and feelings—the analyst can access the understanding and symbolization of the specific nature of the subjective experience of both members and of the intersubjective experience of the analytic pair, in order to verbalize it in the interpretation.

Cesar and Sara Botella

The Botellas centre their conceptions on a detailed study of the event that is the analytic session (the "state of the session") and the "remnants of the session" whose secondary working through can provide new knowledge (Botella & Botella, 2001).

The state of the session is somewhat analogous to an intermediate state between waking and sleep—of an intermediate character, absurd, even monstrous, because of thought regression that approaches that of the dream but does not go as far as hallucination.

The actual neurosis inherent in the state of the session can lead thought, by a regredient route, to cathect the perceptions and visual images that gave birth to it. The analysand tends defensively to hypercathect the object (the analyst), producing in the latter a narcissistic and/or homosexual double. The analyst, because of his/her own formal regression, is confronted with the unknown and resorts to representability, which results in a figure both of representation and of perception.

This precise and detailed study leads us back to notions that have been familiar since Freud (1919h): concepts such as the double and "the uncanny" [*Unheimlich*]—of the psychic double, the auto-erotic double, and the narcissistic double—in order to allude to several aspects of the union between analyst and analysand and the mechanisms shaping it. They add the concept of "double work", which reveals what exists in the analysand in a non-representable state and is finally able to access the quality of a representation thanks to the united work of two complementary psyches.

Also, the concept of representability, referring to the "work of representability", alludes to a metapsychological conception of thought formation, seen as a necessary stage between the first physical, sensorial expressions of the drive and the achievement of its highest forms of concretion: verbalization and sublimation.

Christopher Bollas

Bollas, too, describes an intermediate zone between the subjectivity of patient and analyst, which becomes a vehicle of perception, creativity, and unconscious communication, the analyst sometimes echoing his patient's manifestation without knowing why but, authorizing him/herself to react in a deeply subjective way, creating a surprising amount of information (Bollas, 1976, p. 246).

The analyst, with a capacity for unconscious psychic work, incarnates the role of a transformational object, imitating in the analytic situation the mother's transformational function for the baby (Winnicott).

In another text, C. Bollas describes

> the secret idiom of mother and infant, communication by the route of affect . . . that resorts to a syntax made out of sounds, gestures and, even more, by the way the mother and child use each other (as well as other objects) to express themselves.

> Psychoanalytic therapy offers patients a space and a relation that facilitates sharing the secret mother–child culture . . . inside the analytic space, transference and counter-transference become a discourse that allows . . . the re-emergence of the mother–child secret . . . all analysis develops on this pre-verbal basis. [2001]

This description of modes of mother–infant communication leads naturally to a particularly understandable aspect of field theory.

Thought transmission: communication between unconsciouses

In "Recommendations to Physicians Practising Psycho-Analysis" (1912e), Freud indicated how the doctor must place his mind in evenly suspended attention (the second fundamental rule) in order to avoid interfering with the reception and understanding of the unconscious concealed in the patient's manifestations:

> He must adjust himself to the patient as a telephone receiver is adjusted to the transmitting microphone. Just as the receiver converts back into sound-waves the electric oscillations in the telephone line which were set up by sound waves, so the doctor's unconscious is able, from the derivatives of the unconscious which are communicated to him, to reconstruct that unconscious, which has determined the patient's free associations. [1912e, pp. 115–116]

He refers to the possibility of re-translating what has been discerned beyond the discourse into the patient's language. It is "unconscious-to-unconscious" communication, which is also termed preverbal or paraverbal communication.

Freud himself as early as 1890, in "Psychical (or Mental) Treatment", had pointed out some mechanisms of this communication:

> the relation between body and mind . . . is a reciprocal one [p. 284]

> . . . These concomitant physical changes are for the most part of no advantage to the person concerned; on the contrary, they often stand in his way if he wishes to conceal his mental processes from other people. But they serve these other people as trustworthy indications from which his mental processes can be inferred

> and in which more confidence can be placed than in any simultaneous verbal expressions that may be made deliberately. [p. 286]
>
> . . . The affects in the narrower sense are, it is true, characterized by a quite special connection with somatic processes; but, strictly speaking, all mental states, including those that we usually regard as "processes of thought", are to some degree "affective", and not one of them is without its physical manifestations . . . [p. 288]

The perception of these physical signs, not necessarily conscious, has always been valued beyond, concurrently with, and sometimes in contradiction to the patient's verbal discourse: associated or vicarious language sources that provide a different route to access the patient's internal world; in the analytic situation seen as a field, they also reveal secret aspects of the analyst to the patient. This type of communication is attributed to intuition and empathy.

Bion (1961) considers that it is effected by a pro-mental system, where physical and mental attitudes cannot be differentiated, found outside the field of generally recognized psychological investigation.

Julia Kristeva (1993) speaks of

> communication from unconscious to unconscious, from pre-psychic to pre-psychic, a dolphin communication, if I may use the word, to suggest forcefully that it is "semiotic", pre-verbal, and yet mobilizes our rhetorical capacities so that we can give it a communicable formulation . . . We know about the two moments of drive and sensory overflow that accompany the transference–counter-transference and its conjunction with the work of formulating the interpretation. . . . I am sure that the analyst's evenly suspended attention proceeds by identification with the unconscious, and beyond, with what Merleau-Ponty calls "the flesh" . . . an identification with the patient's flesh, a very strange basis for the art, but which we can reach at some point,—speaking of that bi-univocal immersion that is the transference–counter-transference.

Kristeva refers to the semiotics already mentioned by Freud. He also thought that an intense unconscious wish was what was transmitted to the receiver, precisely at the moment when the representation emerges from the unconscious on its way from primary process to secondary process.

In today's clinical work, it is assumed that these pre-psychic elements impose themselves when resistances impede their transformation into representation and word.

Among these occult phenomena, Freud was particularly interested in apparently supernatural phenomena such as telepathy and psychic predictions. His rationality resisted considering them as possible, but some such phenomena were undeniable.

In cases of psychic predictions, we may think that the medium or the psychic reader is specifically gifted or trained to re-establish images or thoughts from signs that are imperceptible to others.

But telepathy, when "an event which occurs at a particular time comes at about the same moment to the consciousness of someone distant in space, without the paths of communication that are familiar to us coming into question" (Freud, 1933a, p. 36), requires a different hypothesis.

Freud assumed that this transmission could insert "the unconscious between what is physical and what was previously called 'psychical' . . . the original, archaic method of communication between individuals [while] . . . the older method might have persisted in the background and still be able to put itself into effect under certain conditions." He compares it to "how the common purpose comes about in the great insect communities" (p. 55).

In field theory, we consider that persons with strong emotional ties may participate in the same affective structure organized by a "basic unconscious phantasy", which tends to become manifest in shared worries, memories, and representations—perhaps more frequently so when the people are separated. I understand that for scientific investigations of the transmission of data or other information—as was done, for example, in the Soviet Union—generally subjects are used whose lives or affects are linked in some way: mother and child, two siblings, or persons in other types of intimate relationships.

Returning to the analytic situation, we could mention other coincidences, few of which are mentioned in the literature, supposedly because of analysts' reluctance to reveal anything about their countertransference, such as complementary or mirror dreams of analyst and patient. In Argentina, we know of a case published some time ago by Luis Rascovsky (1976). It is my belief, gained from analysts' and patients' comments and in seminars and supervisions, as well as my personal experience, that such cases occur fairly frequently. I consider that analyst and patient, even outside the session, belong unconsciously to the common structure of the analytic relation. In certain circumstances—often just before or during a separation—the "basic unconscious phantasy" leads both to express in dream images contents that clearly refer to a shared experience of loss or abandonment.

Brief clinical complement

The analytic relation varies with the personality and characteristics of its two members. We know empirically that not just any patient can function with any analyst and, reciprocally, that not all analysts work well with all patients, even though their previous analysis may have broadened their intuition and capacity for understanding. Mutual adaptation by analyst and patient is needed for the formation of the field and the creation of the shared basic unconscious phantasy. A subject may visit two or more analysts before finding one with whom he/she can settle into the analysis and initiate a psychoanalytic process. "The analytic object is formed by a homologous and complementary relation between analyst and patient" (Green, 1990a, p. 88).

When I was in training, I was taught that in the preliminary interviews we should try to make, beyond or together with the psychopathological diagnosis, a diagnosis–prognosis of the way the analytic relation would be constituted. This, too, can be viewed as a problem of the field and of the possibility of creating a basic unconscious phantasy wherewith to organize its structure.

The confrontation between generations as a dynamic field

Luis Kancyper

> In brief, it is exciting that adolescence has become vocal and active, but the adolescent striving that makes itself felt over the whole world today needs to be met, needs to be given reality by an act of confrontation. Confrontation must be personal. Adults are needed if adolescents are to have life and liveliness. Confrontation belongs to containment that is non-retaliatory, without vindictiveness, but having its own strength. . . . Let the young alter society and teach grown-ups how to see the world afresh; but, where there is the challenge of the growing boy or girl, there let an adult meet the challenge. And it will not necessarily be nice.
>
> In the unconscious fantasy these are matters of life and death.
>
> D. W. Winnicott, 1971, p. 150

The confrontation between generations is essential to the acquisition of identity. Its primary precondition is the presence of an other who is neither soft nor arbitrary and who makes a tension of differences between opposites possible, while both parties acknowledge that being opponents is not tantamount to being enemies.

Without this arch of tension, the dialectics of identifications, disidentifications, and re-identifications that extend throughout the life span but are particularly in the foreground during adolescence—characterized, in turn, by the mental letting-go of the parents through the overcoming of the Oedipus complex and the end of sexual development—are paralysed.

Just as parents are much needed for access to the Oedipus complex, they are equally important in enabling it to be left behind, so that the child can choose sexual objects that are neither incestuous nor parricidal and can have access to new vocational interests beyond parental mandates.

This is a long, difficult, and tortuous path, where many stop before they reach the finish-line.

Dolto points out that adolescence is a movement full of strength, of life promises, of expansion, and that there are no adolescents without problems, without suffering: it is perhaps the most painful period of life, though it is, at the same time, the period where joy is most intense (Dolto, 1989, p. 19). It also represents a period of the most intense grief, anxiety, and joy for the adolescent's parents, who, because of the sometimes tragic reactivation and resignification, at a time that coincides with menopause and ageing, of their own long-bygone adolescence, must go through a complex psychic readjustment.

Relinquishing the narcissistic desires of immortality and completeness invested in the child by the parents, the pygmalionic desires (Kancyper, 1990) related to fantasies of making and modelling an other in the Maker's own image so as to exercise an absolute and omniscient power over the product fathered by them, gives rise to anxiety and demands to be mourned. Moreover, parents must admit the child's blooming sexuality and the difference in developing strength between the child who is growing up and the parents who are getting old.

Parents must wage several battles on different fronts at the same time, in order to be able not only to demystify the Narcissus, Pygmalion, and Oedipus who take shelter in different degrees in every parent's soul, but also to dismantle Cronos, who devours his own offspring. It is a painful and complex task for the adolescent's parents to admit the inexorable irreversibility of the arrow of time, as well as the final prohibition of the devouring re-appropriation of children.

However, what happens when the father of the adolescent cannot let go of his own adolescence and cannot, in consequence, carry out his paternal function? Or when he cannot go through all these mourning processes, which are characterized by a complex, multiple causality? The difference between generations fades, and the necessary oedipal rivalry becomes a tragic narcissistic struggle. There is no confrontation: there is, instead, provocation, avoidance, or disavowal of the generation gap, hindering the development of individual identity.

Confrontation between generations and dynamic field

Confrontation between generations needs to be considered as a whole, as a product of an intersubjective relationship in which parents and their children define each other, involved as they are in a dynamic field.

The field as a structure is different from the sum of its parts—just as a melody is different from the sum of its notes—and it gives rise to a basic unconscious phantasy, which, being a field product, is rooted in the unconscious of each of the members (M. Baranger, 1992).

But why introduce the concept of dynamic field into the description of the act of confrontation between generations?

The concept of field has antecedents in Gestalt psychology and in Kurt Lewin's work; it was later reformulated by Merleau-Ponty in order to establish a psychology of man "in his situation"—that is to say, able to notice and to understand psychic facts by means of their significance in the context of intersubjective relations.

Madeleine and Willy Baranger (1961–62; Baranger, Baranger, & Mom, 1978) incorporated this concept to view the analytic situation as a bipersonal field:

> The analytic field is a shared ground between patient and analyst that gives rise to original phenomena, different both from what can be observed in each of the members and from the sum of what each of them contributes to it.
>
> In this perspective, the object of study is neither the patient, nor his interaction with the analyst, but the field of the analytic situation as a producer of original phenomena and pathologies.
>
> In consequence, we aim at revealing the movements that take place in this field, mostly unconsciously, and which shall be the

> starting point of our clinical and theoretical formulations. [Baranger & Baranger, 1961–62, p. 129]

In this chapter I extend the concept of field out of the analytic situation and into the dynamics of the confrontation between parents and children and between siblings as well.

We can describe or understand parent–child relationships and those between siblings when involved in an act of confrontation not as isolated individuals, but as a structured totality, the dynamics of which result from the interaction of the members with each other and with the overarching situation in a reciprocal causation within the same dynamic process.

This other view makes possible a better understanding of the increasing levels of complexity that can be ascribed to the progressive and regressive phenomena that appear in the interweaving of the generations, to the dynamics originated between intrasubjectivity and intersubjectivity, and to their effects on the structuring and destructuring of each of the members' psychic agencies.

The functionality of the field of confrontation between generations demands a radical asymmetry between paternal and filial functions; but both parents and child are required to go through different and complex processes of psychic working through:

1. mourning processes in the narcissistic, oedipal, and pygmalionic dimensions (Kancyper, 1995);
2. mourning for the irreversibility of time, which implies the ageing parents' progressive fall from immortality and omnipotence and their admission of the new generation's growing strength as well as the latter's questioning of previous certainties and of dominating relationships within the family, institutions, and society;
3. gradual or paroxystic loss of the child's idealized image of wonderful parents and of the wonderful child who can manage to fulfil parental ideals (Kancyper, 1985);
4. reorganizing of identifications and of resignification, both in the parents and in the child (Baranger, Goldstein, & Goldstein, 1989).

The concept of field permits an approach to many problems in the confrontation between generations as manifestations of the presence of pathology specific to that structure, where both parents and children take part to varying degrees and complementarily.

This intergenerational dynamic field depends, on the one hand, on the effects emerging from parental and filial narcissistic systems, which are not symmetrical, together with their fantasmatic configurations of immortality, omnipotence, idealization, and of the double, and, on the other hand, on the incestuous, parricidal, and filicidal fantasies that arise from the Oedipus complex and the furtive excommunication and confraternity fantasies belonging to fraternal complexes. I would like to emphasize that the fraternal complex is not a mere consequence of the Oedipus complex; rather, it has its own specificity and may—or may not—be articulated with the nodular complex of neurosis (Kancyper, 1991).

We can classify various distortions in the dynamic field of generational and fraternal confrontation according to the predominance of (a) stifling, (b) disavowal, (c) paralysis, (d) inversion, (e) provocation, (f) avoidance of generational interweaving.

These different dynamic fields are conditioned by the singular simultaneous interaction displayed between characteristics of the child and those of the parents: (a) "do-all", (b) "*puer aeternis*" [eternal child], (c) authoritarian, (d) soft, (e) parent–sibling, (f) "blind-eyed", and (g) servile.

Dynamic field pathology in generational and fraternal conflict

I give the term "field" to the structure created between parents and child, or between siblings, which allows the development of generational and fraternal confrontation.

This field has three aspects:

1. *a formal aspect* or rule of the game (the presence of a differentiated other who allows the tension between opposites);
2. *a dynamic aspect*: the evolution of parent–child and fraternal relationships as the various changes and conflicts inherent in successive evolutionary stages start to appear;
3. *a functional aspect*, as the dynamics of the field allow a recognition of the difference, as well as the display and the evolution of the conflict, between generations and between siblings.

A dynamic field that is not working may be one in which the confrontation process is paralysed or has been replaced in one way or another, hindering the identity process.

Perversion is established within the field of generational and fraternal confrontation when the structuring aim of the conflict has essentially become a perverse activity that puts to one side the main objective of the act of confrontation, which is to tend to the growing assumption of similarity, difference, and complementarity between participants.

This takes place when confrontation is experienced and administered in ways that gratify perverse traits of the parent–child or fraternal couples by means of a thanatic defiance, leading to pseudo-individuation.

The perverse trait in sadomasochistic or voyeuristic–exhibitionistic fields is often intellectualized by parents and their children or among siblings—for example, the theory that extols the virtues of tolerance and altruism so as to smother masochistic, self-sacrificing satisfaction, or the one in which the entrenchment of liberating spontaneity and transparency masks a perverse exhibitionistic satisfaction; both find support in theoretical approaches that at the same time consolidate the crystallization of the "bastion".

> The "bastion" is an immobilized structure which hinders or paralyses the process.
>
> None of the participants is ever aware of it, as this structure manifests itself by indirect effects: it stems from the complicity between both participants in unawareness and in silence in order to protect a bond that must not be disclosed. This situation culminates in the partial crystallization of the field, in a neo-formation built around a shared fantasmatic set-up where important aspects of the histories of both participants are involved, and which assigns each a stereotyped imaginary role.
>
> Sometimes the bastion remains as a static alien body while the process apparently follows its course. At other times, the whole field becomes pathological as the bastion completely invades the field and removes all functionality from the process. [Baranger, Baranger, & Mom, 1978, p. 1102]

I consider that Baranger's concept of field tends to be wrongly seen as an equivalent to the mere existence of transference in the analysand and of countertransference in the analyst. It amounts to more than that: the field creates an original fantasmatic whole, a basic unconscious phantasy. This concept awakens much resistance among analysts—but how is this phantasy different from others?

The phantasy emerges within the analytic process created by the field situation, and events follow through it. It is not the consequence of unconscious communication, nor of a mechanical interweaving of projective and introjective identifications; rather, it is the precondition of these identifications. The basic unconscious phantasy is an original production; it originates in the field, and its dynamics are structured through it. It includes important aspects of each member's personal history, and each assumes a stereotyped, imaginary role.

This phantasy does not derive its existence out of the field situation, although it is rooted in the unconscious of each of the members.

Starting from this field, unconscious phantasy, the psychic functioning and the intra-subjective history of each of the members can begin to be unravelled: from intersubjectivity to intrasubjectivity, from "*hic et nunc*" to the past and the future, from this apparently atemporal precipitate to the temporality of resignification.

Admission of the status of the basic unconscious phantasy of the field is conditioned by the overcoming of several obstacles:

1. This concept inflicts a new wound upon the analyst's narcissism and power, because of the loss, once again, of the illusion of omnipotence and self-sufficiency. In the relationship with the other and with others, the phantasy created in and because of the field situation "spreads its wings": it is autonomous and exercises its own influence over the individuals, like the unconscious, which has its own rules and psychodynamics, independent of rational and conscious control.
2. Accepting the presence of this concept in every stable and long-term relationship demands the inevitable assumption of complex additional work. The analyst cannot go on maintaining his position as a passive observer of a situation that is unfairly alienating and frustrating; rather, a shift in position is required. Through his/her own psychic functioning, conditioned by his/her own complemental series, the analyst too has a part, in asymmetrical degrees, in the outcome of the relation's trophic or destructive destinies.
3. The extra psychic work imposes the relinquishing of an automatic

> tendency to place in others the torrent of projections and projective identifications or onto oneself the massive return of these, in order to admit that, in the end, each of the participants in the field has a part in the production of the intersubjective phantasy and, furthermore, that the latter is original and originated by that particular field situation.

The fruitfulness of this concept opens up new paths, such as the advent of oneness, correlative to the consolidation of otherness; it allows the revision of the individual's own history as well as that of the other, and the admission of points of similarity, difference, and complementarity between participants (Kancyper, 1995).

Narcissism and sadomasochism

Sadomasochistic relationships between parents and their children give rise to a perverse dynamic field, where confrontation and confirmation are replaced by the act of provocation. This provocation holds back the participants in the field in a thanatic defiance, which blocks the separation–individuation processes as well as the complementary support between generations.

These relationships present a bi-directional movement. Although in the great majority of cases the accent of sadistic polarity relies on authoritative parents, because of the exercise, use, and abuse of an asymmetrical relationship of control conditioned by the biological, psychic, and social dependence of the child, in other cases it is the children themselves—regardless of their real age—who act as domestic tyrants to their parents, the latter ultimately becoming mere servile slaves of their master–children within a relationship of sadistic complementarity.

I shall describe three distinct categories of parents who satisfy their own sadomasochistic and narcissistic drives while carrying out their parental functions.

From a clinical point of view, they present conspicuous differences from each other. According to the perspective of the dynamics of narcissism and its link to the masochistic component and to the establishing of the different kinds of fields they constitute along with their children, I shall classify them as (a) servile parents, (b) parents who "turn a blind eye", and (c) "do-all–sur-dying" parents.

Servile parents

Servile parents tend to satisfy their own masochistic needs for punishment, and they obtain a narcissistic gain through the fulfilment of an ideal that is governed by the logic of the tragic hero's sacrifice.

They are self-denying and long-suffering parents, who can put up with anything and who, in addition, intellectualize their excessive unconditional service with the entrenchment of an ideology that extols the virtue of unlimited altruism but which, in fact, masks an economic gain of suffering in their parent–child relationships. The more they suffer, the better they feel they are as parents, both before themselves and before others: the narcissistic secondary gain of parental masochism.

Servile parents usually suffer from "delusions of insignificance"—precisely as Freud describes the *Selbstgefühl* of the melancholic in "Mourning and Melancholia" (1917e [1915]). They consider themselves unworthy of any respect or consideration on their children's part. They suffer from various outstanding debts that drive these guilt-ridden parents to acts of compulsive reparation, and their children often take advantage—either consciously or unconsciously—of the feelings of anxiety and guilt of these "deficient parents", assuming the complementary role of home-executioners and predators who ill-treat the self-sacrificing parents.

Through their children's sadism, these "servile parents" bring to life, morally and/or erotogenically, their own masochistic fantasies from "A child–parent is being beaten". They operate as unconditional servants, carrying out strict ceremonials—genuflecting, observing rules of courtesy, and offering various gifts—in order to win their wonderful children's favour and ill-treatment: the princes and counts who live at the mansion, enjoying every privilege and having no duties. A pathology of the dynamic field—the perverse sadomasochistic field—comes into being.

Parents who "turn a blind eye"

Parents who "turn a blind eye" constitute a pathological field along with their children. They keep with the latter a "pact of silence" that turns out to be the by-product of a narcissistic collusion between the parents and the children.

An alliance is established between both of them, in order not to speak, not to hear, and not to see. The main active mechanism of this dynamic field is not indifference but ignorance. What prevails is not so much guilt as anxiety, which often manifests itself through severe symptoms in the participants.

Both servile and "sightless" parents are gagged before their own children. But there is a conspicuous difference between them with regard to the act of intergenerational confrontation. While in the former confrontation is replaced by the act of provocation that subjugates and ill-treats each of the participants of the perverse field through a thanatic defiance (Dora's case history: Freud, 1905e [1901]), in the case of the latter—"sightless"—parents we are witness to the paralysis of the act of confrontation.

The bipersonal basic phantasy in the dynamic field formed by "sightless" parents and children is "escape and flight" (for example: "I don't say anything, because if I do, I'll get out of control, or I'll hit or kill him, or he'll kill me in retaliation"), and children tend to experience this parental inhibition as if it were carelessness on their part, while the parents, in their turn, often suffer anxiety because they cannot break the wall of silence. In cases such as these, there can even be established a field of extreme avoidance that paralyses the intergenerational confrontation.

Let us remember that in the case of homosexuality in a woman described by Freud (1920a), the adolescent "retired in favour" of her mother and her brother and "turned away" from her father; instead of confronting them, she tried, by means of revenge—and through sadomasochism—to provoke her father and run away from the "sightless" mother who was narcissistically competing with her own daughter.

It could be said that what had taken shape between them was a particular field phenomenon and, furthermore, a bipersonal phantasy rooted in the unconscious of each of the participants—the phantasy of "retiring in favour of someone else".

> The girl we are considering had in any case altogether little cause to feel affection for her mother. The latter, still youthful herself, saw in her rapidly developing daughter an inconvenient competitor; she favoured the sons at her expense, limited her independence as much as possible, and kept an especially strict watch against any close relationship between the girl and her father. A

> yearning from the beginning for a kinder mother would, therefore, have been quite intelligible. [Freud, 1920a, p. 157]
>
> The mother herself still attached great value to the attentions and to the admiration of men. If, then, the girl became homosexual and left men to her mother (in other words, "retired in favour of" her mother), she would remove something which had hitherto had been partly responsible for her mother's dislike. [pp. 158–159]

In another paragraph belonging to the same case history, Freud points out:

> The mother was tolerant, as though she appreciated her daughter's "retirement" as a favour to her; the father was furious, as though he realised the deliberate revenge directed against himself. [p. 160]
>
> Furiously resentful and embittered, she turned away from her father and from men altogether.
>
> After this great reverse she forswore her womanhood and sought another goal for her libido. [p. 157]

Freud points out in a footnote to this paper the essential role of generational and fraternal confrontation in constructing the adolescent's identity. He underlines that "retiring in favour of someone else" instead of confronting the parents on the one hand and siblings on the other discloses very complicated conditions in the mind, which take part not only in erotic choice, but also in the sphere of vocational interests (Kancyper, 1991, 1992).

In this case history (Freud, 1920a), we can see a pathology in the field dynamics—a perverse field through the revengeful provocation of the father ("to turn away from the father") and a "blind-eyed bastion" along with the mother and the brother ("to retire in favour of someone else").

The pact of silence between the homosexual's mother and her daughter constituted an obstacle to generational confrontation. It stemmed from collusion between certain traits of the mother and corresponding aspects in the daughter's unconscious. A sphere of unawareness had been created in which both participants took part, as if they had agreed not to see what was going on with the daughter. It could be said that between them a "link" had been created, an intersubjective "sightless bastion"—the concept of bastion as described by the Barangers, which refers, as I mentioned earlier, to an artificial formation and is a by-product of analytic technique, but can also be extended to the bipersonal field between parents and their children and among siblings.

The "do-all-sur-dying parents" (Kancyper, 1994)

The "do-all" parents position themselves simultaneously in a narcissistic and masochistic dimension. They are chronic debtors to the ideal agencies of their own personality: ideal ego–ego ideal–superego. They adopt an attitude of sacrifice before their children, offering themselves as a magical substance that can resolve any conflict; at the same time, however, they block in the other the origination and development of true desire, cancelling, furthermore, the essential function of anxiety as a signal–affect to detect danger.

This signal anxiety is a device activated by the ego, as if it were a sensory organ specialized in perceiving internal and external realities; this function needs to be exercised and developed by each individual. But "do-all" parents tend to assume this function in their children's name, depriving them of this alarm-signal that alerts and organizes, similar to the symbolic function of thought that allows the weighing up of tensions in the external and internal worlds.

These parents conceal behind an apparent omnipotence their own acute anxieties, which stem from imaginary situations of uncertainty, from the potential danger of their children abandoning them because of catastrophic fatalities: illness, accident, kidnapping, or death. Due to the interchanging of roles, certain children often exercise an abusive power that exploits precisely those manifest and latent anxieties and feelings of guilt in their all-powerful parents, who become beggars subjected to the tyranny of their own creatures.

"Do-all" parents are also "*sur*-dying"[1] because they build their view of the world on the defensive foundations of escape, control, and attack mechanisms in order to protect themselves from castration/death; because in this family environment anxieties and feelings of guilt are the central axes of the members' psychic life. They live to save themselves through permanent reassurance in order not to suffer. But they pay for their right to existence through constant suffering: *dolo ergo sum.* They prefer avoiding displeasure to seeking pleasure, but they cannot stop suffering (Kancyper, 2000, p. 125).

And it is precisely this tension of uncertainty, which stems from the mortification caused by the action of uncanny anxieties, that protects them from the absolute lack of tension characteristic of the Nirvana principle—paraphrasing the poets: "Dying life, living death".

"Do-all-sur-dying" parents generate addictive relationships with their children, and they enslave each other, creating a retaliating pendulum that sustains itself because of the validity of this link between uncanny anxiety and power (Kancyper, 1994).

These parents exercise their power by means of "spells" and fascination techniques and through compulsive offerings—material, verbal, and affective—in order to keep the threats stemming from their own anxieties neutralized, with the aim of guaranteeing the unconditional presence of their children–objects so that they will never leave.

The "do-all-sur-dying" parents position themselves as deities who perfectly assist their children, fulfilling every *Ananké.* They are placed in a phallic position and consider their child as a helpless anti-anxiety object who is always there in order to guarantee the presence of a mirror-like and marvellous other, so that, when the father mirrors himself in his own "work", he reflects his own omnipotence as the "Maker"—the pygmalionic father who models and creates his own creature. The repetition of these parental anxieties turns "do-all" parents—although wrapped, before themselves and others, in the disguise of "demi-god" parents—into domestic slaves, into unconditional servants to demanding children.

In this aspect "do-all-sur-dying" parents are different from the other parents described earlier, because from the very beginning they occupy the place, of the ideal ego, of the all-powerful parents: the "Three Wise Men" who magically provide a world without conflict, struggling to combine infantile narcissistic perfection with their facile denial of a world that is, in reality, quite unpleasant, and the psychic existence of destructive and self-destructive drives that are essentially incompatible with narcissistic happiness.

The "do-all" parents' need to feel that they are above everyone else is so intense that it allows them to disavow the very high costs of suffering and displeasure that result from their masochistic behaviour, so as to keep sustaining the phallic logic of narcissism in their relationship with their children. I propose to apply the term "masochistic dimension of parental narcissism" to the relationship between narcissism and the thanatic component between "do-all-sur-dying" parents and their children, whereas "narcissistic dimension of parental sadomasochism" applies to the relationship between servile and "unseeing" parents and their children (Kancyper, 1998, p. 13).

From subjection to generational confrontation: the fathers of silence

Bezoari and Ferro, speaking of the unconscious phantasy organizing the analytic field described by the Barangers, point out: (a) that it is a bipersonal phantasy that cannot be reduced to the classic conception of unconscious phantasy (for example, that of Susan Isaacs)—that is to say, as the expression of the individual's instinctual life; and (b) that the unconscious bipersonal phantasy is formed by the interweaving of groups of projective identifications in which both analyst and analysand are involved (Bezoari & Ferro, 1990).

> Assuming this radically bipersonal model, that of projective identification, also produces important changes in the conception of transference and countertransference dynamics. According to the Barangers, what is classically conceived of as transference-neurosis (or psychosis) shall have to be considered within the notion of field as transference–countertransference neurosis (or psychosis), that is to say, as a function of the couple. The patient's pathology does not enter the field as such, but only in relation to the analyst, who in turn actively contributes (although, it is to be hoped, to a lesser degree) to the constitution of that field pathology which shall be the objective of analytic working over. [Ferro, 2001, p. 193]

Along the same lines of thought, we can study the obstacles in the process of generational confrontation as a dynamic field that involves, as a whole, mourning processes and the reordering of identifications and resignifications, both in the growing child and in the ageing parents. Between them, a field phenomenon is created—one that could only be created between that child and those parents (Kancyper, 1983). Metaphorically speaking, a precipitate is formed between these interacting elements, and a blocking or a paralysis of the field dynamics occurs.

Final reflections

Generational confrontation requires consideration as a whole, as a product of an intersubjective relationship in which parents and children define each other, involved, as they are, in a dynamic field.

As I have already pointed out, here I extend the concept of field out of the analytic situation and into the confrontation between parents and children as well as between siblings. We cannot describe or understand parent–child and siblings relationships when involved in the act of confrontation as conflict between isolated individuals, but as a structured totality, the dynamics of which result from the interaction of the members with each other and from the situation overarching both in a reciprocal causation within the same dynamic process.

This other view makes possible a better understanding of the growing complexity that can be ascribed to the progressive and regressive phenomena that appear in the generational interweaving.

The functionality of the field of generational confrontation demands a radical asymmetry between paternal and filial functions. But both parents and child are required to go through different complex processes of psychic working through.

From a clinical point of view, the individuals can be grouped into three categories:

1. those who are unable to confront their parents and siblings;
2. those who perpetuate an endless confrontation through a thanatic defiance (the perverse field);
3. those who have put behind them the thanatic defiance and have managed to engage in a trophic challenge, obtaining all the structuring benefits for the construction of identity from the generational and fraternal confrontation.

Notes

Translated from Spanish by Valeria Muscio <valeriamuscio@yahoo. co.uk>.

1. Sur-dying: neologism that refers to a particular psychic functioning that, instead of being governed by the pleasure principle, is governed by the flight from illness or death.

Commentary

Antonino Ferro

It is with great interest and pleasure that I have read these admirable papers by Madeleine Baranger and Luis Kancyper.

I think that the authors, constructing a metaphorical image of a solid and fertile tree, succeed very well in showing clearly the roots, the trunk, the branches and fruits of the concept of field, which has been refined over the years, since it was first introduced in the famous work *La situación analítica como campo dinámico* (Baranger & Baranger, 1961–62).

The application of the concept of *field* to the study of psychic phenomena has a well-known history, anticipated by Gestalt psychology and Kurt Lewin's work, where it acquires a greater epistemological autonomy, freeing itself from any residual physicalist traces. Not so well known, perhaps, is Merleau-Ponty's reworking of this notion. (The latter has greatly influenced the Barangers' philosophical education). Merleau-Ponty adopts the notion of *field* within the theoretical framework put forward by Koffa and Lewin, as a useful foundation for a psychology of *man in his situation,* facilitating the observation and understanding of the meaning of psychic processes within the context of intersubjective relationships. This formulation would thus offer a solution to the age-old conflict between naturalistic objectification and solipsistic introspection (Bezoari & Ferro, 1991).

The concept of field has brought about a momentous qualitative leap and a "catastrophic" change within psychoanalytic theory.

Madeleine Baranger shows us how this concept owes its origins to the very notions of transference and countertransference and to the Kleinian formulation of projective identification. She also claims that the notion of field was created "in the field"—if you would excuse my play on words—as it was born, in fact, from the clinical problems raised within contexts of supervision and from our daily work with patients.

The movement from previous formulations in terms of a one-person psychology to a radically new two-person perspective on what goes on in the consulting-room indeed constitutes a new paradigm. Together, patient and analyst structure a field that is a function of the inner lives of both participants, brought together by a shared basic unconscious phantasy, which develops at that very moment when the setting is constituted.

It goes without saying that there is a certain degree of asymmetry, and that is what confers on the analyst the mandate to take "a second look", in order to work through that area of cross-resistance, defined as "bastion", to the creation of which the analyst him/herself has contributed.

The continuous interplay of bastion formations—second-look metabolization of the bastions—and, again, new bastion formations, represents a kind of breathing process for the field, which, ultimately, must become ill—first with the same illness as that of the patient and then with the patient's and analyst's joint illness—to be able finally to get better. Moreover, the recovery of the field triggers a transformation of the internal worlds as well as the biographical histories of patient and analyst alike, through a succession of continuous *après coups*. In this respect, I wish to recall the other two seminal papers "Process and Non-Process in the Analytic Work" (Baranger, Baranger, & Mom, 1983) and "The Infantile Psychic Trauma from Us to Freud" (Baranger, Baranger, & Mom, 1987).

Furthermore, I find the new developments in Madeleine Baranger's latest work, and above all, her references to Bion, worthy of comment.

In particular, I am interested in the link with Bion's thought, which seems to go beyond his work with groups and extend to his formulations of the analytic situation as such. Bion, in fact, talks about the "patient as best colleague" (1978); he emphasizes the centrality of the continuous interplay between projective identifications and reverie as the essential driving force of analysis, and he also develops the fundamental concept of "waking-dream thought", a by-product of the alpha-function.

The concept of "waking-dream thought", of "beta-elements" (proto-sensory elements) not yet transformed into alpha-elements (proto-visual thought elements), can be explicitly married to field theory, so much so that we can conceptualize a field alpha-function, field beta-elements, and a field waking-dream thought. They all are a joint creation of patient and analyst, with the understanding that the latter occupies a position of relative asymmetry, being the holder of the clinical responsibility for what goes on in the session (Ferro, 2002).

Given these premises, it follows that the Barangers see insight as an experience of the analytic couple, not reducible to the introspective self-knowledge that individuals can acquire of their own psychic reality. Within the analytic situation, insight obtains when analyst and patient reach a shared understanding of the unconscious fantasies active in the field, at any given time. This coincides with a re-structuring of the field itself, because the possibility to think and communicate—both affectively and cognitively—extends to areas previously occupied by bastions, which are thus immobilized and dissolved. What had previously been split off and deposited in the bastions by the couple in a confused manner can now be integrated, symbolized, and discriminated, and this allows both analyst and analysand to see themselves more clearly in relation to one another. That self-recognition will be "conscious and silent" within the analyst, "conscious and manifested" for the analysand (Baranger, Baranger, & Mom, 1983).

Another extremely interesting point of the Madeleine Baranger's reflection is her reference to the most significant developments in contemporary psychoanalysis. While she is close to some of those contributions, from others she departs considerably. She clarifies important issues in relation to intersubjectivist theories, from which field theory represents a much more radical departure, as it posits a shared basic functioning of the analytic dyad, as a foundation of the field.

It is also significant that the notion of field has "travelled" well, instigating fertile new advances in psychoanalytic theory—first of all in South America: in Uruguay, Argentina, Brazil—and at this point it suffices to briefly mention the existence of a large quantity of works inspired by this theory. It has also travelled through Europe, and in Italy it has creatively influenced Francesco Corrao's thinking. Corrao (1986) defines the field "as a function whose value depends on its position in space–time; it is a system with an infinite number of degrees of freedom, resulting from the infinite possible determinations assumed by it at every point in space and at every instant in time" (quoted in Ferro, 2002).

Corrao had previously suggested a psychoanalytic reading of some of the characteristics of the model of field advanced by modern physics. One of these features is located in the crisis of the assumed clear-cut distinction between the observer and the object of observation, whereas in quantum physics, as Heisenberg has demonstrated, it is not possible to decide—except perhaps arbitrarily—which objects are to be seen as belonging to the observed system and which are, instead, part and parcel of the apparatus for observation. Incidentally, as we might all remember, Heisenberg's famous principle of indeterminacy is founded on the acknowledgement of a mutual interaction between the observer and the observed object. Unlike classical theories, modern physics does not view this interaction as so negligible, or so small, or, at any rate, so controllable as to be able to eliminate its influence through calculations.

Equally fruitful have been the applications of field theory to child analysis (where it has permitted both the dynamics in the session and the movements pertaining to the wider field, which includes the parents' fantasies to be captured more accurately), serious pathologies, and the institutional domain.

Luis Kancyper is a very prolific and creative writer who has, over the years, been consistently making very significant contributions to the notion of field. His theory exerts an original and essential function, in that it promotes a very clear and strong distinction between the field model and others that, favouring the transference–countertransference axis, would qualify more as intersubjective. The field model is characterized by a basic couple unconscious phantasy, which emerges precisely when the field is structured.

To look at the interactions between patient and analyst is very different from the formulation of a field as a new structure, with its own pathological nuclei. In some way, the field operates irrespective of the sum of the two functioning minds, inasmuch as it is something new and different, which strongly reminds me of Bion's "basic assumptions", Ogden's "analytic third", and the notion of "functional aggregates" developed by Bezoari and myself (Bezoari & Ferro, 1991).

This work of Kancyper's presents some original and innovative applications of the concept of field, with all its peculiarities, which he extends from the strictly therapeutic context to the confrontation between generations. He points out how the conflict between parents and children generates a "field" that is a function of both parties while, at the same time, not belonging exclusively to either.

Kancyper had previously shown the usefulness of the notion of field in child analysis, which can be conceptualized as a triadic field, including the young patient, the child's parents, and the analyst. Needless to say, he also demonstrates the invaluable modifications of technique that necessarily accompany this new model.

In the present work, Kancyper considers adolescence as a critical phase that cannot be resolved unless we widen our horizon to encompass the dipole constituted by adolescents and their parents. Temporally, a child's adolescence is located at the intersection of two "pivotal age-crises" (Ferro, 2002b): the children's developmental crisis and the crisis of the parents' decline.

In this text is also featured one of Kancyper's favourite concepts: the "fraternal complex", which is as significant as the Oedipus complex to the structuring of the individual's identity.

I believe, however, that what Kancyper describes as an external application of the concept of field can also be brought back into the strictly analytic field. When he talks about the different perversions the field can acquire in the confrontation between generations, describing with unsurpassed astuteness all the possible articulations of these pathologies, he could also be indicating that similar pathologies might develop in the "generational confrontation" that occurs within any analysis, between progressive and regressive aspects and new and obsolete ones, between mature, adolescent, and infantile features.

This is why the rich variety of models that the author gives us with invaluable depth (the formation of the "bastion", which stifles any possibility of transformation; servile, distracted, or pygmalionic parents) can also aptly describe the dysfunctional aspects that can beset any analysis, to the point of paralysing the field or causing field malfunctioning (interminable analyses, negative therapeutic reaction, etc.).

Moreover, Kancyper (1989, 1991) has shown us the pitfalls of the abuse of models, when they are utilized as if they were orthodoxy: the patient who is always right or always wrong, the one who cannot live without the analysis, the one who marries the analyst's model, to which he/she has become enslaved.

I may be right in saying that the implications of this work go even beyond the author's intentions, as they reveal not only the heuristic fruitfulness of the application of the field concept outside the consulting-room, to understand better a complex reality like generational confrontation, but also, conversely, that what is seen as pertaining "outside" can be brought back into any analysis—not to mention the usefulness of this model to enhance our understanding of the drawbacks of an excessively rigid adherence to some psychoanalytic theories.

Of the many hypotheses put forward, I would like to pick out the self-castrating way of withdrawing from conflict through an act of renunciation, which seems to be the diametric opposite of an oedipal conflict, leading to death. It is, in fact, an avoidance of something feared to be terribly explosive, which could only result in a solution like "*mors tua vita mea*" or, conversely, "*mors mea vita tua*". It is between those two extreme possible mental scenarios—between Scilla and Carybdis—that the creative confrontation between patient and analyst is located, and likewise the confrontation between supervisor and supervisee or between psychoanalytic models.

Luis Kancyper seems to personify Bion's concept that defines analysis as a probe that constantly expands the field that it explores. In fact, he talks about those very themes and knotty problems that we all try to address and solve, every day, in our analyses, supervisions, or, indeed, in our lives. In this respect, I believe that health consists in being aware of our illness and trying to balance one well-known illness with a different one. Sometimes it also feels healthy to stick our heads outside the field with its pathology, even just for a short time, and breathe the pleasurable fresh air of our separate, unique identity as mortal beings.

What I would like to emphasize, above all, are the clinical implications of the concept of field (some already pointed out here by Madeleine Baranger, and others to be found in her numerous previous works). Before I do that, I wish to express my profound gratitude to Willy and Madeleine Baranger and Luis Kancyper and implicitly to all those who have creatively addressed the subject of the analytic field.

Clinical implications

A corollary of field theory is that the criteria of analysability and termination of analysis are freed of any misconceived "objectivity". Somehow, within this perspective, both the alpha and the omega of our analytic work are changed. The possibility of beginning an analysis, carrying it through, and concluding it (and at what given point it can be terminated) derives no longer from criteria related to the patient's pathology; rather, it is specific to that individual couple.

The analytic process thus acquires characteristics idiosyncratic to the functioning of "that" analytic couple at work, and the idea of a natural process wanes. Each couple will have their particular way of proceeding through the analytic work, and even the events of an analysis—the negative therapeutic reactions, psychotic transference, and countertransference—will belong to that individual couple. Naturally, there needs to be a limit to a possible subjectivistic drift, which is, indeed, bounded by the analyst's ethicality, personal analysis, and training, but also by the latter's responsibility to metabolize only those narrated facts in need of urgent "alpha-bet-ization" by the analytic couple, and not others. In this respect, some concepts deriving from narratology, such as the "limit of interpretation" and "limit of the opening of all possible worlds", can provide significant assistance in setting boundaries.

It goes without saying that field theory requires that analysts need to be continually vigilant and to maintain in good working order their main tool: their mental life.

The analyst co-determines the development of the analysis, the process of which also depends on the analyst's mental functioning (which will co-constitute the field), on his or her capacity to contain the patient's anxieties and projective identifications. Naturally, we have to take into account the possibility that the analyst's functioning might be temporarily compromised or that s/he might even reverse the flow of projective identifications.

Field theory radically changes how we listen to the patient's communication, which will be seen as also a product of the quality of the analyst's mental functioning or malfunctioning. At the same time, this is also very helpful inasmuch as the patient always functions as a mirror and reflects any movement of the analyst, when s/he comes too close or moves too far away. The analyst will thus be able to make use, among other things, of what the patient signals, to change his or her interpretative attitude.

The concept of field noticeably widens the idea of a relationship, extending it so as to encompass the analytic situation as a whole, including the setting and the rules. This offers us the possibility of thinking that many analytic events "belong in the consulting-room", before they can be referred to the relationship. The analytic space thus becomes a kind of intermediate area where scenes and characters that would otherwise remain immobilized and imprisoned can come to life and find embodiment. Within this framework, the analytic relationship is one of the functions of the field itself.

Clearly, the age-old dilemma between internal and external reality becomes somewhat irrelevant, because what matters are the phenomena occurring within the transitional space of the field, to borrow Winnicott's language.

Moreover, I would like to point out once again how fruitfully we can match these conceptualizations relative to the field with Bion's thought. For instance, it might be possible to describe a field as a hyper-beta field, with an insufficient alpha-function, which leads to ruptures of the setting or acting-out phenomena.

Conversely, we might have a well-functioning field, with a relative balance of beta-elements belonging to the field and a capacity of the alpha-function to transform them and to form alpha-elements.

The *field*, thus defined, acquires the following characteristics:

- it is transformed into a spatiotemporal dimension where the emotional turbulence activated by the analytic encounter occurs;
- it is a function in relation to both members of the couple, with a very high degree of unsaturation;
- it becomes a space–time context, aiming to foster the narration of stories that represent the "alphabetization" of the proto-emotions within the couple.

The *transformations of the field* take place through a constant labour of co-narration carried out by analyst and patient together, who become "two authors in search of characters" (Ferro, 1992) and who "alphabetize" their proto-emotions, thus permitting them to evolve.

In the *field,* the semantic scope of the concept of interpretation widens so as to include all the unsaturated conversational interventions of the analyst.

An essential element of the field is the *analyst's reverie*—that is, the analyst's capacity to get in touch with his/her waking-dream thought, and its constituting sub-units, the alpha-elements, which can then be narrated verbally and so activate the transformational elements of the field. No less central, however, are the narrative derivatives of the patient's waking-dream thought and the alpha-elements that make them up.

Within this framework, we could conceptualize the patient's narrative as an endless re-narration of how s/he "photograms" aspects, events, and forces within the field. What follows from this is that there is no patient's discourse that does not pertain to the field.

The analyst's *attention,* previously turned to the observation of the patient's communication and the countertransference, is now focused on the characters that come alive within the field and continuously bring news about its life and state.

To the complexity of the *present, horizontal field,* alive in the *here-and-now,* I would add the evenly matched complexity of the *vertical field,* which includes the transgenerational: this is how time enters the consulting-room.

We thus approach not merely the geometry formed by the "internal world" and the "relationship", but also the geometry of stories and their transmission. Present in the consulting-room are not just patient and analyst with their two-dimensional "photos" of parents, aunts and uncles, or grandparents that will be interpreted and revealed in transference interpretations: rather, there will be three-dimensional characters, from different temporal dimensions, demanding or needing, in any event, to be able to come on stage autonomously. At this point any interpretation made within the field becomes a transference interpretation.

I believe that the analyst, within this dimension, needs to allow him/herself to be occupied by these transgenerational "freeze-dried" elements, awaiting the sap of the containment provided by the field to come alive and acquire the temporal depth of history.

The scene that comes alive in the consulting-room operates not only along a spatial axis, but also along a temporal one: "undigested facts", "pockets of beta-elements", as well as "packets of alpha-elements" enter the room.

Thus we are faced with a web of complex experiences that we are not always equipped for, and so we feel as if we were in "Tonight we improvise" or, if you prefer, in "authors in search of characters" by Pirandello.

In this regard, I could suggest many other interesting areas for further exploration: for instance, how the narrative function within the field might give a containing form to pockets of unthinkable contents:

- the analyst's transgenerational legacy enters the consulting-room as that which concerns the person of the analyst and *as that which concerns the transmission of the analytic function,* including his/her blind spots (which hopefully the field, if appropriately monitored, can point out!).
- We can trace back our history, even our own history as psychoanalysts, not just as an empty ritual, but also as a way of discovering our *transgenerational legacy.*
- We can open up new vistas on the concept of projective identification and emotional turbulence. With recourse to a cinematic image, we could think of the opening shot of *Jurassic Park* with fragments of DNA still included and conclude that our mental development cannot occur without a certain re-actualization of what had been split off.

The "double multiple personality" (Baranger, Baranger, & Mom, 1983) of analyst and patient have previously unlocked for us a myriad possible universes located on the spatial axis, whereas now it can also show us its ramifications in time. We could say, with Borges, that we see "a growing network of times coming close, branching off, intersecting, ignoring one another"[1]—a world of the Ucronies, of the utopias of history. The opening up of these possibilities is a mere exercise as far as the history of civilization is concerned (if Custer had won at Little Big Horn), whereas in our personal history, through the *après coup,* new future realities and—why not—new past realities can also be made thinkable.

Notes

This commentary has been translated by Pina Antinucci.

1. From Jorge Luis Borges, "The Garden of Forking Paths".

4

Psychoanalysis and linguistics: is dialogue possible?

Susana Vinocur-Fischbein

The invitation to write a chapter on "Psychoanalysis and Linguistics" devoted to Latin American contributions to psychoanalysis implies dealing with a wide and quite complex conceptual field. This subject refers to the various connections and exchanges that took place, from their beginnings and throughout their own histories as scientific disciplines, between psychoanalysis—either as a theory on psychic processes, their genesis and vicissitudes or as therapeutic method—and the different structuralist and post-structuralist linguistic theories that followed upon De Saussure's work (1916).

Psychoanalysis and linguistics, thus coupled, call for an interdisciplinary perspective well delimited in its extension and boundaries.[1] So far, the interdisciplinary relationship has been grounded not on the suppression of their mutual specificities, but on a gradual and increasingly intricate task of establishing feasible bonds between their discourses, while acknowledging the differences in the nature and ways of approaching their respective objects of study. The object "language" of psychoanalysis is ordinary speech transformed by the intersubjective psychoanalytic field, whereas the "*langue*", the object studied by linguistics for decades, is the abstract formal system that has shunned motivation, affect, and the subjective acquisition of meaning.

The first section of this chapter, "Psychoanalysis and language theories", aims to delimit the influence of linguistics on certain areas of psychoanalytic development.[2]

The second section, "Language, symbol formation processes, and linguistics in Río de la Plata psychoanalysis", briefly presents the general lines of thought dealt with by some of the most relevant psychoanalytic papers in this area that have considered linguistic phenomena through taking into account the described areas of influence.

The third section, "New perspectives: from transformational grammar to linguistic pragmatics, from sentence to discourse", puts forward the contributions of linguistic pragmatics and discourse analysis that may be employed as *complementary tools to understand different types of discourse that handle extra-linguistic realities.*

A fourth section, "Psychoanalysis and pragmatics: moving towards a shared interest", examines some recent Río de la Plata metapsychological revisions regarding the heterogeneous nature of mental functioning, as well as new directions in linguistic research concerned with the pragmatic abilities that allow verbal interaction to be produced and understood. The latter's acknowledgement of the complex heterogeneity of the mental processes at play paves the way to a common frontier-ground that is propitious for mutual exchanges concerning the hypotheses on the genesis and the role of language in psychic functioning as well as the origin and development of symbol formation.

Finally, in a fifth section, "The dream narrative: discourse and subjectivity", I propose a personal area of work devoted to research into the value of the narration of the manifest content of dreams. To approach dream reports through textual analysis relates to an attempt to categorize this type of discourse and show how linguistic pragmatics, founded on the philosophy of language and analytic semiotics, may be applied through a functional perspective (Vinocur-Fischbein, 2003, 2004).

Psychoanalysis and language theories

Various theories about language, either as an organizer of psychic structuring or as a crucial element in communication, have trodden their own paths with few encounters for decades, in psychoanalysis and in linguistics. Therefore, the mutual influence exerted by the two disciplines is still to some extent a controversial topic: determining whether (a) linguistic theories have been of potential usefulness for psychoanalytic theories on mental processes, whether certain linguistic concepts have influenced psychoanalytic notions regarding the subjective and/or social use of language, and (b) whether psychoanalytic theories on psychic functioning and on the patient's and the analyst's roles concerning their verbal performances, both as senders and receivers—conceived neither as identical nor as overlapping in the asymmetric dialogue of the session—have been or are of interest, and to what extent, for past linguistic developments, especially for the latest ones.

The rigorous research into language as a system (De Saussure, 1916)—initiated by the formalist linguistic trends that emerged with structuralism and that later accompanied the revolution introduced by transformational grammar in the 1950s (Chomsky, 1957, 1965)—was devoted to looking for universal abstractions that could only incidentally be associated with the psychoanalytic position as regards the subject being radically decentred from his discourse. From the psychoanalytic vertex, the many reflections on language in the literature—both theoretical and clinical–technical—from Freud onwards, have not evidenced a genuinely psychoanalytic theory of language (Anzieu, 1981; Green, 1984, 1995b) that could either articulate the therapeutic effect of interpretation with the other acknowledged language functions (Jakobson, 1963) or be taken into account by linguists. In the main, linguists have been reluctant to admit the existence of repression and/or splitting at the core of the dynamic unconscious submitted to the interplay of drives, as well as to consider the inclusion of affect expression and the intra- and intersubjective assignment of meaning in their own theories.[3]

It may be pointed out that a joint exploration by psychoanalysts, sociologists, and linguists to achieve "a deeper understanding of the complex meaning processes in language" and of "the unconscious structure of behaviour", as proposed by Benveniste (1966), has taken place far less frequently and intensively than might have been expected, in spite of the promise implied in Lacan's (1953, 1957) works for a major encounter between linguistics and psychoanalysis.[4]

In an attempt to systematize the contributions of linguistics to psychoanalysis as comprehensively as possible, it may be suggested that, generally speaking, linguistics has influenced at least three relevant areas of psychoanalytic theory and practice (Vinocur-Fischbein, 1996).[5] The first of these areas refers to the endeavours to produce a psychoanalytic psycholinguistic theory that would comprise symbol formation and symbolic processes as well as theories on language acquisition and disturbances in its performance—that is, theories on both *competence* and *performance,* in Chomskyan terms. A second area is geared to the search for the role of language in psychic structuring at phonological, syntactic, and semantic levels. This would encompass primary and secondary processes, the mechanisms of condensation and displacement with their rhetorical correlates (metaphor and metonymy), and the relationship between thought and language, not excluding language as a function and/or as psychic structure. Though partially overlapping thematically with the first area, psychoanalytic writings dealing with this one have been far more numerous, and they may be fairly distinguishable according to schools of thought.[6] The third and final area includes the uses to which language is put and the problem of meaning in clinical practice—that is, language as a working tool. In this case, even more than in the previous ones, it would be almost impossible to detail the literature on the subject. Any type of selection would inevitably be incomplete and arbitrary, for there is scarcely a paper that does not mention, at least indirectly, language use in clinical practice.[7]

Language, symbol formation processes, and linguistics in Río de la Plata psychoanalysis

As far as the first area referred to above is concerned, E. Rodrigué's writings, which followed Susan Langer's ideas (1953), have been significant in our region. In his opinion, her work on the logic of "presentational (non-discursive) symbolism" provided the necessary logical frame for a psychoanalytic theory of symbols and narrowed the gap between the psychological and epistemological views regarding the way symbols function. He suggested revising the topic in the light of Melanie Klein's specific contributions, since Rodrigué agreed with her that in the case of patients with symbolic alterations, the problem is how symbols are dealt with, not their content (Rodrigué, 1956, p. 147).

Arminda Aberastury (1958) also displayed her ideas about language and symbolization in child psychoanalysis, taking as a starting point Melanie Klein's (1929) and Hanna Segal's writings (1957). For the most part, she supported their ideas on symbol formation and the subsequent emergence of speech, which both paves the way to the working-through of the depressive anxieties increased by the advent of teeth and serves as an instrument "permitting the magic reconstruction of objects" (Aberastury, 1958, p. 167).

In more recent years, E. Del Valle (1998–99, 2003) has dealt with theories about symbolism in psychoanalysis, primarily taking into account the concepts put forward by the English School. She has emphasized particularly the prevailing conceptual misunderstanding between symbolic deficit and lack of representations, rooted in an indiscriminate use of the notion of "non-presentable" and in the improper extension of the concept of symbol to any type of psychic registration.

In Uruguay, M. Casas de Pereda (1999) has attempted to articulate, in her essays on body and symbolization, Winnicott's ideas on the (unconscious) subject's need to create and lose the (transitional) object, together with Lacan's conceptualization of the role of the Other and the three elements—*body*-sensation and perception, *object*, and *interpretant*—in Peirce's model.

In the field of semiotics and structuralism, a development of the second area is conspicuously represented within the Argentine psychoanalytic movement by I. Berenstein's works, whose paradigm was that of A. Greimas's structural semantics (1966). In his paper "On the Manifest Content of Dreams", Berenstein (1974) formalizes some unconscious structures that group semantic universals; and in his study on the Oedipus complex, he depicts the three models—identifications, object-choices, and object-realizations—of which this structure is composed (Berenstein, 1975b).

Finally, two prominent pioneers concerned with the third area, Luisa Álvarez de Toledo and David Liberman, are to be cited. During the 1970s and 1980s, there were many writings concerning a semiotic reading of clinical materials, which, from different perspectives, took into account linguistic and paralinguistic phenomena. Though these were written by Liberman's followers, the nucleus of his findings was not systematically applied until after his death, except for D. Maldavsky's researches.[8]

Luisa Álvarez de Toledo's (1996) ground-breaking essay, "The Analysis of 'Associating', 'Interpreting' and 'Words'", may be in-tion of language and symbolism; it was essentially triggered by Melanie Klein's theory, though incorporating Langer's Saussurean ideas on sign and symbol and Piaget's theories on the genesis of children's knowledge. Developed in an independent way, her views on speech were remarkably close to what would, years later, be the pragmatic theoreticians' concern: the notion of speech act as a discursive event that goes beyond the verbal text (Austin, 1957; Searle, 1969).

David Liberman's works (1962, 1970–72) developed a wide conceptual framework to integrate communication and linguistic theories into psychoanalytic clinical research. As opposed to Álvarez de Toledo, Liberman has been one of the psychoanalysts who have taken most into account the advances of linguistic theory. He found support in communication theory (Morris, 1938) and then in Chomsky's transformational grammar. According to Liberman (1976, p. 101), psychoanalysis is "a basic science that consists in investigating the evolution of analytic dialogue in and out of the session". It was this position that led him to look for the confluence of various disciplines that could be *instrumentally* formulated. Liberman's proposal on interpretive and complementary styles to be used in the analyst–analysand interaction constitutes his most fruitful research programme. He amalgamated a subject usually relevant to the Argentine school concerning the contents and form of interpretations in the analytic dialogue with ideas sparked off by communication theory and semiotics. Liberman reformulated psychoanalytic psychopathology in terms of syntactic, semantic, or pragmatic disorders. (He followed Ruesch's [1957] classification based on people's modes of communicating: demonstrative, scared and evasive, logical, impulsive, depressive, infantile, and observing but not taking part.) He later depicted psychopathological categories in terms of *communicative styles*, according to a grouping based on Freud's and Abraham's theory of libido stages; in a further development, he also incorporated the *ego* functions as well as the capacity of the ego for communication and object reparation (Liberman, 1962, 1970–72). Liberman distinguished six styles: reflexive, epic, lyrical, narrative, aesthetic, and suspenseful. A survey of changes in the analysand's styles would give us an objective indicator to assess advances in the process and the patient's psychic changes (Winograd, 1985). Liberman's contribution becomes remarkable inasmuch as he introduces the notion of *options*, which is complementary to that of communication thought of as just an encoding and decoding process, this being the prevailing theory at the time: "I also assign to the receiver the competence to make options in the special case of an analyst carrying out his therapeutic function" (Liberman, 1970–72, p. 147). The larger a psychoanalyst's repertoire of styles, the greater will be the possibilities to develop her/his work. In acknowledging that in the process of understanding a patient there are more "codes" at play than the verbal one, this author anticipates what the theory of relevance would postulate on the topic of *style* years later (Sperber & Wilson, 1986, p. 217). (This notion is explained further in the following section.)

New perspectives: from transformational grammar to linguistic pragmatics, from sentence to discourse

In its theoretical and philosophical aspects, the latest linguistic research is focused on the mental mechanisms involved in the inference and interpretation of the speaker's meanings (Carruthers, 2003; Sperber, 1994; Wilson, 2003); whereas the studies dedicated to the analysis of various types of discourse—defined here, in its widest sense, as *text + context*, in an attempt to encompass its three main dimensions: *language use, communication of beliefs, and social interaction*—usually pay attention to discourse genres, speech used as action, and the implementation of argumentation strategies (Anscombre & Ducrot, 1988; Van Dijk, 1997).

The appearance in the 1950s of *transformational grammar* (Chomsky, 1957, 1965)[9] meant a radical change in linguistic scientific direction, owing to two reasons: (a) it was the starting point for a relevant research programme in cognitive sciences; (b) it was the first scientific programme in linguistics that formulated the hypothesis of natural languages as formal systems. The even more forceful thesis endorsed by *generative semanticists*, who attempted to complete the above programme, was that natural languages could be defined as *interpreted formal systems* (Bach, 1989). Converging with the above Chomskyan research programme, *formal semantics* acquired great importance in the development of new logical instruments. However, in its search for a desired but ultimately not found logical structure in natural languages, comparable to a semantic structure, this trend completely neglected those aspects concerning its use in connection with context.

These conceptualizations are worth mentioning because from the outset transformational grammar and generative semantics stimulated some Argentine analysts (Bleichmar, 1983; Liberman, 1970–72) to correlate data, inasmuch as linguistic theory, like psychoanalysis, was stating that the source of meaning was to be found not in surface manifestations but in deep structures and the passage from the latter to the former involved transformation processes. This theoretical similitude was basically apparent since, as already mentioned, linguistic models did not take into account either the unconscious or the role played by repression in psychic functioning.

Oxford philosophies, founded on the so-called later Wittgenstein (1953), whence the contemporary pragmatics successfully evolved within linguistics in the last 20 years derives, have concluded that word relationships with the world are inextricably established through the use of language, and this is essentially defined by its communicative approach.[10] In the place of words or grammatical sentences, utterances become the units of meaning. Words do not have inherent meaning but are defined by their collocation in a sentence/utterance and by their relationship to other words and sentences/utterances.[11]

Grice's notion of implicature, one of the single most important ideas in pragmatics, and the four maxims of the cooperative principle[12]—quantity, quality, relevance, and manner—have paved the way for a communication theory the corollary of which is the attempt to account for the fact that what the speaker means is characteristically far richer than what she/he directly says, in the strict sense of Grice's *meaning: nn* (non-natural meaning), not only sustained by what is explicitly uttered—that is, referential information—but also by what is *inferred*: expressive information (Grice, 1957, 1967). This kind of inference, called *implicature* (what is not said but meant), both *conventional* (overt) and *conversational* (covert), and then extended to the notion of *explicature* (the multiple meanings of what is said), involves incorporating an inferential model into the classical code model of communication,[13] this being an instance of the power of pragmatic explanations concerning linguistic phenomena, especially with relation to those aspects of meaning not dealt with by semantic theory (Vinocur-Fischbein, 2003).

While Grice was developing his alternative theory, showing that both explicit and implicit verbal communication enclose substantial inferential intention recognition, the attention of linguists became increasingly focused on the analysis of context dependence, both in pragmatics (the contextual interpretation of utterances) and in semantics (the analysis of particular context-dependent expressions, such as deixis, quantifiers, modals, comparatives, and so on).

Sperber and Wilson (1986) contributed to pragmatic theory with the "relevance principle",[14] and they have criticized Grice's cooperative principle. However, they state that speakers cannot avoid being relevant in some way or other, even if that had not been their intention; moreover, utterances are stimuli different from others in that they involve communicative intentions that have an impact on the hearer's task when processing and interpreting the received information. They have proposed both a cognitive and a communicative principle in an attempt to expand the inferential theory of communication to a *relevance comprehension theory* that may be articulated with the semantic analyses of linguistic expressions (Sperber & Wilson, 1995; Wilson, 2000).[15]

André Green admits that pragmatics has opened a significant field of reflection; however, he considers that this theoretical position, supported by the act of speech theory, favours the social polarity of language, which he judges to be a source of ambiguity and misunderstanding. In his review, Green also delves into the use of language in the analytic setting. In psychoanalysis, doing is saying: if something is said because it cannot be done, language becomes a symbolic substitution for acting. Saying would no longer be a mode of action. Though analysts may recognize the emergence of speech acts in their analysands' discourses, they do not look into them but listen to the substitute value of language (Green, 1984).[16]

However, it would be appropriate to speculate on the scope of the "substitute value of language" and the extent to which its pragmatic dimension is encompassed in the psychoanalytic method. A brief fragment from the "Analysis of a Phobia in a Five-Year-Old Boy" (Freud, 1909b), the episode of a visit to Freud by Hans and his father, persuasively illustrates how the analyst's words attain illocutionary force and perlocutionary effect in a speech event such as a psychoanalytic session or interview. However, in such cases interpretations may be expressed as a narrative, a genre usually considered as comprising not a perlocutionary but a constative value, because it supposedly depicts a state of affairs or a series of events.

> I then disclosed to him that he was afraid of his father, precisely because he was so fond of his mother. . . . Long before he was in the world, I went on, I had known that a little Hans would come who would be so fond of his mother that he would be bound to be afraid of his father because of it; and I had told his father this. "But why do you think I'm angry with you?" *his father interrupted me at this point*; "have I ever scolded you or hit you?" Hans *corrected him*: "Oh yes! You have hit me." "That's not true. When was it anyhow?" "This morning", answered the little boy. [Freud, 1909b, p. 42; emphasis added]

Freud could not but acknowledge the important outcome of his words when he concluded:

> From the date of this consultation I received almost daily reports of the alterations in the little patient's condition . . . But it became apparent that a possibility had now been offered him of bringing forward his unconscious productions and of unfolding his phobia. [p. 43, emphasis added]

Another argument in favour of the interest this language perspective may assume for the psychoanalyst is the already mentioned fact that the domain of linguistic pragmatics would cover all those aspects of meaning not captured by a restricted semantic theory. Therefore, understanding an utterance involves a great deal more than knowing the meaning of the articulated words and the grammatical relations between them. This type of comprehension implies the making of *inferences* that will connect what is said to what is mutually presupposed or to what has already been said—that is, its aim is to bridge the gap between textual meanings and the resulting comprehension of the dialogue. Linguistic pragmatics deals with the *resources and strategies used for doing through words, for expressing one's ideas vaguely, for making understatements, for leaving the possibility open to withdrawing what one has said* (Lavandera et al., 1987). We generally acknowledge that in the clinical context we understand the patient's discourse on the basis of our "evenly suspended theorization", which neither is explicit nor refers merely to a theoretical background but to its complex interrelationship with both the patient's historical reality (sifted through psychic reality) and her/his transference history—that is, those elements that allow us to produce hypotheses beyond the uttered discourse.[17]

Emphasis on the inferential processes in this new communication paradigm, which may be interpreted as one of the psychic workings of the unconscious, not only highlights the predominance of interpretive creativity with relation to the automatism of the previous model but also checkmates the idea of inevitable symmetry as the notion of subjectivity at play pervades discursive activity. Proof of these changes in linguists' position is the use of dialogism and polyphony (Bakhtin, 1984)[18], at first in the analyses of literary discourse, these theories being later reintroduced, developed, and improved by certain linguists who, having devoted themselves to enunciation and argumentation, expanded their use to even the most ordinary forms of discursive productions. If, in the late 1970s, some pragmatists could still be criticized because of their refusal to question the "unity of the speaking subject", two decades later the situation turned out to be utterly different, especially if we take into account the linguists who follow the Francophile trend. Not only have their concerns travelled along new routes, but their writings have also been permeated by French psychoanalysis. According to them, the cases in which one speaker is said to cover several enunciators have multiplied almost uncontrollably (Anscombre & Ducrot, 1988; Authier-Revuz, 1974; Ducrot, 1984; Kerbrat-Orecchioni, 1996).[19]

The notion of subjectivity as characterized by enunciation, that is, by the linguistic activity performed by the speaker at the time of speaking—a definition completed by Kerbrat-Orecchioni (1996, p. 124) by saying: "also performed by the listener at the time she/he listens"—and the study of the speaker's traces at the heart of her/his utterances bring linguists closer to the clinical field in unprecedented ways. Here, the intricacies of dialogues show that not only are conceptual words—those words liable to substitution along the paradigmatic axis—significant, but so are some other linguistic elements—e.g., *hardly/almost/somewhat/not very; but, however/therefore*—because of their coordinating function and their power to determine the semantic relationships between the elements connected along the syntagmatic axis.

Some of the above issues can be illustrated with well-known clinical material: three brief pieces of dialogue quoted from the long conversations between Hans and his father. In this case, they are talking about "playing at horses", which might have coincided with "the nonsense" beginning.

> I: "Were you often the horse?"
>
> HANS: "Oh, yes."
>
> I: "And that was how you got the nonsense?"
>
> HANS: "Because they kept on saying "'cos of the horse", "'cos of the horse" (he put a stress on the "'cos"; so perhaps I got the nonsense because they talked like that; "'cos of the horse"). [Freud, 1909b, p. 59]

In his footnote, Freud very appropriately underlines what was not perceived by paternal insight: Hans' insistent emphasis on "*wegen dem Pferd*" ["'cos of the horse"] did not mean that the nonsense had begun at that time, as his father wanted to show, but "in that connection"—that is, "owing to the horse" (father).

Through a double semantic liaison, the little word *wegen* [because of] points at the origin and persistence of phobic symptoms. Along the syntagmatic axis, this lexical item introduces causality: "because of this motive" (the horse), he has "got the *nonsense*", whereas along the paradigmatic axis, on the basis of the homophonous *wegen/Wägen*, the phobia extends from the horse (the father's symbolic substitute) to vehicles. Even if Freud continues: "It must never be forgotten how much more *concretely* children treat words than grown-up people do, and consequently how much more significant for them are similarities of sounds in words" (ibid, p. 59, footnote, added emphasis), we could also enquire about pragmatic abilities—not only those of adults, but Hans's as well, given that he succeeds in communicating his thoughts to the Professor. (Freud states in the same footnote: "*I may at the same time complete what the child was unable to express* . . ."—emphasis added.)

Could we say, then, that it is just a question of a sort of radical ambivalence registered in language itself, as Laplanche suggests (1970–73, p. 105): "as if certain ordinary language words might enclose a stratification of this ambivalence?" or are we, rather, *vis-à-vis* pragmatic abilities subjectively involved in language and set in motion by anxiety and drives? A few lines further on, Hans gives new proof of his ability when eluding his father's inquisitive questions with indirect answers bearing implicit meanings (*conversational implicatures*):

I: "And when she widdled did you look on?"

HE: "She used to go to the W.C."

I: "And you were curious?"

HE: "I was inside the W.C. when she was in it." [Freud, 1909b, p. 61]

A bit earlier, Hans had also shown his excellent pragmatic competence in responding to his father's questioning either with the use of negation or with indefinite expressions (explicatures), the semantic ambiguity of which Hans's father is compelled to solve with his own interpretation—hence, the insistent questions that follow:

I: "But you and the others were often in the stables. You must surely have talked about horses there."

HANS: "We didn't." [We haven't talked at all; we haven't talked about any subject that might interest you; we haven't dealt with the subjects you are asking me about; we haven't particularly talked about horses.]

I: "What did you talk about?" [His father has inferred that the negation does not refer to the act of speaking but to the topic.]

HANS: "*Nothing.*" [No subject has been talked about, or none that Daddy may be so very interested in?]

I: "Such a lot of children and *nothing* to talk about?"

HANS: "We did talk about *something* but not about horses." [Repetitive use of indefinite pronouns so as not to say exactly what is meant, and a scalar implicature: *nothing, something, much*]

I: "Well, what was it?"

HANS: "I *don't remember anymore.*" [Did he remember before? When? According to Grice, Hans breaches the Maxim of Quality.] [Freud, 1909b, p. 60]

There can also be no doubt about the value of linguistic pragmatics for interpreting and elucidating the sense of severely disturbed patients' discourse. Analytic practice with these patients entails a disposition to hold and transform their unbearable experiences (Canestri, 1994, 2002), as well as alterations in *standard analytic listening.* Adequate understanding of their discourse underlines the importance of ideas that may account for the complexity of linguistic activity while considering in addition the multiplicity of the semiotic systems used in the production and recognition of the analytic dialogue.

Some of the changes needed in analytic listening may be correlated with a kind of psychic functioning that allows a given content to gain access to consciousness, while in the case of psychoneurotic patients this content would have remained unconscious until grasped through analytic work (Picollo, 1994). Listening is focused on manifest discourse rather than on latent content in a traditional sense. It is a type of listening geared to a use of language that has lost its inner-world-evocative quality and that copes with it as if it were an external reference. The verbal expressions that detach us from the so-called metaphorical interpretations by leading us to interpret apparent discourse "literality" are those instances the ambiguity of which—literal/non-literal—we solve by means of a process of selective assignment of context-dependent semantic value (Recanati, 1995).

An appropriate example would be the one expounded by Bion regarding the schizophrenic employment of language as a mode of action. According to Bion, this mode—different from the use of language as a method of communication or as a mode of thought—is in the service of either splitting the object or projective identification.

> The patient comes into the room, shakes me *warmly* by the hand, and looking *piercingly* into my eyes says, "I think the sessions are not for a long while *but* stop me ever going out." I know from previous experience that this patient has a grievance that the sessions are too few and that they interfere with his free time. He intended to split me by making me give *two opposite interpretations at once,* and this was shown by his next association when he said, "How does the lift know *what to do when I press two buttons at once?*" [Bion, 1967, p. 24, emphasis added]

Let us also analyse this example from a pragmatic perspective. Bion emphasizes the patient's paradoxical attitude shown by the contrast between shaking hands *warmly* and looking *piercingly* into the analyst's eyes. In addition, the sense of the grammatically correct utterance the patient uses to express himself may be understood as a contradiction. As an argumentative connector, the conjunction "*but*" links (at the semantic level) two contrary arguments that reveal the covert existence of two different enunciators under the same speaker (Kerbrat-Orecchioni, 1991). If we accept that these divergent voices refer to the patient's (speaker) perception of his own mental state, then the enunciating voices may attain the value of a reflection made on his split self. The same procedure may be noticed in the next associated utterance, articulated in the interrogative form to introduce another conflicting voice. One enunciator asserts: "*I press two buttons at once*", while the other asks: "*How can I come to know what I do?*"

The above examples show how pragmatics, understood not merely as another level of analysis that may be added to the phonological, syntactic, and semantic ones but as a view integrating the former linguistic elements with the paralinguistic ones that occur in a speech-event context, may cooperate in a relational conception of communication and may allow the statement that there can be no speaking that is not accompanied by and integrated into listening. If the unconscious exploitation of language resources makes up each subject's *style*, we could also add the idiosyncratic *style* of each analytic couple, in keeping with the revision made by the theory of relevance. [*It is sometimes said that the style is the man. We would rather say that style is the relationship*" (Sperber & Wilson, 1986, p. 217).] Style would be an outcome of the speaker's tailoring the linguistic form to suit the hearer: that is, it would reflect the speaker's assumptions about the hearer's ability to infer the conveyed meanings. Thus, a relationship would be established between the speaker and her/his communicative intentions, on the one hand, and the hearer and her/his interpretive abilities, on the other.

A corollary is that choices are *over-determined* by the search for relevance; hence, this conceptualization differs from the usual ones that consider *style* as the creation of the speaker's free choice among the various possibilities offered by any natural language. This description of style is quite compatible with psychoanalytic proposals regarding analyst–analysand communication. The way the analyst listens to the patient's speeches, the way she/he formulates interpretations in order to be understood: all these facts are highly dependent on meaning assignment, which, in turn, is subordinated not only to the analyst's code—i.e. the theories employed—but to context as well, to the analyst's unique outlook on the analytic setting either as an area restricted to the display of subjectivity or as an expanded ground that includes intersubjectivity, as considered by *dynamic bipersonal field* theory (Baranger, 1992; Baranger & Baranger, 1969a).

Psychoanalysis and pragmatics: moving towards a shared interest

Beyond the use of discourse analysis in clinical practice, it is now appropriate to turn to a potential rapprochement in recent years between psychoanalytic searches concerning psychic functioning and those carried out in the field of pragmatics—the latter being basically supported by investigations carried out by the cognitive sciences and the various philosophical trends that deal with language.

a. Some Río de la Plata authors, whose writings deal with some of the most important ideas developed by psychoanalytic thought during the second half of the twentieth century, are deeply involved in revising standard psychoanalytic metapsychology and clinical tenets without neglecting advances in other disciplines also devoted to mental processing. This group of psychoanalysts maintains that there is a need for models that may encompass the multiplicity of heterogeneous psychic agencies and zones to approach phenomena that are scarcely displayed in the field of representations but proliferate in current psychopathology and clinical practice.[20]

I would specifically mention:

- The *tertiary processes* depicted by H. Fiorini (1995) in connection with creative thought: this tertiary organization is polyvalent, able to shelter different modes of thought and to hold various logical processes; the design of these tertiary processes is comparable to the architecture of a Gothic cathedral.
- A notion of unconscious consistent with the *logic of coexistence* that gives support to R. Zuckerfeld's "third topography" (2000), formulated as a mind model where two main types of functioning coexist: that of the final psychic apparatus (Freud, 1933a) and that corresponding to the *split unconscious,* which constitutes its hard core.
- The concept of superimposed psychic "zones or areas" functioning simultaneously developed by N. Marucco (2003a), which both account for the structuring of the mental apparatus from different perspectives and are disclosed through the complexities of psychopathological configurations.
- The studies on psychosomatic disorders that deal with the failure of psychic symbolizing activity owing to excess or impairment, and the

subsequent lack of organization of mnemic traces in an inner world able to hold fantasies, thus hindering the developmental step of the passage from a perceptual to a representational universe (J. Fischbein, 1999, 2000). Alterations in the register of intero- and exteroceptive sensations produce failure in the constitution of representations (the unthinkable), in their being bound to words (the unmentionable), and in their severance from the associative paths owing to splitting processes (the unspeakable) (D'Alvia, 2003). Deprived of the bindings granted by words, mnemic traces are prone to be discharged in acts or in the soma, and these are precisely the ones requiring our countertransference resonance to build up representations (Aisemberg, 1998–99).

- The approach to a "theory of mental modularity" (Chomsky, 1984), according to which H. Bleichmar (1997) proposes a more general form of psychic structuring and functioning, resulting from the coordination of different sectors or modules that may be self-regulating regarding the qualities of their components and their organizing laws. It is formulated as a model able to deconstruct the dimensions of affects, drives, desires, anxieties, and defences *vis-à-vis* psychic pain while simultaneously keeping the mind quality in its entirety.

If we acknowledge that in explaining the multiple ways of unconscious existence, the above conceptualizations reject reductionism, we may surmise that one of the paradigms of today's epistemological horizon that allows for feasible rapprochements to the psychoanalytic description of the psyche as a complex system is precisely that of linguistic pragmatics, as this discipline is also confronted with the need to describe complex systems of great interest for our psychoanalytic theoretic and clinical work.

b. The introduction of the inferential theory of communication and its corollaries within the general principle of relevance gave rise to still unresolved debates in current theoretic pragmatics. These issues deal with the relationship between language, consciousness, and cognition, with special reference to the nature and functioning of the mental mechanisms employed in the cognitive and inferential processes associated with the comprehension of meaning.[21] It is beyond the scope of this paper to delve into these controversies more deeply. The leading idea is to review only some aspects of the hypotheses concerning the nature and distinctive features of human cognition processes involved in the language "faculty" and use, which may be of heuristic relevance for psychoanalysis and has become the subject of research in developmental psychology, neurobiology, and philosophy of the mind. Basically, the fundamental concern is to shed light on the enigma of the relationship between natural language and thinking: its role in mental architecture and human cognition—whether language is a necessary condition for certain kinds of cognitive processes, whether language and speech serve as a crucial scaffold for the development of conceptual thinking, and what determines its *flexibility* and *creativity* of content and the *abductive inferences* that may be performed upon such contents. Moreover, the goal is to find out what the relation is (from one completely context-independent to one of increasing contextual dependence) between (a) the pragmatic abilities employed in the interpretation of communicative behaviour and in reasoning, and (b) the more general mental abilities used in assigning intentions and beliefs and forming *thoughts* about *attributed thoughts* and therefore being able to interpret the speakers' communicative behaviour—a process that has been called *mind-reading* (it is also known as *theory of mind*) (Carruthers, 2003). This expression connotes a sort of *grasping aptitude or inferential comprehension*, but pragmatists disagree whether it precedes or follows human ability to communicate verbally.

According to the classical version of the modularity thesis as outlined by J. Fodor (1983), there are two main types of cognitive systems: *input* modules, which are inferential only in a general sense, and central systems, which are conceptual but not at all modular; yet, the latter show an inferential ability whose workings are "mysterious". Amalgamating a broad Chomskyan view of language with a broad Gricean view of pragmatics, Fodor (1983) maintains that language is an autonomous, domain-specific modular system and pragmatics a domain-general central system because its outcome depends on "global" factors such as free access to memorized information.[22] Modular processes, on the contrary, are *local, encapsulated,* and very constrained as regards the type or source of contextual information on which they may draw (Wilson, 2003). What makes a fundamental difference between them is not merely that pragmatics is inferential while language is not, but the fact that pragmatic inferences are highly context-dependent, and for pragmatists there is no *theoretically grounded limit* on the type of contextual information that may be required or the source from which it may come.[23]

It is to be noted that the so-called Fodor's Problem—namely, the riddle of how human cognition is distinctively built up out of a (massive) modularity postulated for mental workings such as perception, vision, audition, language processing, and motor control—is constantly the subject of deep discussions in the field of pragmatics. *Vis-à-vis* Fodor's scepticism about the possibility that this "mystery" may be resolved in a foreseeable future, the pragmatists, who ultimately defend an exclusively modular conception of the human mind and try to make some progress in explaining the problem from an evolutionary perspective, hold that inferential comprehension is a hypothesis construction and evaluation process about the speaker's meaning, an interpretation process called "metapsychological" (Sperber & Wilson, 2002). In fact, the real question amounts not simply to whether the processes involved are local or global, but whether they are performed by general-purpose mechanisms or by autonomous, special-purpose mechanisms, attuned to regularities existing in specific domains. Does the comprehension and interpretation of the speaker's utterances and intentions depend on the application of general mind-reading abilities to a particular communicative domain, or are we to suppose that there is a *meta-communicative* module with its own specific principles and mechanisms?

Verbal communication constitutes a special case presenting regularities not found in other domains, which may have led to the development of a module, even a set of sub-modules, devoted to comprehension precisely with their own special-purpose principles and mechanisms.[24] Thus, there is developmental and neuropsychological evidence that seems to favour a view of mind-reading as a domain-specific modular system rather than a central, reflective one (Wilson, 2003).[25] Moreover, it has been discovered not only that there are parallels between the breakdown of mind-reading abilities and the breakdown of inferential communication abilities, but also that clear dissociations exist between mind-reading abilities and general reasoning abilities.[26]

In short, given the complexity of the mind-reading process used in the interpretation of verbal communication and the variety of tasks it has to perform, it is safe to assume that *mind-reading is not a single, relatively homogeneous system, but a collection of autonomous mecha-*

nisms or sub-modules articulated together in an evolved "mental organ". This position means that modules are no longer conceived as encapsulated or isolated (they can be altered through some way of learning, or through changes in belief elsewhere in the mind), but as interactive, and that *natural language syntax is crucially necessary for intermodular integration* (Carruthers, 2002, 2003, p. 4). This would also highlight a converging trend in the heretofore opposing set of hypotheses in the cognitive sciences.[27]

At a time when mental mechanisms that transform visual, acoustic, and linguistic representations are acknowledged to be heterogeneous, when interpretation of verbal communication is recognized to require (clearly unconscious) meta-representational comprehension strategies not retrievable by introspection (Sperber, 1994), it is very significant that pragmatists have resorted to a vocabulary with psychoanalytic resonance. Caution tells us that so far this lexical adoption implies only that the aforementioned hypotheses on both the construction and assessment of speaker's meanings are used exclusively in pragmatics to discriminate the types of unconscious thought mechanisms involved in the pragmatic aspects of speech processing and in the attribution of beliefs and intentions—that is, recognition of the other's mental states on the basis of behaviour observation.

However, in this sphere a wide field of research and even of mutual integration may open in the near future concerning psychoanalytic theories on the genesis of language and the latter's role in psychic structuring, as well as on the origin and development of symbol formation.

The dream narrative: discourse and subjectivity

As has already been stated, pragmatic theories concerning mental architecture and functioning are mainly supported by developments that are radically different from those of psychoanalysis inasmuch as the latter proposes the joint study of human thought and drives.

However, current clinical work challenges us to confront the need to generate a suitable technique with patients categorized as non-neurotic (Green, 1976), who present with various impairments in symbol formation. Their oneiric activity and fantasizing ability may be partially absent or altered. In the case of patients with psychosomatic disorders, this lack or failure from a functional viewpoint parallels the growth of a mental life in which the prevailing type of thought duplicates things and/or action, thus showing an *operative* quality [*pensée operatoire*] (Marty & M'Uzan, 1983). Such patients' discourse is usually restricted to factually communicating events within a limited time frame. Their use of language to express the experiences and imaginary aspects of psychic reality is inherently meagre. As the oneiric function is also altered, dreaming is infrequent or, at least, these subjects show a noticeable inability to convey their dreams. The function of dreams would be less focused on expressing unconscious wishes than on representing their inner world state. It may even be said that dreaming constitutes an attempt at reflection. Although these dreams are supposed to engage drive cathexes, the almost complete lack of associations accompanying them prevents us from proceeding in the same technical way as with psychoneurotics.

Under these circumstances, the emerging dream life constitutes an exceptional field of exploration where both disciplines could cooperate. The complex relationship between dreams and language justifies the inclusion of an inferential view of communication and of the processes of meaning production as contributions to the metapsychological consideration and interpretation of dreams.

In recent years I have been developing an original proposal of research into the narrative of the manifest content of dreams in patients with psychosomatic disorders. Owing to their infrequent appearance, these may significantly pave the way to a type of unconscious functioning the drive modality of which is detached from representations and dream working-through. Notwithstanding the fact that the manifest content is the outcome of preconscious processing, its narrative reveals the interdependence of all the systems involved in psychic functioning.

Dream narration constitutes the retroactive *translation* of dream content, this being, in turn, the pictographic transcription of dream wishes. Therefore, such recounting entails the difficulty of establishing, either by inference or by deduction, the *original* that underlies the translation, through retracing the distorting censorship steps that create secondary revision (Freud, 1900a).

It is worth while to point out that the transformation of dream-thoughts into visual images that are then put into words and organized through the retelling of the manifest content entails a series of options performed in the intricate relationship between different semiotic modes of expression. Gaining access to a dream means basically translating the various raw materials of the dream that the dream-work has succeeded in expressing through a pictorial mode to a verbal code (including prosodic features) and communicating this new formation in the context of a session, which signals its actualization as speech act with illocutionary force and perlocutionary effect (Austin, 1962; Vinocur-Fischbein, 2004).

The theoretical psychoanalytic bases that validate taking the narrative of dream manifest content as a legitimate unit of analysis with non-neurotic patients are most notably found in Freudian writings on dream metapsychology and dream interpretation (Freud, 1900a, 1917d [1915], 1916–17, 1920g, 1925i, 1933a). Post-Freudian developments, which deal with the significance of oneiric life, not only as proof of symbolic work but also with relation to their function within the frame of psychic life, are to be highlighted as well (Bion, 1992; Meltzer, 1984). I would include among these essential contributions Willy Baranger's ideas on dreams as intentional communicative signs within the analytic situation, in addition to his theories on the intersubjective dynamic field. Baranger regarded dreaming as an activity the connotation of which exceeds "the meaning of dreams"—that is, his conception went beyond considering them as a set of visual images structured by wish. With a semiotic view, he assigned this psychic activity the function of "a language whose choice among other multiple possible languages is itself significant" (Baranger, 1969, p. 185).

P. Marty (1984) correlates an impaired psychic structuring with various types of somatic disorders. The preconscious, a central part of psychosomatic patients' mental life, governs both oneiric and somatic mechanisms. Therefore, the quality of dream activity constitutes one of the most important points of reference with regard to psychic disorganization and reorganization movements.[28] The absence of dreams or the appearance of repetitive, operative, or "raw" dreams during a psychoanalytic treatment would suggest the impact of a new trauma on the psyche.[29]

The above leads us to conclude that dreams may act as indicators of subjective psychic structuring and of somatic health. Consequently, a careful textual analysis, which may include their formal elements—the polysemic (or literal) nature of words, the particular employment of deixis, the individuality of syntax, phonology, or even typography (if communicated in written form)—would allow us to explore the genesis of subjective symbol-formation processes and hypothesize whether there is any correlation between semantic content and narrative form (Mahoney, 1987).

Up to the present time, dream narrative has seldom been described in terms of its enunciation. My thesis is that dream narrative exhibits certain features that make it recognizable as a specific discursive strategy. The following is an attempt to list these features, though not exhaustively:

1. Enunciation occurs in the first person as it is retold by the dreamer.
2. There is usually some homogeneity in time reference. The present tense prevails at significant moments, eventually alternating with past verbal forms.
3. There may be a fragmentary development of the narrative structure. It may be a very short or unfinished text, which may merely describe an action or scene.
4. There is no explicit argumentative positioning.
5. There are omissions and inaccuracies that illustrate the restrictions that repression imposes on the narrator's "cognitive abilities".
6. There may be a possible overlapping of situations, facts, or scenes. The increase of referential sources produces a "collage" effect (rebus), which notably distinguishes this narrative from everyday statements.
7. There is a signalling of the dream account through generally well-defined opening and closing sequences.

Dreams may also be dramatized: they may have a beginning, an unfolding, and a *dénouement*; they may possess scenarios and characters. It is on each of these aspects where the narrator–analysand stamps her/his subjective discursive traces. Even in the analysis of apparently identical repetitive dreams, it would be possible to find distinctive elements introduced by the idiosyncratic use of linguistic options. Moreover, the articulation of the manifest content in the form of a narrative with subsequent associations and interpretations (when these arise in the heart of a session) organize and assign meaning to evocative episodes. By not intruding as isolated memories, these evocative episodes favour the gradual spatial and temporal integration of subjective structuring, since the narrator becomes the author. The dream is *about something, about someone,* and is enunciated *by someone, so as to elicit the other's response.* The highly subjective meanings conjured up by the analysand's words under the influence of the transference can hardly get a more specialized listener than the analyst, and in what other ways could these be summoned and bound but by the latter's interpretations, through the intercession of countertransference?

Closing remarks

It is not always possible to respond in depth to the difficult problems introduced by current psychoanalytic practice from a unique theoretical view, and in widening its frontiers to include those pathologies not clearly recognized as belonging either to the field of neuroses or to that of psychoses, the precise boundaries of traditional theoretical psychoanalytic foundations have had to be traversed. Hence, the inevitable interlocution with other theories (e.g. neuroscience, neurobiology, biology, anthropology, linguistics, etc.) that hold other viewpoints is fruitful even at the risk of collisions or misunderstandings, inasmuch as this may lead psychoanalysis to an innovative position such as the one embraced at its beginnings.

We are rarely faced these days with symptoms representative of symbolizing psychic work: that is, symptoms that bear latent meanings involved in lexical polysemy or homophony, symptoms revealed through slips of the tongue or exposed by symptomatic acts. The conveyed "messages" usually lack preconscious sophisticated transformation. Hence, some of the questions posed by pragmatic theories concerning the relationship between explicit and implicit communication of meaning, the enigma of conceptual registration, and the construction of intention during the speakers' interaction cannot but arouse our interest. By taking into consideration the conditions surrounding discourse production and expression, we expand our "conceptual and operative frame of reference" in the analysis of the contextual construction of sense (Pichon Rivière, 1979, p. 99).

New directions in pragmatic researches dealing with the mutually dependent status of thought and language as well as the revisions in psychoanalytic metapsychology may pave the way for an encounter of shared and even compatible interests in the field of language: that is, the role of language in psychic structuring and especially its function as intermediary and interpreter of any semiotic system. The frontier thus created could give rise to progress in both disciplines.

Notes

This chapter has been translated by the author herself.

1. As regards the above statement, the following definition of inter-discipline has been considered: "The generation of an object of study in the intersection of at least two sciences, requiring new knowledge with inherent sense. This meaning can only be supplied by the involved disciplines through the development of a theoretic–methodological apparatus created to that end" (Pardo, 1996, p. 28).

2. In the presentation of some relationships between psychoanalysis and linguistics, I leave aside certain epistemological issues and consider as equally relevant concepts coming from linguistics and semiotics as well as contributions from the theory of communication and the philosophy of language.

3. However, some very well-known exceptions (Benveniste, 1966; Jakobson, 1963; Ivan Fonagy, 1970–71; Labov & Fanshell, 1977; and, in recent years, Authier-Revuz, 1984; and Kerbrat-Orecchioni, 1996) may be quoted.

4. Lacan's "linguistic turn" was clearly inspired by Lévi-Strauss's anthropological works and by structural linguistics, which supplied him with a paradigm. His ideas, almost exclusively based on De Saussure and Jakobson, used certain linguistic concepts to expand psychoanalytic theory through the well-known formula that shows the power of language to constitute and simultaneously decentre the individual as subject (Lacan, 1953, 1957).

5. According to B. Litowitz, theories about language used by analysts were taken out of the continuum that represents the history of linguistics, though in certain cases a series of theories that replaced one another engaged some psychoanalytic writers with outdated ideas. On the other hand, there have also been psychoanalysts who were aware of changes in linguistic models but preferred previous ones (Litowitz & Litowitz, 1977).

6. In the first area, Freud's ideas have been deepened and extended by writers as important as S. Ferenczi, J. Lacan, D. Anzieu, J. Laplanche, A. Green, E. Jones, M. Klein, S. Isaacs, H. Segal, W. Bion, V. Rosen, and C. Rycroft. With relation to the second aspect, the names of J. Kristeva, I. Fonagy, P. Luquet, G. Rosolato, and P. Marty may be added to the previous ones. In the American school, the names of R. M. Lowenstein, E. Sharpe, H. Edelheit, and M. Edelson have become relevant. In the British school, the writings of Donald Meltzer have developed Melanie Klein's and W. R. Bion's ideas on the relations between thought and language.

7. Among the psychoanalytic writers who have recently emphasized the significance of the use of language in clinical practice, it is possible to

mention T. Shapiro and B. Litowitz in the United States and A. Green and J. Canestri in Europe. In Latin America, we may find the writings of D. Gil, S. A. de Mendilaharsu, M. Casas de Pereda, and A. Vares in Uruguay; whereas in Argentina, David Liberman's followers, such as B. Winograd, S. Dupetit, and D. Maldavsky; and also, introducing a personal line of thought, E. Liendo, A. Picollo, and this author in a type of approach based on linguistic pragmatics and discourse analysis.

8. As a former associate of Liberman's in his beginnings in the 1970s, D. Maldavsky's works are framed in the context of systematic research in psychoanalysis. His aim has been to examine how erogeneity and defences are expressed in language, and to that purpose he has coined the term "languages of erotism" rooted in Freudian thought. His main goal has been to develop a method called the David Liberman Algorithm (ADL), which may systematically connect metapsychology with clinical practice (Maldavsky, 2001, 2003).

9. Chomsky has repeatedly stated that linguistics is a branch of psychology; however, he has also emphasized the fact that the language domain should include the cognitive system involved in an adequate linguistic theory on its acquisition: how the child/speaker–listener manages to produce sentences never before uttered or heard. Language creativity is only made possible through behaviour governed by a finite number of universal rules and by transformations inherent in each language that allow for utterance variation and flexibility.

10. These philosophical schools of thought are critical of the idea that utterances communicate only propositions that describe states of affairs, propositions that may only be validated by their conditions of truth or falsity.

11. The difference depends on whether we speak of philosophical or literary texts, written or oral discourses. These developments, such as the well-known act of speech theory (Austin, 1957; Searle, 1969, 1979), the theory of implicatures (Grice, 1981), as well as enunciation and argumentation theories (Anscombre & Ducrot, 1988; Ducrot, 1984) revolve around the explanation of the prevalence of *sociability* in the attribution of meaning. Moreover, argumentation theories in particular attempt to provide the foundation for a semantic theory.

12. The cooperative principle says: "make your contribution such as is required, at the stage at which it occurs, by the accepted purpose or direction of the talk exchange in which you are engaged" (Grice, 1967).

13. The *code model* considers that communication involves a sender, a receiver, a set of observable signals, a set of unobservable messages, and a code that relates the two; that is, a set of rules or proceedings that pair messages with signals. The sender selects a message and transmits the corresponding signal, which is received and decoded at the other end; if all goes well, the result is the reproduction in the receiver of a message identical with the original one. The *inferential model of communication* includes central mental processes: namely, thought processes at the input and output of the message, followed by coded and then decoded acoustic signals, which are finally transformed into thought processes. Therefore, there is a gap, filled by inference, between the semantic representation of sentences and the thoughts actually communicated by utterances (Sperber & Wilson, 1986).

14. They share a Chomskyan formalistic view of language in stating that communication is a secondary function of language.

15. According to the first principle, human cognition tends to be geared to the maximization of relevance; the second principle states that every enunciation, or any other act of manifest communication, communicates a presumption of its own relevance. The speaker, by the very act of addressing someone, is communicating that her/his utterance is relevant enough to be worth the processing effort. These principles may be very useful to take into account when, in clinical practice based on certain theoretical frames of reference, some patients' speeches are qualified as "non-communicative" and merely "evacuative" or the expression of "resistance".

16. André Green asserts that there is a sort of incompatibility or an unbridgeable gap between psychoanalysis and linguistics, essentially as regards the conceptions about two basic elements: representations and affect (Green, 1984, 1995).

17. A. Duarte is correct in asserting: "During sessions, the analyst listens and observes, decodes, selects, organizes into a hierarchy, arranges in a specific order, compares, relates, and remembers linguistic and paralinguistic messages; associates, looks for recurrent and divergent topics and situations, integrates, anticipates, and, being alert to the patient's textual polysemy, more than once delves into the different associative trains of thought" (Duarte, 2000, p. 101)

18. Every dialogue implies a differential relation between the enunciating voices in two dimensions: the conversational dimension, which implies the interacting presence of two distinctive voices pertaining to different speakers, and the dialogic dimension, which refers to the presence in one discourse of divergent and even contradictory voices embodied in just one enunciator.

19. It is considered that referred discourse, proverbs, the way of functioning of certain connectors, interrogative and negative statements, figures of speech, and so on belong into the domain of polyphony.

20. Without ignoring the theoretical foundations Freud himself provided for this exploration, these writers consider the valuable contributions of Bion, Winnicott, Lacan, Aulagnier, Green, McDougall, Marty, M'Uzan, and Botella—specifically, those related to "multiple psychic persons", what is split, "nameless dread", and the inassimilable beta-elements, the threat of annihilation, the real, what cannot be symbolized, the primordial mind, the work of the negative, "tertiary processes", "archaic hysteria", "operative thinking" [*pensée operatoire*], the repetition of the identical, what cannot acquire "figurability", and so on.

21. Grice was non-committal in the ensuing controversies on the source of pragmatic abilities for communication and on the form of the comprehension process, and he engaged even less in the discussions on their place in the overall architecture of the mind.

22. The issue of memory systems is one of the more revised subjects in current psychoanalysis in the light of neuroscience (for a specialized bibliography see Amati-Mehler, Canestri, & Argentieri, 1990; Bleichmar, 2001).

23. That is, the interpretation of prior discourse, observation of the physical environment, encyclopaedic memory, knowledge of the speaker, cultural, scientific, or religious beliefs, fantasy life, and so on. We may see that precisely the reverse takes place in the psychoanalytic field, where the metapsychological and psychopathological theories provide a wide conceptual and contextual frame of reference.

24. Recent researches in developmental psychology and neuropsychology suggest, among other things, that word learning in children typically entails monitoring the speaker's referential intentions by checking the direction of his or her gaze. Autistic children, on the contrary, make a purely mechanical association between word and object and fail to monitor the speaker's inferential intentions through checking gaze direction. Their difficulties are not restricted to mind-reading abilities but also extend to other actions linked to nonverbal communication. Some studies comparing the interpretation of metaphor and verbal irony in children with normal development and people with autism have shown that their respective comprehension is tied to different levels of mental work.

25. However, philosophers have described mind-reading as an exercise in reflective reasoning (a central process, in Fodor's terms) involving the application of general reasoning abilities to premises based on explicit assumptions about the relations between mental states and behaviour.

26. Subjects with Williams Syndrome, for instance, have good mind-reading and communication abilities but poor general reasoning abilities, whereas subjects with Asperger's syndrome may have good general reasoning abilities combined with serious impairments in mind-reading abilities.

27. Up to now, research has focused mainly on the production rather than the comprehension side, given that this may be more difficult to study because general mind-reading abilities might compensate to some extent for specifically pragmatic impairments (Bishop, 1997).

28. Disorganization movements may revive previous somatizations or determine the appearance of new illness; organization movements may be linked to the decrease of somatic pathology.

29. "Raw" dreams depict, through direct scenes, the fulfilment of instinctual aims; their distortion is so minimal that it would be possible to think that they present a sort of photograph of the unconscious.

Commentary

Jorge Canestri

From the very beginning, the author of this excellent and comprehensive chapter clearly explains the extent and complexity of the conceptual field in which we must move in order to understand the relationships between linguistics and psychoanalysis. This is due not only to the intrinsic complexity of the guiding theories of contemporary linguistics and psychoanalysis and to the ever-problematic delineation of an interdisciplinary area, but also, and perhaps above all, to the fact that this dialogue is not one between just two interlocutors—psychoanalysis and linguistics—but between many: semiotics, philosophy of language, cognitive theories, philosophy of mind, theories on mentalization, psycholinguistics, and neurolinguistics. It is particularly difficult to exclude any of these disciplines when discussing the relationships that exist between language and the theory and practice of psychoanalysis.

Susana Vinocur-Fischbein takes this into account when stating that "The object 'language' of psychoanalysis is ordinary speech transformed by the intersubjective psychoanalytic field, whereas the '*langue*', the object studied by linguistics for decades, is the abstract formal system that has shunned motivation, affect, and the subjective acquisition of meaning." This difference is essential for distinguishing the object that is interesting for psychoanalytic reflection and for constructing an interdisciplinary dialogue. The object "language" that psychoanalysis confronts is certainly closer to the linguistic activities of subjects (Canestri, 2000) than to the abstraction of the "*langue*".

The division of the work into five sections is a valuable help for readers: they are led by the hand through a variegated panorama dense with useful information to then enter a terrain that is unfamiliar to most psychoanalysts—although the same could be said about linguists as far as our discipline is concerned, even though in both cases there are a few, but significant, exceptions. Despite the fact that Freud defined our discipline as a "talking cure" and that the father of psychoanalysis made a fundamental contribution to what we can today say about the language-psychoanalysis relationship, there is a lack of proportion between the results so far obtained in the psychoanalytic study of language, and its recognized importance in theory and in practice.

In the *first section,* "Psychoanalysis and Language Theories", Vinocur-Fischbein deals with these questions, underlining the incompatibility between the structural linguistics of De Saussure and Chomsky's transformational grammar with their universalistic abstractions, and the "subject" of psychoanalysis. But she also identifies the absence of a "genuinely psychoanalytic theory of language (Anzieu, 1980; Green, 1984, 1995)"—a theory that, in my opinion, is unlikely to see the light of day considering the present status of our knowledge and our dialogue with the specialists in the above-mentioned disciplines.

I agree with the helpful division that Vinocur-Fischbein proposes between the three areas of influence that linguistics exerts on psychoanalysis. The interested reader will find it useful (and compatible with the classification proposed by the author) to consult the work of the psychoanalyst and linguist L. Danon-Boileau (1987), who, as well as offering a rich and productive interweaving of the two disciplines, presents a well-articulated panorama of what has been explored in psychoanalytic reflections about language.

One of the many good points of Vinocur-Fischbein 's work is her examination, in the *second section,* "Language, Symbol Formation Processes, and Linguistics in Río de la Plata psychoanalysis", of the contribution—let me say pioneering—to our argument made by Río de la Plata psychoanalysis. It is no mystery that the so-called imperialism of the English language (today's Latin) offers many advantages for communication between cultures, as did Latin in the cultural world until the seventeenth century. But we are also aware that, with a few exceptions, nothing remaining outside the sphere of influence of the English language has much chance of spreading through the field of international psychoanalysis. One of the clearest examples is what the author rightly considers Luisa Álvarez de Toledo's (1954) ground-breaking essay: "The Analysis of 'Associating', 'Interpreting' and 'Words'". This work, written in 1954, was translated into English and published in the *International Journal of Psychoanalysis* 42 years later. It anticipates by three years the famous text by Austin (1957) and by 15 years J. Searle's (1969) similarly well-known book on all that concerns the favourite theme of pragmatic theoreticians, namely "the notion of Speech Act as a discursive event that goes beyond the verbal text" (Vinocur-Fischbein). It precedes by almost 40 years the growing interest on the part of contemporary psychoanalysis for the "pragmatic turn" in linguistics and philosophy of language. And what about the enormous lot of work done by David Liberman, who attempted to integrate communication, Chomskian linguistic theory, and psychoanalytic theory, defining psychoanalysis as "a basic science that consists in investigating the evolution of analytic dialogue in and out of sessions" (Liberman, 1976, p. 101, quoted by Vinocur-Fischbein)? This work, contained in three volumes and written in Spanish, has still not been translated into English. This is one of the many reasons to welcome the publication of this volume by the IPA Library of Psychoanalysis.

However, the exploration of the psychoanalytic universe linked to reflections on the incidence of language and of linguistic theories on our theory and our practice is certainly not limited to these two major names. In Susana Vinocur-Fischbein's chapter the reader will find an accurate description of the different researches leading us from the past to the present-day state of the art in Río de la Plata psychoanalysis. They range from the ideas of E. Rodrigué, A. Aberastury, E. Del Valle, and M. Casas de Pereda on symbolization, symbolic deficit, and lack of representations, the elaborations by I. Berenstein in the wake of Greimas's structural semantics, and the pioneering work of Liberman on interpretive and complementary styles and on reformulations of psychoanalytic psychopathology in terms of communicative styles, to the recent proposals by Winograd on the possibility of evaluating the psychoanalytic process and the patient's psychic changes following the stylistic changes of the patients themselves and, lastly, to the sophisticated research by D. Maldavsky that has led to the creation of an instrument and method entitled the "David Liberman Algorithm" (ADL), recently published in the *International Journal of Psycho-Analysis.*

The *third section* deals with those changes in the theoretical problems of linguistics, semiotics, and the philosophy of language that make present-day developments possible. The title of the section, "New Perspectives: From Transformational Grammar to Linguistic Pragmatics, from Sentence to Discourse", describes the oscillation by which pragmatics and discourse become the centre of interest of present-day linguistic thinking. It is this difference in viewpoint, as the author rightly emphasizes in her text, that brings linguistic disciplines and semiotics closer to psychoanalysis, since, as we mentioned earlier, the object "language" of psychoanalysis is more intimately linked to the linguistic activity of the subjects implicated in the analytic experience than to the abstraction of the "*langue*".

The fact that, on the basis of the so-called later Wittgenstein, the philosophy of language and linguistics began to consider utterances as units of meaning and language use as the core of the relationships between words and the world gave rise to what we know as the "pragmatic turn".

The philosopher Karl Otto Apel, in his book *Le logos propre au langage humain,* recalls a comment by Karl Popper following Apel's lecture on communication. Popper objected that to pay so much attention to communication was useless, inasmuch as it is what we have in common with animals, and that what is important in human language are propositions. Apel writes that Popper's ideas refer to the classical or propositional paradigm—that is, the semantic–logical–referential of the *logos.* Apel states that the platonic root of *logos* was dialogic (*logos* as language *and* as discourse in conversation). Aristotle, after Plato, introduced a distinction between *semantikòs* logos and *apofantikòs* logos. The semantic logos of language must be conceived as having a wider meaning than that of the representative function of language. *Semantikòs* logos develops its functions of communicative agreement on the world in dialogue. From this point of view, what appears as an essential dimension of this new pragmatic paradigm, in opposition to the classical paradigm, is now the link with a theory of meaning. Pragmatics contributes to the semantic logos: to the intersubjectively valid meaning of the signs of language and to the meaning of theories. In a paper on these subjects I commented that probably

> no psychoanalyst in his clinical practice has never neglected this aspect relative to the contribution of pragmatics in the construction of meaning, inasmuch as Freud, in the third chapter of his rightly famous book "Der Witz", proposes the well known joke: "Two Jews met in a railway carriage at a station in Galicia . . ." (1905, p. 115) . . . what I wish to emphasize in this case is the fact that Freud places pragmatics in the foreground; in fact, in the communication between the two Jews, the truth does not depend on the description of "things as they are", but on what the subjects do with the words. [Canestri, 1999, 2002a]

However, not intuitively neglecting the contribution of pragmatics to the meaning in clinical practice does not, in itself, guarantee either the possibility of conceptualizing it adequately, or of drawing from this new paradigm the greatest possible profit for our discipline.

For this, we must thank the author of this chapter, who leads us with great clarity through the far from simple alternatives that the philosophy of language and linguistics offers us for reflection. Grice's notion of implicature, Sperber and Wilson's contribution with the "relevance principle", inferential models as opposed or complementary to code models, Bakhtin's dialogism, Kerbrat-Orecchioni's conceptualization of enunciation, and so on, are all presented with authority and are applied to a review of some fragments of Freud's *Hans* that are of great interest.

Certain other writers would not be out of place in this list. I would have included the well-known recently deceased philosopher D. Davidson and his theory that emphasizes that in order to understand the meaning of an utterance it is necessary to insert the discourse into the general framework of rational action, and that an utterance directed to an interlocutor has two components: the wish to produce a reaction depending on the semantic characteristics of the utterance, and the belief that the interlocutor has the necessary resources to understand the utterance just as we ourselves intend it (Davidson, 1984). I would also have mentioned the French linguist A. Culioli (1990, 2002) who has outlined three different levels in the treatment of representation, and the work of L. Danon-Boileau (1987) on enunciation. But this does not detract from the comprehensiveness of the work of the author, who has had to condense an immense quantity of information into a space that was necessarily limited.

The *fourth section,* specifically dedicated to "Psychoanalysis and Pragmatics: Towards a Shared Interest", in addition to investigating the previous discussion further, develops a very interesting and topical issue: psychic functioning from the point of view of psychoanalysis and from the perspective of pragmatics, mainly assisted by the Cognitive Sciences. Vinocur-Fischbein foresees certain possible and, for some, desirable convergences between psychoanalysis and pragmatics. This informs the reader about developments in Latin American psychoanalysis that take into account other disciplines dealing with mental processing: the "tertiary process" of H. Fiorini, the "third topography" of R. Zuckerfeld, the concept of superimposed psychic areas of N. Marucco, the study of psychosomatic disorders with failure of symbolization of J. Fischbein, the "unthinkable", the "unmentionable", and the "unspeakable" of R. D'Alvia, and H. Bleichmar's theory of mental modularity as applied to psychoanalysis. Interested readers will find a comprehensive bibliography that also demonstrates the vitality and interest of Río de la Plata psychoanalysis for these arguments.

The second part of this section is dedicated to a particularly difficult and controversial issue: "the relationship between language, consciousness, and cognition, with special reference to the nature and functioning of the mental mechanisms employed in the cognitive and *inferential* processes associated with the comprehension of meaning" (italics added). It is obvious that the change of paradigm relative to the processes of comprehension of the utterances—that is, the passage from a model of codification–decodification to an inferential model that presupposes mental processes in the two interlocutors—directs the researchers' attention and efforts towards attempting to investigate and conceptualize the nature of these processes of "mind-reading". P. Carruthers, mentioned in the text, is one of the active and authoritative researchers in the field of the endless and significant dilemma of the thought–language relationship: another area of research about which, like mind-reading (which is connected to it), psychoanalysis would have something to say. Carruthers, as co-editor of the result of an interdisciplinary project, *Language and Thought* (Carruthers & Boucher, 1998)—which is of great help on these arguments—wrote: "we felt that the issue of language and thought had almost dropped from sight in the cognitive sciences in recent decades, and that the time was ripe for a more fine-grained examination of the issues from an interdisciplinary perspective" (p. xiii). I believe that the same observation would be valid for psychoanalysis: a reflection on the problems relative to the inner language and to the different links between thought and language, between types of representations, etc., would be extremely useful. I will not dwell on this theme, as that would require much more space than has been allotted to me, but I believe the author has done well to call it to the reader's attention.

The *fifth* and final *section,* "The Dream Narrative: Discourse and Subjectivity", deals with one of the author's areas of research: she has developed a project on the narrative of the manifest content of dreams in patients with psychosomatic disorders, a narrative that reveals, following Vinocur-Fischbein, the interdependence of all the systems involved in psychic functioning. Willy Baranger, another well-known Latin American psychoanalyst, contributes—this time with his own ideas, also *ante-literam,* and in line with the theses developed in the chapter about the new paradigm offered by pragmatics—his concept of dreams as "intentional communicative signs within the analytic situation" (Vinocur-Fischbein), "a language whose choice among other multiple possible languages is itself significant" (Baranger, 1969, p. 185, quoted by Vinocur-Fischbein). The thesis of the author is that "dream narrative exhibits certain features [which she lists subsequently] that make it recognizable as a specific discursive strategy" (Vinocur-Fischbein). I agree with this formulation of the problem.

In the "Closing Remarks" it is emphasized that today crossing the boundaries between disciplines is necessary and fruitful, despite the risk of misunderstandings and reductionisms. The construction of areas of reciprocal compatibility cannot be taken for granted, but it certainly needs to be sought. A change of paradigms is desirable, also in the psychoanalytic field.

Before ending these brief comments, which unreservedly acknowledge the quality, interest, and completeness of the work being examined, and being motivated by the understandable insatiability of one who deals with these matters, I must say that I should like to have found a section dealing with the acquisition of language. This is also an immense field in which sharply contrasting theories confront each other and where interdisciplinarity reigns supreme in the clash between neurosciences, psycholinguistics, neuropsychology, cognitive theories, and psychoanalytic theories. However, the theme of the affective mother/environment–child exchange and its relationship with the acquisition of language and with the pathologies revealed in the dyadic constructions (Lieven, 1978) seem to me to be particularly interesting for our discipline. All this makes us anxious to read the continuation of this work.

5

The experience of truth in clinical psychoanalysis

Antonio Muniz de Rezende

The question of truth is central in Bion's psychoanalysis. In various works, he tells us of psychoanalytic practice as being, above all, a search for the truth. However, recognizing that all sciences are a search for true knowledge, in the case of psychoanalysis this *question* presents some very singular characteristics.

Coherence, correspondence, symbolic consensus

Adopting the terminology proposed by Jean Ladrière (1970) of the Catholic University of Louvain, we are reminded of the distinction he established among (a) formal sciences, for which truth is *coherence*; (b) empirical–formal sciences, for which truth is *correspondence*; and (c) the human sciences, for which truth is *symbolic consensus*.

The truth as coherence *in formal sciences and in psychoanalysis, particularly in the case of schizophrenic patients*

The formal sciences, whose paradigm is mathematics, are so called because they are the most abstract that we have knowledge of. Because of this, the discourse of these sciences has a certain autonomy and is rationally confirmed in the way the mathematical entities relate among themselves through signs. Therefore, there are no real mistakes in formal sciences, unless one considers reading mistakes. Hence, formal sciences are also recognized as the more rational and exact, providing ample certainty relative to the knowledge derived from their practice. This is a consequence of the fact that the statements are univocally understood—that is, they have the same permanent meaning, indefinitely. This also means a very special relationship between semantics and semiotics, favouring the latter, with the prevalence of the signs over the symbols themselves. The sign can be univocal, whereas the symbol will always be polysemous. In this way, we speak not of mathematical *interpretation,* but only of *consistency* in coherence. For the formal sciences, the truth is experienced as "*coherence*"—or, more precisely as "*discourse coherence*"—in establishing relationships between various "*propositions*" and their diverse "*elements*". More than just in appearance, we are dealing with *formal logic* in its purest form.

When conceiving his *Grid* as an instrument to follow the development of thought, Bion (1977) did not hesitate to reserve the last category (H) for *algebraic calculus,* in continuation with the *deductive scientific system* (G). This does not mean to say, as has already been suggested, that the Bionian analyst is being invited to practise psychoanalysis as if it were some kind of psychological algebra. It actually means that Bionian psychoanalysis, at its highest form of achievement, implies access to a level of thought in which algebra also becomes possible.

A fine example given by Bion himself (1973) is regarding the way in which he conceives the *container/contained* element. In a way, the Kleinian concept of container is still based on Euclidean geometry, which, in its turn, depends on sensorial perception. The Kleinian container is perceived as a three-dimensional figure—let us say, a cube—with a whole internal space into which the projections are made. Going beyond Euclidean geometry, Bion (1970, 1973) refers us to the algebraic geometry of Rieman and Lobachevski, with the possibility of thinking in a space of more than three dimensions, able to contain psychotic projections thrown into an infinite space.

It was principally Matte Blanco (1981, 1988) who brought back Bion's great intuitions with respect to the logic of the Unconscious, showing how, finally, it is another logic altogether. In fact, Bionian psychoanalysis makes us recognize the presence of two logics—a bilogic, or even a binocular logic—in such a way that the coherence of one does not necessarily coincide with the coherence of the other. And, paradoxically, this also is congruent with the great psychoanalytic discoveries. The Unconscious exists and never fails to surprise the Conscious!

And then we perceive how important the theme of *thought* is in Bion's psychoanalysis. It is not without reason that Matte Blanco wrote *Thinking, Feeling, and Being* (1988), and I myself wrote *Wilfred Ruprecht Bion, Uma Psicanálise do Pensamento* [Wilfred Ruprecht Bion, A Psychoanalysis of Thought] (Rezende, 1995). As for Bion (1956), we can find extremely important texts about thought disturbances, such as in schizophrenia. Apart from the major symptom, which is mental confusion, the schizophrenic is characterized by attacks against the *links* of connection—precisely those that are normally factors of coherence of the discourse: that is, logic. In his article "Attacks on Linking" (1959), Bion shows how the schizophrenic fails to establish links between ideas, and, consequently, this makes his communication more difficult to understand.

The truth as correspondence *in the formal–empirical sciences and in psychoanalysis, particularly in psychotic patients*

The paradigm of the formal–empirical sciences is physics or, more precisely, physics–mathematics. Taking into account the greater *complexity* of physics in relation to mathematics, this way of expressing it marks, on the one hand, the difference and, on the other, the continuity between the formal–empirical sciences and the formal sciences. They are empirical because they are based on experience, but they continue to be formal in their attempt to use mathematical language to *describe* lived experience.

Epistemologically speaking, *correspondence* can be verified at the level of language as well as in relation to the *referring* in question. In the case of the empirical–formal sciences this *referring* is the reality itself as an object of experience. Thus it makes sense that one of the first books written by Bion would be *Learning from Experience* (Bion, 1962a). We learn psychoanalysis through the psychoanalytic experience. However, Bion is not actually an empiricist in the strict sense of the term. He frequently quotes one of Kant's sayings: "*Intuition without concept is blind, concept without intuition is empty.*" This is another way that Bion tells us how he conceives the truth as *correspondence:* a correspondence between intuition and concept, between concept and intuition; neither can exist without the other.

With regard to the formal sciences, psychoanalysis, together with the formal–empirical sciences, introduces a greater *complexity* and recognizes the profound dimension of a dialogue with *complex* contemporary *thought.* The representatives of *complex* contemporary *thought* show us, in a way, the continuity between the science of nature (*Physis*) and all the others, as nature, in all its *complexity,* is the largest *container,* in which all the differences are contained. Edgar Morin (1977) and Ilya Prigogine (1996) have, inevitably, become interlocutors for contemporary psychoanalysts. However, it is not because of this that we can reduce psychoanalysis to only a small case within *complex thought.* I have tried to approach some related questions on this subject in my book, *A psicanálise atual, na interface das novas ciências* [Contemporary psychoanalysis in the interface of new sciences] (Rezende, 2001).

When I speak about contemporary psychoanalysis, I refer to Bion's thoughts, noting especially the distinction established by him among various levels of reality with the respective levels of experience: *physical* reality, *sensorial* reality, *psychic* reality, *pneumatic* or *spiritual* reality, and *ultimate* reality. If we learn from experience, then consequently we learn different things at the various levels of reality. Therefore, the proposal of Bion's (1965) psychoanalysis is that we pass from one level to another, through the necessary *transformations,* but always maintaining ourselves in the *direction* of "O", to be in *agreement* with "O". Furthermore, with the experience of truth as *coherence,* Bion has helped us to reflect about what happens with schizophrenics; with truth as *correspondence,* he has invited us to reflect about *psychotics* and their attacks on reality at various levels.

An important aspect of this reflection is when, expanding Melanie Klein's ideas, Bion shows us how the *envious* person psychopathically attacks the good object, seeing it with bad eyes, to the point of becoming, because of this, a bad observer. If, according to Heisenberg (1969), "the observer is part of the observation", this situation impedes the *envious* person from having access to the truth as *correspondence.* The same can be said of a *liar,* for equally serious reasons: the *liar* knows the truth but does not love it; thus he attacks it, even if, for this reason, he must continue with his lie for the rest of his life. And it is worse when others practise a *psychotic moralist dogma-*

tism, dogmatically imposing on him and others arbitrary criteria of action and values. Nevertheless, the gravest situation is when the psychotic not only attacks, but ends up denying his own mental life, in the worst form of *reductionism*, by making symbols and ideas concrete. *Concrete thought*, in its extreme, invalidates not only the psychoanalytic experience but also its discourse.

The truth as symbolic consensus *in the human sciences and in psychoanalysis, particularly in the case of neurotic patients*

In expanding on Bion's ideas, we recognize that post-paradigmatic psychoanalysis is not merely another case among the other sciences. Moreover, the question has already been raised regarding the originality of the human sciences, particularly because they are more *complex* than the others. Even without drawing an absolute distinction between the human and the natural sciences, we must not forget to affirm the paradox contained in the former: that, for human beings, *culture* is, in fact, *natural* (according to Vygostky, 1984, 1989); it does not, however, reduce itself to a mere physical phenomenon. Even more significantly, *symbolization* is a *natural* process, principally with regard to a healthy human (according to psychoanalysis).

It is this that permits us to also recognize the originality of the experience of truth—as *symbolic consensus*—in the field of human sciences and in psychoanalysis. We can also add, expanding on what we have already said about psychosis, that this consists of an attack against something that is constitutive of the very human condition in its symbolic capacity. By *symbolization*—expanding on Bion as well as Merleau-Ponty (1942, 1945) and Paul Ricoeur (1965, 1969)—I understand the *unified polysemy* present in the diversity of cultures, understood as a historic form of existence. We are equally human, despite living our symbols and values differently. In the adequate treatment of similarities and differences, Bion (1965) invites us to the practice of *transformations*, by means of the use of *symbolic analogy*.

Anthropologists like Lévi-Strauss (1958) became valuable interlocutors of psychoanalysis, not only in dealing with the diversity of languages, but precisely in recognizing different views of the world from the point of view of diverse cultures. With this in mind, Bion makes a valuable contribution, speaking of *common sense* at its diverse levels of achievement: common sense at the level of *senses*, common sense at the level of *emotions*, common sense at the level of *thought*, common sense at the level of *language* and *communication*, common sense at the level of *being* and of *acting*.

Relative to the *sensorial* perceptive system, following an intuition that has come down to us from classical philosophy, Bion (1963) recognizes that there is nothing in the mind that has not first gone through the senses [*nihil est in intellectu quod prius non fuerit in sensu*]. Continuing, he tells us of the truth of the senses, in the way one confirms the other, in a properly *synaesthesic* activity. *Synaesthesia* is the name of *common sense* making an experience of the truth at the very sensitive level.

Moreover, surprisingly, in "A Theory of Thinking" Bion (1962b) even suggests an *emotional* perceptive system, with which we can make another kind of experience of the truth, as *shared emotional experience*. What happens at the level of the senses happens *analogically* at the level of emotions, when one emotion confirms another relative to the same object: a loved but also hated object is recognized as being the same *total* object, emotionally perceived by the same person or by various persons.

Even more profoundly, we can recognize the possibility of a *common sense* at the level of thought, when people meet at the level of intuition and ideas. With regard to both, Bion teaches us, on the one hand, that the very psychic objects are not "*seen*" at the sensorial level but "*intuited*" with intelligence at a deeper level. True *common sense* exists when the psychoanalytic couple share the same intuition with respect to the patient's experiences. This is manifested by means of interpretation, understood precisely as a sharing of intuitions in the communication between analyst and analysand. We can also talk here about truth as *symbolic consensus* in the sharing of intuitions with respect to the experience lived by the analytic couple.

Following this, we have *common sense* in the socio-cultural relationship. The most eloquent example is that of Bion himself, who was born in India, lived in England, frequently visited the European continent, lived in the United States, and travelled several times to South America: an authentic citizen of the universe. We can say that Bion had the opportunity to establish a dialogue with various cultures and, at this level, to experience the truth as symbolic consensus in a socio-cultural *common sense*.

As an example, we can verify, above all, the privileged place that he attributes to myths. Moreover, in *Learning from Experience* (1962a) and *Elements of Psychoanalysis* (1963) he recognizes that dealing with objects and elements of psychoanalysis extends itself towards the dominion of the senses, of *myths,* and of passions; as in the *Grid* (1977), Category C is reserved for dreams and *myths,* of which he affirms that "the *myth* is like the dream of humanity", therefore concerning all of us. Myths show something in common among men. It is probably regarding the myths that Jung spoke of a *collective unconscious,* in whose field the experience of truth becomes possible in a myth-symbolic consensus, in a new form of *common sense.*

In this way, Bion not only shows respect for his origins, but he recognizes his links with Hindu culture in the way he quotes the *Mahabharata,* especially from the Baghavad Gita chapter (*The sublime chant*), in which the characters of Arjuna and Krishna invite us to change levels: Arjuna representing humanity and its conflicts, Krishna sending us on to another level, where conflicts are resolved. I believe it can be said that Bion's emphasis on changing levels in the psychoanalytic experience is another sign of what he learned from Hindu myths and culture.

I also think that it is in this context that we find Bion's (1970) great intuitions with respect to the relations between the mystic and the group. In an extremely simple phrase, he summarizes the situation: "The group needs the mystic, the mystic needs the group." And in saying this, at the same time he recognizes how and how far *common sense* can become difficult within the group, in a true experience of truth as *symbolic consensus.* The difficulty occurs precisely because of the fact that the mystic is an exceptional, *gifted* individual, with talents that are not always shared within the group. Regarding these talents, Bion mentions three different situations in relation to the *genius,* the *messiah,* and the *mystic.* Making use of a language inspired by Spinoza, I believe I can say that the genius is characterized by the *new idea,* the messiah by the *promising idea,* and the mystic by the *true idea.* Owing to the exceptionally gifted individual's talents, many difficulties could appear within the group, obstructing the establishment of a true group *common sense,* even—or particularly—when dealing with a group of psychoanalysts. This all indicates that Bion was talking about his own experience in the bosom of the British Psychoanalytical Society, of which, notwithstanding, he became President.

In the same volume of *Attention and Interpretation* (1970), apart from speaking of the mystic and the group, he also tells us of the container/contained and of the difficulties that the group might find in *containing* the exceptional individual. *Genius, messiah,* and *mystic* have experiences that do not combine with the conservatism of the Establishment and its *dominant castes* (especially in the Training Institutes). It is not easy to arrive at a *symbolic consensus* in an institutional *common sense*! Because of this, Bion does not hesitate to speak about a *moralist psychotic dogmatism* making the symbolic communion difficult and, indeed, impeding it among the members themselves. I keep asking myself whether, as Bionian analysts, we should not take up again the Frankfurt Critic School's proposal to establish a criticism of the unconscious *ideology* that is present and active in groups formed by psychoanalysts. We must especially be alert to the possibility of an *ideological common sense* among psychoanalysts—as has been denounced recently by Slavoj Zizek (1989), speaking about the sublime object of the ideology.

This is also what allows us to analyse the religious problem, not so much in its mystical and ethical context, but, rather in the context of the *myth–poetic–religious* experience. In *Caesura* (1977), speaking of the *cairotic* (from Greek *kairós*) moments that separate our existence, Bion suggests two significant cuts, one at the beginning, the other at the end, connoting the religious creation myths and the eschatology.

I could not end these considerations about *common sense* without evoking the place that Bion reserved for Meister Eckhart [1260–1327], mystic theologian of fourteenth-century Rhineland. On the one hand, and surprisingly, there are many shared points between Hindu thought and Meister Eckhart's thought; on the other hand, the latter seems to have given Bion (1965) some precious intuitions with which he managed to go beyond the impasse suggested by Kant's famous phrase: "*Intuition without concept is blind, concept without intuition is empty.*"

Starting from the Eckhartian distinction between God and Godhead, Bion also recognizes that God is everything we say about "Him", but it is not about "Her". We have concepts about God but not about Godhead. It is for this reason we can go beyond Kant and recognize that, in this case, we have an intuition without concept, which is not empty because of the presence of Godhead. It is Meister Eckhart who helps us to understand the paradox, by emphasizing the primacy of faith relative to the presence of Ultimate Reality. In the same way, psychoanalysis is everything we say about the mind, but is not the mind itself. In this respect, Bion poetically says that psychoanalysis "more than container, is a probe", for which, he adds, we must keep our receivers open in order to capture the signals of the Ultimate Reality, wherever they come from. In the same way as Meister Eckhart spoke of the presence of an invisible Godhead, Bion tells us of the presence of "O", *void, formless, infinite, unnameable,* no longer as an object of knowledge but one of faith, from which comes his profession of fundamental faith: "*I believe in the Ultimate Reality as a primordial fact.*" The mystic model, for Bion, is the richest of all, and also the most mysterious, with the possibility of *At-one-ment* with "O".

Unveiling, recollection, concordance

The three new modalities of the experience of truth in the psychoanalytic clinic concern the greatest *complexity* of psychoanalysis: the truth as *unveiling,* as *recollection,* and as *concordance.*

The truth as unveiling in the psychoanalytic clinic

Apart from an experience of truth from the dialogue with other sciences, psychoanalysis, being more *complex,* has the possibility to give us an experience typical of the truth as *unveiling* [*desvelamento*]. This must be said taking into account, what Freud teaches us about the *concealing defences,* as well as the fact that the very word *truth*—in Greek, *alétheia*—has a principal meaning of *uncovering* that which had been covered. From this point of view, psychoanalytic clinical activity can be considered as an attempt to *unveil* that which the patient has covered in a defensive attitude of repression. In my volume on the question of truth in psychoanalytic investigation (Rezende, 1999a), I point out five moments of this first clinical experience of truth: *denuding, unmasking, the breaking of the mirror, iconoclasm,* and *catastrophic change.*

Denuding becomes necessary because, with the aim of protecting himself, the patient covers, consciously or even unconsciously but almost always guided by the feeling of guilt, what was causing the inconvenience. Writing about the truth, Heidegger (1951–52) teaches us how discreet it is, "showing and hiding itself at the same time". Real truth never totally unveils itself. Using another metaphor, Heidegger says that truth turns its back on us because it walks ahead, showing us the direction to follow. The same should happen with the couple in the analytic situation: both alert to the signals of truth, but with the full respect for the secrets of the other.

Unmasking is an experience of the truth of the personality, taking into account the patient's attempts to favour the personage and the false self, to the detriment of personality. Furthermore, this is one of the strong points of a Bionian psychoanalysis: the focus on the personality conceived as a structure of relations. By not being aware of the meaning of words, many patients and analysts run the risk of confusing *persona* and personality, disregarding the fact that *persona* in Latin is a translation of *mask* in Etruscan. Bionian psychoanalysis is particularly aware of the truth of personality, starting with the quality of the relations that are established with other personalities. Taking into account what Freud says with regard to "Oedipus as structuring personality", Bion also recognizes the importance of relations and links, from the beginning to the end of life—calling our attention to the *character* resulting from the remarkable relations. In the context of the analysis, we must inquire whether a change *of* personality is possible, although one cannot deny the occurrence of relatively significant changes *in* personality, because of the trans*ferential* and countertrans*ferential* relationship.

The *breaking of the mirror* of Narcissus goes beyond the question of the false self, since what occurs, with the inter*ference* of the mirror, is the impossibility of the appearance of the other as another. In contrast, the other becomes *echo,* and the myth was indeed wise when naming the Nymph as Echo. Facing the mirror, on which he projects his own image, Narcissus does not give any chance to the other (he, she, they), who therefore remains outside his life; alienated, without any chance of access to its own identity, Narcissus sees himself equally incapable of a relationship not *in-himself-ed* with the others. Narcissism is not only a neurotic situation, with detours from ability to love, but also a psychotic disturbance that is close to autism and other forms of encapsulation. The situation is so tragic that it is not at all surprising when you think of it: Narcissus's death could very well be considered a suicide.

Iconoclasm provides a paradoxical experience of truth, expanding on the Oedipus situation, as a criticism of the superego and of the superstructures of the ego. In fact, it is a criticism of the more primitive infantile scheme, under which the child does not really have access to ethics but accommodates itself to models superegoistically imposed by the parents. The myth of the father's death sends us not only to incest taboo as the start of culture and to the symbolic experience characteristic of the human condition, but also precisely to the symbolic statute of ethics as a form developed from human existence inside the creative process. After the death of God, the principal worry of psychoanalysis is with the false gods, promoters of the death of humans: not only sadomasochism, but other diverse forms of destructive aggressiveness, starting with passive aggressiveness, under the direct action of the death instinct.

The truth as *catastrophic change* starts to appear along with the process of *deconstruction, "de fond en comble"*. The most eloquent example that we can give is the deconstruction of the Tower of Babel. Though Bion (1963) often spoke of the Tower of Babel to imply a determined conception of God as zealous with his own power and knowledge, there is a clear allusion to the competitive spirit of those who intend to become omnipotent to the point of overcoming any threat of death. More than just a simple confrontation with a greedy God, the Tower of Babel again puts the myths of omniscience, omnipotence, and immortality in front of us. When he invites us to *think* of tolerance to frustration, Bion speaks about such tolerance as being derived from the force in the fight for life, with creativity and hope, based principally on the possibility of good alliances. Regarding this, I like to point out, with respect both to the Deluge and the Tower of Babel, that the *rainbow* was present as a sign of, and an invitation to, the Alliance. (Bion does not appear to have perceived how the true impasse of the Tower of Babel was the denial of the Alliance.)

The truth as recollection in Latin languages

Though having formulated the *without memory, without desire, without comprehension* principle, Bion (1970) does not forget to distinguish, in *Attention and Interpretation,* between *memory* and *recollection* [*recordação*]. The first signifies a repetitive form of dependency on the past, the second means a present experience of the *link,* by way of *gratitude.* Without doubt, this is one of the most important points of Melanie Klein's (1957) influence over Bion.

Personally, I think it very significant to establish a relation between Bion and Heidegger, through the mediation of Melanie Klein, concerning one of the richest themes in the psychoanalysis of both.

Bion recognizes the importance of *thought* in the clinical practice of his psychoanalysis; Heidegger (1951–52), having queried the meaning of *to think* ["*Was heisst Denken?*"], answers by saying that *thinking* means *being grateful* ["*Denken heisst Danken*"]. Melanie Klein (1957) counters, in "Envy and Gratitude", by recognizing in the latter, a very rich capacity of relationship with the other and with reality.

An important consequence of this introduction of gratitude into the process of thinking is a significant expansion of Bion's ideas. Not only is thought conceived as tolerance to frustration (with force of resolution and creativity . . .) but, "Kleinianly" and "Heideggerianly", it is placed in relationship with gratitude and recollection. It is not only tolerance to frustration that permits thought, but—in the same way as Ricoeur (1965) tells us that the symbol makes us think [*le symbole donne à penser*]—so also does gratitude, principally due to the strengthening of links.

The primitive meaning among the Greeks of the word *truth* as not-forgetfulness [*a-létheia*] was analysed by Detienne (1981) in his book entitled *Les Maîtres de Vérité dans la Grêce archaïque* [The masters of the truth in ancient Greece]. In Bion's perspective, it is a matter of, on the one hand, recognizing the importance of psychoanalytic investigation as archaeological investigation, and, on the other, showing the necessity of going deep, with the sense of us reaching the core of the present structure of the personality. In his trilogy *A Memoir of the Future* (1991), Bion does not only play a game of words in the titles of the three volumes—*The Dream, The Past Presented* (principally), and *Dawn of Oblivion*— but also, by using the onion model, he shows us how the "archaeological" is also the "nuclear", which, as such, continues to the present, to the point of being able to be analysed. In this way, Bion is very close to Lacan (1953) when the latter tells us that it is not the past that gives meaning to the present, but it is the present that gives meaning to the past—a symbolic re-meaning [*ressignification après coup*].

It is interesting how, in Detienne's interpretation, this role of *master of truth* is attributed principally to the poet—mainly at the time when society was formed by great number of illiterates. However, until today, the scholars of Greek culture are unanimous in recognizing that Homer, in fact, narrated the history of Greece, in a way that no other citizen could allege not recognizing it in its most important details. The Greeks quote Homer, Bion quotes the *Mahabharata* and Shakespeare!

In some way we also go in search of an analyst who has this poetical function developed to the point of not allowing us to forget the origin of our foundation, helping us to think of it using the resource of the proto-myths of humanity and of each individual. Once again, Bion is profoundly correct in recognizing that *myths are like the dream of humanity, the dream like the myth of the individual.*

One of the more significant and beautiful aspects in the elaboration of the depressive position, the way I usually describe it with the help of the parable of the Prodigal Son, is when he, after reaching the depths of the abyss, comes to his senses and thinking, he recollects and rediscovers the *links* he had with his father, and these permit him to return and so to rediscover his own identity.

The Bionian aspect of the question has everything to do with the conception of personality as a structure of remarkable relations; this can be understood as relations that constitute the character, up to a point that it is by means of them that each one is recognized and identified. Remarkable relations are those that establish *links*—the more significant, the more durable. In this sense, our truth is *the truth of our links.* This shows us Bion's originality when he tells us of the third element of psychoanalysis as being LH–K. Love and hate are link generators that permit a certain type of knowledge and interrelation of personalities, be it in the shape of *recognizing* [*reconhecimento*] or *ignorance* [*desconhecimento*]—that is, in terms of love and hate. Principally, in Latin languages, the verb *to recognize* [*reconhecer*] means both being grateful and actually identifying someone. Finally, in a Bionian–Kleinian context, only gratitude recognizes, to the point of knowing the truth in each one. In the same way, it is hate that does not recognize, impeding recognition [*reconhecimento*] in K and favouring the ignorance [*desconhecimento*] in –K.

All of this makes us recognize the elaboration of two positions (as the second element of psychoanalysis), stating from the beginning that elaboration of PEP can be considered an indispensable stage before the elaboration of PD. Some have already suggested that, among Kleinians, there would be a certain leaning towards PD—something that, according to them, Bion would have had difficulties in admitting. However, a deep examination of his thinking shows, on the contrary, the importance that he attributed to the oscillation of two positions and of the interaction that is established between them throughout life, and particularly throughout analysis. Surprisingly, however, we cannot fail to recognize, in Bion, how the elaboration of the defences of the paranoid-schizoid position makes us confirm positive aspects of a constructive aggressiveness, at the disposal of the life instinct. Love of life makes us fight for life, appealing to a constructive aggressiveness to be used with creativity, including the establishing of good alliances—and the unmaking of perverse ones. Frequently it is necessary to *sunder* in order to be able to *decide*, in a healthy way, in terms of a *caesura* in which we define our own personality. Thus, well defined, we resolve to elaborate the depressive position, with all its possibilities of strengthening the links in the establishing of new alliances and in the practice of a symbolic attitude, integrative of differences and able to commemorate the deepest meetings. It is in this way that the possibility of an ultimate experience of the truth arises in Bion's psychoanalytic clinic, in the shape of *concordance*, and in the terms of a transformation into "O".

The truth as concordance

This is the most *complex* form of the experience of truth in psychoanalysis, in expanding everything that has been said about the others, from truth as *coherence* to truth as *correspondence*; from those to the truth as *symbolic consensus* among the various forms of *common sense*; from truth as *unveiling* to truth as *recollection* [*recordação*]; and from this, finally, to truth as *concordance*.

I would start by emphasizing the larger grid of the complexity of experience and of psychoanalytic knowledge. In Bion's Grid, we go from the more complex (*beta*-elements) to the simpler, with algebraic calculus and the deductive scientific system. In my proposal, we go from the simpler (H and G categories) to the more complex, in a progressive and paradoxical discovery of the presence of the Unconscious, not only in linguistic and formal terms, but in the existential and lived sense. In the words of André Green (1973), we go from the analysis of the discourse to the analysis of the *life* of the discourse. We recognize not only that the Unconscious structures itself as language, but that language is an expression of the life of the Unconscious, as representation and affect—in the emotional *choice* of feeling and in the *connection* of the chosen feeling to a determined meaning (in the chain of meanings—"*dans la chaîne des signifiants*")

In this way, Green (1998) himself helps us to suddenly become aware of the *birth of the symbol* in the very bosom of the Unconscious, when he shows us (in his paper "On Discriminating and Not Discriminating between Affect and Representation", presented at the International Congress in Santiago) how the symbolic conjunction of representation and affect comes about. Going back to, and going further into, very important issues that have already been mentioned in *Le discours vivant* [Live *Discourse*] (1973), Green allows us, finally, to elaborate a new psychoanalytic theory of the symbol—that is, a theory that conjoins representation and affect, or, more precisely, knowledge and life, or, even more precisely, *meaning and existence* in the field of the Unconscious.

The most important conclusion from this is with regard to the *truth as concordance.* It is considered not as a logic concordance, neither linguistic nor grammatical, but as a *live concordance* for which the experience of *being* is prior to all others. Nevertheless, "*Being*" now becomes the most complex experience of which we are capable. It is this that leads Bion, finally, to privilege the truth of Being and, even more so, the truth of Being "O"—*infinite, amorphous, unnameable*—not only at the level of mathematical meanings, as he appears to have thought in the first chapters of *Transformations* (1965), but also at the level of existence itself, in an ethic–mystic context, as he proposes in the last chapters of the same volume. Furthermore, in the same way, in *Attention and Interpretation* (1970) he recognizes the greater originality of the mystics, not only when they speak of what they experiment with, but also when they recognize that the *negative capability* is that which best corresponds to everything that can to be said, and which we cannot manage.

Finally, paraphrasing Shakespeare, Bion recognizes—and invites us to recognize—that there are more things between heaven and earth than our vain *psychoanalysis* suspects. Once again, the truth turns its back on us by going on ahead, showing the way. And, following behind, we discover our own name while finding the road that we follow—in the words of Antonio Machado:

> "Walker, there is no path, the path is made as you walk."
>
> [*Caminante no hay camino, el camino se hace al andar.*]
>
> [Machado, 1969, p. 189]

Commentary

James S. Grotstein

Professor Muniz de Rezende's contribution brilliantly and sentiently anticipates a new era in Bion scholarship, that of the unravelling of the hidden order in Bion's radical metatheory for psychoanalysis, the fundamentally organizing and ultimately defining existence of *Truth*, and not just Truth, but the *evolution* (Bianchedi, 2004) of impersonal Truth, "O", to become personal (personally accepted) truth as alpha-element and *its* symbolic descendants.

We have all been long familiar with Bion's better-known concepts of container/contained, alpha-function, alpha- and beta-elements, L, H, and K linkages, and many other such concepts in the same lineage. We also have become familiar, moreover, with the shifts and progressions in Bion's background assumptions as his explorations continued—that is, his initial clinical interest in and punctilious observations of the phenomenology of psychotic patients, and then his "second thoughts" about his observations, which marked the launching of his epistemological period. The latter was characterized by his formulation of a daunting psychoanalytic ontological epistemology (a theory of emotional thinking) that can be epitomized as a protocol for "learning from experience"—*by daring to experience the truth,* as we shall soon see. This meta-concept brought to bear the formidable vertices of empirical science, formal logic, and mathematics as useful analogues with which to calibrate emotional life "scientifically"—that is, rationally. What became more and more apparent as he was progressing on this tack, however, was that he was re-routing and reorienting the psychoanalytic focus from the instinctual drives to emotions (L [loving], H [hating], and K [knowing] as *emotional linkages* between self and objects) and establishing an extraordinary transformational protocol or flowchart to account for the epigenesis of emotional development from the most basic and inchoate experience of "O", which yielded the unmentalized beta-element's (proto-emotion) progression to a mentalized alpha-element (mentally acceptable emotion), which could be felt by the mind.

All the while, Bion alluded to the importance of truth ("the mind needs truth as the body needs food"), but he never really integrated it within his metatheory. With extraordinary synchronicity, Muniz de Rezende and I have each, independently and simultaneously but from different vertices, become involved with studying the fundamental importance of truth as the underlying common denominator that functions as the "Ariadne's thread" that courses its way through the entirety of Bion's work and has often been hidden under the name of its better known alter ego, its twin: *"reality"*. My own assessment of the importance Bion assigns to truth is embedded in my two contributions about the *"truth drive"* (Grotstein, 2004a, 2004b). In the latter contribution I also proffer the notion of a *"truth principle"* to correspond to the reality principle. I shall now examine the vertices Muniz de Rezende has used to reveal the importance with which Bion invests truth.

He initially cites Bion's (1977) reference to truth in *Two Papers: The Grid and Caesura*:

> . . . whatever the discipline, there is a primitive, fundamental, unalterable and basic line—the truth—in which it is based and which restricts the work of the scientist, the religious and the artist . . . that is what we are concerned with—inescapably and unavoidably—even if we have no idea what is true and what is not. [1977, p. 43]

As Muniz de Rezende points out, this work was written at a new era in Bion's thinking, his post-mathematical, post-"scientific", and post-logical attempts to create a new language for psychoanalysis. Today, we might call this attempt his effort to find a neutral *analogue* language. Beginning in 1965, he seemed to veer on a new tack, that of *mystical uncertainty*, had uncovered "O", and now invoked the use of multiple vertices from which to apprehend "O"—that is, the aesthetic, the scientific, the religious, the psychoanalytic, and so on—and was in pursuit of yet a newer language for psychoanalysis, the "language of achievement", the reverie-induced, spontaneously evoked language of intuition, of resonant inner emotional truth.

The author's careful research reveals that Bion (1963) first referred to the subject of truth as a subject in its own right in *Elements of Psycho-Analysis,* when he referred to Oedipus's arrogant determination to learn at all costs the truth about what lay behind the plague in Thebes. Bion implied here, and in other myths, such as those of the Garden of Eden and the Tower of Babel, that the deity was opposed to man's quest for truth—where "truth" was conceived of as God's Truth, which we would now call "O". Parenthetically, it would seem that God's injunction against man's search for truth could be interpreted from the adaptive or pragmatic vertex as a statement about the need for defences (God's injunction) against the blinding glare of "O", the Absolute Truth about Ultimate Reality. Put another way, the Absolute Truth is too much for man. God's injunction against truth is merely a way of stating from the religio-mythical vertex what can be more pragmatically expressed from the scientific vertex: that man needs a transformational semiotic filter to intercept the blinding glare of "O". One is also reminded here of the myth of Prometheus, who stole fire (Knowledge, Truth) from Zeus and suffered the consequences.

The author next cites a later passage in Bion's (1970) *Attention and Interpretation* in which the latter refers to the distinction in practising psychoanalysis or reading his book in which the analyst or reader may resort to acquiring "knowledge about" the subject at hand rather than immersing him/herself in the experience. What I believe Muniz de Rezende is strongly implying is that, according to Bion, there exists a constant conjunction between experiencing one's experience and the experience of truth itself.

The author returns to Bion's allusion to the vertices of art, science, and religion but reconfigures them as three epistemological models: (a) the aesthetic–artistic, (b) the scientific–philosophic, and (c) the religious. These three vertices are to be consulted in elaborating psychoanalytic theories and in undertaking clinical practice. Muniz de Rezende then reminds us that these epistemological models, which derive from other disciplines, are to be consulted as vertices, but ultimately Bionian psychoanalysis departs from these models to become a "post-paradigmatic science in its own right": what Bion would call "mystical science", a science of uncertainty, or what others would call the "non-linear science of complexity", the authentic housing of Truth. The author thereupon reminds us of the three forms of truth found in the practice of science, according to Ladrière (1970): (a) truth as *coherence* in the formal sciences, (b) truth as *correspondence* in the empirical–formal sciences, and (c) truth as *symbolic consensus* in the human sciences. I consider this "truth troika" to be a fascinating and highly useful idea to help us triangulate the most cogent aspect of truth that we may be considering at any given moment.

I believe that it is important to compare the concept of truth with that of reality because in common usage the boundaries are often blurred. Reality constitutes the verdict of the senses ("common sense"), whereas truth constitutes our emotional acceptance of that verdict. Just as the concept of reality has two major connotations, that of the external and that of the internal worlds, respectively, so does the concept of truth have two connotations. One is that of the ontological (emotional) experience or recognition of truth, and the other is the acceptance of an epistemic truth about the relationship between objects in reality. Reality *is*; truth is our recognition of what is.

What the author has effectively done is to give complexity and multidimentionality (multiple vertices) to the concept of truth. Truth as coherence, correspondence, and symbolic consensus, however, constrains the idea of truth to judgements in reference to reality. Even Bion allowed himself to constrain truth to reality judgements when, in describing "O", he listed the "Absolute Truth" alongside "Ultimate Reality". *I* believe that it is more apposite to refer to the "Absolute Truth *about* an Ultimate Reality" that is ever-evolving. What I am trying to say is that I believe psychoanalytic truth exists orthogonally to reality and constitutes *emotional truth* about psychic reality and its evolutions. Put another way, could we state that truth is the ontology that must confront the reality of the symbolic (epistemology), the results of which fall into the realm of phenomenology? Yet being in agreement with "O", according to Muniz de Rezende, constitutes our fundamental calibration. What I am getting at is that I believe that Bion may have mistakenly conflated Absolute Truth with Ultimate Reality rather than considering that Absolute Truth is always impersonal, indifferent, and extraterritorial to the subject's experience. It is only when the subject experiences "O", which *I* define as Ultimate Reality, that the subject's inchoate phenomenologically experienced *personal, subjective* sense of Absolute Truth, as a property inherent in the subject, becomes activated and ontologically operant. In other words, "O" does not consist of the Absolute Truth: it is the property of the subject who confronts Ultimate Reality, "O", and is associated with alpha-function and unconscious consciousness—that is, "attention" or "intuition".

After discussing the parallel works of Vygotsky, Merleau-Ponty, and Ricoeur, the author conflates their contributions with those of Bion, particularly in regard to his work, *Transformations* (1965). When we read this work, we usually have in mind that he is designating transformation as an observational as well as a semiotic process whereby Absolute Truth *and* Ultimate Reality (ever-evolving "O") intersect the subject's emotional frontier to create beta-element impressions, which then undergo a series of progressive semiotic transformations conducted by alpha-function whereby the infinity of the content of the message becomes transduced to binary-oppositional derivatives (e.g. "good" versus "bad") that are practically manageable. What Bion hinted at but never fully enough explicated was the idea that the process of transformation can be seen from the vertex of shifts of perspective as a process designating how the subject him/herself becomes transformed by accepting the verdicts of truth. That is how they "learn (evolve) from experience".

Furthermore, when we consider what the cargo is that is to undergo transformation, we realize that truth, "O", can never, in itself, be transformed. What undergoes transformation, in addition to the self becoming transformed by truth (as I have just discussed), is the semiotic processor, the internal container (including alpha-function), which must undergo a transformation to accommodate to the demands of truth. I should like to proceed one step further to consider the relationship between truth and emotion. The truth is always the truth, but our acceptance of it constitutes an emotional phenomenon. Moreover, I should like to suggest that the ultimate importance of emotions is that they are the vehicles, the carriers of truth. Emotions, as the container of truth, undergo transformations of necessity, truth never.

I found the author's discussion of "common sense" and synaesthesia to be of great interest. It seems that the author is stating that that Bion is suggesting that a sense of truth is arrived at not only by the consensus of the senses responsive to external reality but also by the sense organ of consciousness responsive to psychic reality—that is, at the level of intuition which, in other words, constitutes an emotional perceptive system for the apprehension and relaying of emotional truth. The author states that Bion (1962b):

> even suggests an *emotional* perceptive system, with which we can make another kind of experience of the truth, as *shared emotional experience.* What happens at the level of the senses happens *analogically* at the level of emotions, when one emotion confirms another relative to the same object: a loved but also hated object is recognized as being the same *total* object, emotionally perceived by the same person or by various persons. . . . *common sense* . . . [or] symbolic [emotional] consensus.

The preceding is a fine epitomization of Bion's style of "binocular vision"—that is, thinking along parallel or dual tracks and also thinking in terms of analogues. The author next links this theme with Bion's theory of myths. Bion states that the analytic object is apprehensible by the triangulation of sense, myth, and passion and that "the *myth* is like the dream of humanity"—or the group dream. The author then connects the theme of myths with that of Bion's theory of the mystic: "Making use of a language inspired by Spinoza, I believe I can say that the genius is characterized by the *new idea,* the messiah by the *promising idea,* and the mystic by the *true idea.*"

I believe that the author has given us a highly useful and credible distinction between the types of messages being proffered by these three different aspects of the mythically exceptional individual, yet we can also begin to believe that they, compositely, comprise each of us as latent potentials. They each are agents of the truth. If we were otherwise to personify alpha-function, we might call it a "preternatural presence", "mystic", "messiah", "genius", or "hero"—or the "ineffable subject of the unconscious" (Grotstein, 2000), the ultimate agent of truth reception and truth transmission (what Bion calls "publication").

After skilfully expositing Bion's theory of the mystic and its connection with the "godhead", which Bion derived from Meister

Eckhart, Muniz de Rezende posits the "five moments of this first clinical experience of truth: *denuding, unmasking, the breaking of the mirror, iconoclasm, catastrophic change*", to which he appends *truth as reflection,* and *truth* [*aletheia*] as non-forgetfulness. In regard to denuding, the author cites Heidegger: "Heidegger says that truth turns its back on us because it walks ahead, showing us the direction to follow. The same should happen with the couple in the analytic situation: both alert to the signals of truth, but with the full respect for the secrets of the other." Unmasking refers to the emergence of the personality through the veil of the defensive persona. The breaking of the mirror refers to the need to break the narcissistic encapsulation of the self inherent to the mirror so as to be able to emerge as a true self.

"*Iconoclasm* provides a paradoxical experience of truth, expanding on the Oedipus situation, as a criticism of the superego and of the superstructures of the ego." Truth as catastrophic change refers not only to the truth of change itself but also to the truth that is emergent in the deconstruction of a myth—that is, the Tower of Babel myth, where one's belief in one's omnipotence and omniscience is exposed. The truth as recollection refers to the distinction Bion makes between memory, which is to be eschewed, and recollection, which is spontaneous and to be respected. Furthermore, the latter derives from gratitude towards one's objects and allows for the tolerance of frustration upon which thinking and recollection depend. The truth as *aletheia* is the truth after is has been "archaeologically" unconcealed or uncovered, a situation in which one has reached the true core of the self.

Once again the author has provided us with a multi-tasked, multidimensional approach to the differing vertices of truth in the analytic situation. Investigating truth, according to the author, requires that we state the context of the truth. Comparing Bion with Lacan, the author states: "Bion is very close to Lacan . . . when the latter tells us that it is not the past that gives meaning to the present, but it is the present that gives meaning to the past—a symbolic re-meaning".

Muniz de Rezende then comments that: "Our truth is the truth of our links" in other words, our L, H, and K links when properly aligned (with mitigation of H) give us a window into the truthfulness and authenticity of our being. We *are* and we *become* what we feel about our objects! In his discussion of truth as concordance, the author seems to be implying a concordance between representation and affect, or epistemology and ontology, the latter of which seems to confirm the "felt truth" and authenticity of the former. Together, they constitute the symbol. From this hypothesis the author then invokes the notion of *being*. Citing Bion, he discusses that the epitome of Bion's metatheory for psychoanalysis is the "truth of being O", our "*Dasein*", our "*aletheia*".

In summary, I found this to be a remarkable, multi-disciplinary, and highly credible, if not highly cogent, exploration of the subject of truth from an expanded psychoanalytic perspective. The author casts a brilliant and unique light on an entity rarely discussed in our field, an entity that had hitherto been lost under the rubric of "reality". The truths that he presents about truth are as valuable in theory as they are clinically. His ideas complement my own conception that there exists a truth instinctual drive in human beings, which always brings the awareness of truth towards us.

6

External reality/internal reality: a real dichotomy?

Juan Francisco Jordán-Moore

> If we dreamt the same thing every night, it would affect us as much as the objects we see every day. And if an artisan were sure to dream every night for twelve hours' duration that he was a king, I believe he would be almost as happy as a king, who should dream every night for twelve hours on end that he was an artisan. If we were to dream every night that we were pursued by enemies and harassed by these painful phantoms, or that we passed every day in different occupations, as in making a voyage, we should suffer almost as much as if it were real, and should fear to sleep, as we fear to wake when we dread in fact to enter on such mishaps. And, indeed, it would cause pretty nearly the same discomforts as the reality. But since dreams are all different, and each single one is diversified, what is seen in them affect us much less than what we see when awake, because of its continuity, which is not, however, so continuous and level as not to change too; but it changes less abruptly, except rarely, as when we travel, and then we say, "It seems to me I am dreaming." For life is a dream a little less inconstant.
>
> Blaise Pascal

Freud's abandonment of the seduction theory and the substitution of memories of real traumatic events for fantasies as a determining factor in the aetiology of hysterical symptoms established a division between internal and external reality as separate areas of human existence. The discovery of psychic reality can be understood as a birth that is related to a corresponding caesura in the understanding of human existence. The discovery of an internal reality opened enormous possibilities in understanding the normal and pathological workings of the mind. Nonetheless, this generated a new problem, which was how to keep these two realities united. Diverse theoretical developments have addressed the issue of reuniting what was separated, taking into account, in a new synthesis, the unique reality that Freud illuminated with the discovery of the unconscious.

The concept of transitional space underscores that the place in which we live is neither internal reality nor external reality, but an intermediate area of experience (Winnicott, 1971). Clifford Scott's (1948, 1949) concept of body scheme points at something similar. He states that dichotomic terms such as mind/body, psychic ego/body ego, ego/non-ego can be considered to be an illness resulting from the splitting of an integrated experience that he designates the body scheme. Scott's disease can be best thought of as corresponding to the human mind's inherent ability to discriminate and one that, in its pathological extreme, turns into the disintegration of a reality that is also felt as an indissoluble integrate.

Latin American writers such as Ignacio Matte Blanco (1975, 1988), with his concepts of symmetrical and asymmetrical being, and Héctor Garbarino (1990), with his concept of narcissistic being and narcissism of the ego, have tried to clarify the same paradox of existence, a reality that is experienced as an indivisible whole and as constituted of parts.

Other Latin American writers have also generated theories that describe the mind, perhaps without an explicit purpose, in terms that permit a reunion of internal and external reality to be acknowledged. The most outstanding aspect of these theories is the acknowledgment of the vincular structure of the analytic situation.

In these developments we can observe descriptions of the way in which time and space are experienced and how they subvert the daily, conscious way in which they are lived. It has also been necessary to look into the function of language and its vincular nature in the psychoanalytic situation. It seems that only thus has it been possible to do justice to the nature of the analytic experience, an experience of the unconscious.

In what follows, I concentrate on Latin American writers who are considered classic today, whose theoretical developments are still valid, and who have made substantial contributions to the relationship between external and internal reality, as can be seen in the analytic situation, although they have never established a dialogue on the subject. I refer to the relationship between the theories of Matte Blanco and those of the Río de la Plata group. From these developments we can observe the difficulties encountered when we try to investigate a reality in which the *a priori*, fixed concepts of the internal and the external are not sufficient to give a full account of the entire human experience, taking into consideration the antinomy that is created when establishing an internal reality—the unconscious—in which there can be no boundaries between internal and external because there are no temporo-spatial categories to establish this discrimination. This is, then, a reality that cannot account for its supposed inwardness on its own. Nevertheless, we cannot but resort to the concepts of time and space to imagine this reality.

In this chapter, the notions of external and internal are related to what is experienced as belonging or not belonging to the self. According to Freud (1927c), in the beginning the ego contains everything, but later it goes on to segregate an external world. This differentiation process can be considered an ongoing development throughout the course of a lifetime, for which the relationship with others is indispensable, especially when it comes to integrating unpleasant experiences. The ego cannot segregate an external world from itself and by itself, it needs the other to be able to recognize self and non-self.

In this process of delimitation the way projective processes are understood is extremely important. The thesis of this chapter is that projective processes, and therefore what can be recognized as belonging or not belonging to the self, are relational meanings. These boundaries are negotiated in the interaction to account for the emotional experience between both participants. This negotiating process supposes the existence of an epistemological symmetry between patient and analyst—in other words, it supposes that neither of them has a privileged access to reality (Renik, 1995). This symmetry by no means implies ignoring or reducing the importance of the asymmetry in the functions or roles that the analytic contract establishes for both members of the partnership.

Language, time, space, and the psychoanalytic field

Luisa Álvarez de Toledo (1954) writes that underneath the conscious performance of analyst and patient the paranoid anxieties and persecutorial fears of *both of them* are synchronized. The *background* in which the session is structured and carried out is made up of the interweaving of the unconscious projective and introjective identification processes of both participants. This interweaving comes about by means of words and the voice—articulated sound. As the latter, when it pours out of the mouth and enters the ears, comes from the outside and is heard inside, it is capable of sustaining the primitive subject/object, external world/internal world identity. Words, in their capacity as intermediary objects that join and separate, not only transmit their semantic meaning—the meaning expressed in their contents—but they are also the medium through which unconscious fantasies are transmitted in the measure that words acquire meanings that are attached to the act of speech. In this way, the many speech acts involved in the patient's association and in the analyst's interpretations mean concrete acts such as biting and destroying the analyst, emptying the analyst, or feeding the analyst or receiving from the analyst good and bad—milk, faeces, and urine.

On their part, Madeleine and Willy Baranger (1961–62) consider that the analytic situation is continually defined by a dynamic bipersonal field, structured by the analytic contract, the manifest transactions between patient and analyst, together with the role that the analyst plays at this level, and the unconscious phantasy that emerges, which is bipersonal in nature and the object of interpretation. They agree with Álvarez de Toledo's basic definition of the analytic relationship, in the sense that the field consists of the interplay of the projective and introjective identificatory processes and of the counteridentifications established by both participants, although these are more limited in the analyst and have different functions and features in each of the two participants. They agree with Álvarez de Toledo because they also consider words as media that support extremely primitive object relations and emotions. Nonetheless, they do not forget the discriminatory function of language. In this way, they agree with the process of symbol formation as conceived by Klein that establishes that words can equate symbol with symbolized and also discriminate between the two. The lack of either of these aspects of symbolization in the analytic process constitutes an important impediment for the effect of interpretations.

Integrating Racker's studies on countertransference, they define a basic core of the field, which is the transference–countertransference neurosis. This basic configuration conditions the emergence of recurrent unconscious fantasies and can also immobilize or stop the field mobility, in what becomes an unconscious retreat of powerful omnipotence fantasies, which they call the "bastion". Although it is not explicitly stated, there would appear to be a reference to certain more unconscious levels in the structure of the field: for example, the basic nucleus is described as a situation that is more permanent or fixed, more resistant to the analyst's interpretations, than the recurrent unconscious fantasies. This nucleus seems to be the outcome of the interweaving of the subjectivity of the analyst and the patient.

It is important to point out how these writers describe the temporal and spatial configuration in the analytic field. They describe the field as essentially ambiguous. The authors place an emphasis on the ambiguity of the temporality and spatiality of the analytic situation. This temporality is similar to that of dreams. It has a condensation of present, past, and future, in which all the temporal dimensions are mixed. On the basis of this ambiguous temporality, the subject can become part of a different, less fixed temporality that has more of a future. The space of the analytic field is also ambiguous. It involves the superposition of two spaces in order to create a common space, without one of the spaces being completely substituted by the other. This common space is similar to the space that exists in dreams in which the geometrical scandal of ubiquity becomes the rule. The specific reality of the analytic session does not obey the logical principles of identity, avoidance of contradiction and causality, it obeys the law of "participation" as defined by Lévy-Bruhl.[1]

The work of these writers shows the powerful influence that the Kleinian concepts had on Latin American psychoanalysis in the 1950s and 1960s; this is especially true in the case of the concept of projective identification and the idea of mental growth or arrest as the result of virtuous or vicious circles of projection or introjection. Although they postulate that the analytic situation is configured by both participants, many clinical descriptions present the analyst as a rather passive receptacle of the patient's projective identifications. For example, the latter's "desperate projective identification" ultimately creates a transferential–countertransferential psychosis during the session.

The field is thought of as definitely structured by the continuous interweaving of projective and introjective identifications. Klein's original concept (1946) of projective identification states that it is a typically unconscious aggressive phantasy, by means of which certain aspects of the self are placed within the object in order to control and destroy it. When the concept is applied to the analytic situation, projective identification is interpersonalized. It is a way of understanding the structuring of the unconscious aspect of a significant link such as the analytic relationship or the relationship between partners. Although in the former the way in which the contract structures the analytic link leads us to believe that the projective processes will be less intense in the case of the analyst, the analytic partners are constantly threatened to act as a couple in ordinary daily life. In this way, projective identification turns into a phantasy that has concrete emotional effects on the person who receives the projection. Nonetheless, it is still a phantasy, which apparently is not taken into account when theorizing on the constitution of the field. In this way, insufficient attention is paid to fact that the processes that are postulated as structuring the unconscious bipersonal phantasy of the field are themselves an unconscious phantasy that may or may not be shared by both partners. This phantasy considers that inherent aspects of one of the partners migrate towards the mind and body of the other with diverse objectives and intentions.

From a perspective that totally takes into account the contribution of the analyst to the configuration of the field, the theory of projective identification—as sustained by the analyst—should be taken as an important contribution of the latter to the appointment of a meaning to the field events. In this sense, the analyst's theory would be part of his/her mental reality—an external reality that is all-important to the patient. We should also consider up to what point the analyst contributes to generating in the patient desire or rejection, the possibility or impossibility of projecting in the analyst, and vice versa.

For example, Racker (1960) states that the analyst should be actively open to receive projections. He establishes that the subject's internal reality echoes in the internal reality of the analyst.

> We tend to identify, and identification is a partially active mental process that also implies the reproduction of the psychological activity of the object. We let the material penetrate and we occasionally feel the vibration of the chord that was "touched"; but there are other times when this reception must be followed by an active process in which we "touch" and detect the penetration with our unconscious feelings and thoughts, in order to finally be able to join it. [p. 50]

In this case, the accent is placed on the analyst's active reception of the patient's projections rather than on the patient's ability to invade the analyst's feelings, and so the analyst's activities make the patient's projection effective, in the sense of providing him/her with self-knowledge. Rather than invade the analyst, the projection is related to what the interaction activates in the analyst.

Racker's analyst is fully immersed in the relationship with his patients. One of the metaphors he proposes is that of a woman who is actively receptive during the sexual act—an image that is contrasted with the analyst, whose excessive passiveness transforms him/her into the frigid wife who fulfils the wedding contract but is incapable of psychological feeling, of responding, and of reaching a climax. This image is far removed from the Freudian image of the analyst as a mirror or from the image of the surgeon or even from the radio-set metaphor, because a radio has no desires. If we follow the metaphor proposed by Racker, we might believe that an actively receptive analyst would be similar to the wife who actively wishes for penetration and would generate a bipersonal field and dialogue that is very different from the analyst who acts as a reflecting mirror. At the same time, this would affect the intensity of the projective processes. In this way, an analyst who is perceived as impenetrable might generate intense desires of penetration in the patient.

Along the same lines, Jiménez (1992) has said that the fact that a projective identification has a communicative or evacuative intention does not constitute an *a priori* meaning in the patient's mind—it is, instead, an *a posteriori* meaning resulting from interaction. He furthermore suggests that the projective identification phantasy is a construct resulting from the patient–analyst interaction—in other words, it is also a bipersonal phantasy.

In more recent papers, Madeleine Baranger (1993) posits that the concepts of projective identification and projective counter-identification can try to elude the active participation of the analyst's conscious and unconscious participation in the configuration of the field. She no longer refers to a bipersonal field but to an intersubjective situation. In this intersubjective relationship, we can distinguish the intersubjectivity of the psychoanalytic dialogue and, on another level, the intersubjective field. The latter can be revealed or hidden by the intersubjectivity of the dialogue. This establishes a hierarchy in the intersubjective relationship that indicates two levels of relationship: field and dialogue. I refer to these two levels of the relationship further on.

The concept of projective identification can be taken as a concept that tries to close the caesura between external and internal, considering the eminently communicative quality of affects.[2] These processes of affective communication are difficult to integrate into a metapsychological conception of affect, where it is predominantly conceived as a discharge of energy within the organism. It is a way of conceptualizing unconscious processes of mutual affective regulation between patient and analyst or mother and child. Its application to the concept of dynamic field determines that the specific location of unconscious fantasies becomes rather blurred, and their inner or outer position becomes relative. The idea that the unconscious phantasy of the field is a joint creation establishes that the patient's projection is not simply a distortion of the analyst's reality: it also takes into account the participation of the latter, with a specific history to be made manifest in the relationship. Therefore, the analyst's reality is not only limited to his/her material reality: it also includes his/her psychic reality and subjectivity, the latter being the more important reality for the patient (Aron, 1996).

Horacio Etchegoyen (1986) states that for Klein, development refers to projection and introjection processes that operate from the beginning of life. Projective processes condition the relationship with the external object and external reality, and introjective processes condition the relationship with internal reality and psychic reality. According to Klein (1935), internal objects—meanings of experience that are created from the life and death instincts—are at the beginning fantastically distorted images of the real objects on which they are based. Projection places these distorted objects in the external world, and incorporation takes them to the internal world.

Benign circuits that depend on the primacy of the libido, an adequate behaviour of the external object and the maturity of the perceptive apparatus slowly correct these distorted images by means of their integration in the depressive position (Hinzner & Noemí, 1986). These archaic images are actualized in the transference by means of projection and introjection. In this way and with maximal intensity at the beginning of the analytic process, the analyst reality is distorted by the patient's projections.

It seems, then, that the way in which projective processes are visualized is essential for the understanding of the relationship with external reality.[3] Does an internal reality project itself over the external world, so that the latter is considerably distorted by the projection? Or is the projection, rather, part of a process that builds a plausible version of the world and its objects? Is projection an exclusively intrapsychic phenomenon, or is it also part of the meaning negotiated in the intersubjective dialogue? And if we totally accept the Freudian intuition that the unconscious has no categories of time and, as Matte Blanco added (1975), no categories of three-dimensional space either, then how can an unconscious process be possible when it necessarily requires internal and external spatial categories in addition to requiring a temporal course in order to be represented in the system unconscious?

Mutative interpretation and bilogic of the sense of reality

These dilemmas are also present in James Strachey's (1934) formulation of the mutative interpretation. In an earlier paper (Jordán, 1992), I suggested that Strachey refers to a paradox when he describes the way in which the patient has an insight by way of the mutative interpretation. He states that the patient's contact with reality will enable him/her to project his/her good archaic object on good real objects and bad archaic object on bad real objects. The mutative interpretation is divided into two phases. In the first, the patient, aided by the psychoanalyst's auxiliary superego function, will project the objects onto the analyst, becoming aware of an id-impulse directed at the latter. In the second phase, the sense of reality will enable the patient to use the transference interpretation to make a distinction between the archaic object that has been projected onto the analyst and the real analyst. An effective mutative interpretation requires that the analyst remove as much as possible his/her own reality from the patient. If the analyst behaves like the good or bad object, then the patient will lack the tools to contrast the projections towards the analyst, who will remain indistinguishable from the fantasized object.

This poses a paradox. The patient who has sufficient sense of reality to discriminate between the projected object and the real analyst should have the same sense of reality that would allow for the projection of his/her internal object onto some real characteristic of the analyst. If reality were fully withdrawn from the patient, then the latter would be unable to project when expected to have enough sense of reality so as to be able to discriminate between the projected object and the analyst—in other words to discriminate between internal reality and external reality. If reality were totally removed from the patient—something impossible in any case—this would mean striking a harsh blow to the sense of reality that was originally demanded of the patient.

Strachey points out that removal of reality refers to the fact that the analyst should not behave like the archaic good and bad internal objects that project onto the external object. The analyst must refrain from gratifying the patient or from applying the eye-for-an-eye/tooth-for-a-tooth law and must remain neutral. This might be impossible, as it is impossible to know beforehand how the patient will interpret the analyst's behaviour. Thus the analyst defines what is real or unreal, especially in terms of a self-evaluation to determine his/her own reality, and what part of this reality the patient distorts, and what is "really" neutral for the patient. The analyst defines an *a priori* meaning of neutral/non-neutral aspects of his/her own behaviour. This position seems difficult if, on the one hand, we accept that unconscious processes also operate in the analyst because the analyst cannot know beforehand the meaning of all his/her acts and, on the other hand, the analyst is unable to control the unconscious meanings that the patient will give to his/her acts.

Following Matte Blanco, I proposed that Strachey's paradox could be resolved by resorting to a bilogical conception of the sense of reality. The latter appears to have been understood principally in terms of asymmetrical logic that tends to differentiate objects into increasingly discrete units. What has not been considered is the possibility of a symmetrical aspect of a sense of reality—in other words, of the logic that tends to form increasingly general classes and to experience reality as a homogeneous and indivisible unit, in which the difference between a part and whole dissolves, and part and whole are put in a bi-univocal correspondence as happens in the case of infinite sets. In these, for example, even numbers, a part of the set, can by bi-univocally linked with all the other numbers (1–2; 2–4; 3–6 . . .)

Matte Blanco has proposed that mental operations should be considered on the basis of different bilogical structures—different types of relationships between symmetrical and asymmetrical logic. He proposes that the unconscious can only recognize classes, not individuals. A propositional function that defines a class or set is used to classify conscious or unconscious thoughts, persons, and objects into elements of a set, which has the characteristics of infinite sets. The unconscious mind is considered to be in a continuous process of emotional classification. When faced with an object perceived as a set of signals, it will experience this object as something belonging to an infinite set, in which the object can be placed in a bi-univocal correspondence with the entire set: in other words, the part becomes equal to the whole.

Matte Blanco discovered a surprising isomorphism between emotion, the unconscious, and the mathematical concept of infinite. According to this perspective, emotion is taken as a cognitive activity that has its own logic—symmetrical logic, the logic of a mode of being, the symmetrical mode of being that is homogeneous and indivisible. This led Matte Blanco to quote Whitehead, who defined thought as "a propositional emotion".

An example of this logic explains how a patient can feel nurtured by the analyst by receiving an interpretation that makes him/her feel well. From the point of view of emotion, interpretation is classified as another element of all those things that make me feel good: this includes the good food that makes me feel well, so interpretation and food become identical on the basis of a functional proposition such as "*x* makes me feel well". In this way, all the people who feed me can be included in a set that becomes increasingly general and includes the person who feels the emotion, all the thoughts and words that feed my mind and all the material objects that feed my body. So we have, among these elements, the analyst, the mother, thoughts and books that my father gave me, and so on—and myself, as I can feed myself. So, mother's milk, analyst, mother and father, and self become identical: the set becomes symmetrical. If the analyst's interpretation makes me anxious, this corresponds to all the things that can give me displeasure and that I must reject, as would be the case with food that is bad for me and which I must spit out, and this can be identified with mental projection. So spitting and projecting become identical, as Fenichel (1945) said when he declared that projection is the mental representation of spitting, which is a physical act.

Strachey's paradox can be understood in the light of a conception that considers the sense of reality as a bilogical structure that presents an alternation between a symmetrical and an asymmetrical component of the sense of reality. The patient's transference can be understood as the inclusion of the analyst into a symmetrized set.

The subtraction of the analyst's reality creates an ambiguous situation that tends to amplify any perceived aspect of the analyst in order to project a good or bad object. The analyst can be compared to bait. The reader can imagine fishing bait: these are constructed on the basis of the subtraction of the reality of the object they represent. The bait contains nothing but the essential elements that make an object what it is for a given subject. The subject sees the object on the basis of the bait, but if the illusion is to be effective, the bait should also be real, and as an example of this one of its important features would lie in its three-dimensionality. The transference is then understood as a specific illusion (Sandler, Dare, & Holder, 1973).

This illusion is co-constructed on the basis of the bait provided by the analyst and perceived by the patient, and of the latter's fantasies and desires. The analyst provides multiple baits, such as the objects in the analyst's office, his/her clothes, and so on. Nonetheless, the patient's constant conscious and unconscious reading of the analyst's emotion constitutes one of the most important baits provided by the latter. They are, at the beginning of an interaction, and on most occasions, far removed from the patient's conscious sphere. The fact that language allows for lies has refined the capacity of human beings to read the affects of others in order to infer whether or not verbal communications are true.

Projection is understood as the attribution to the analyst of the characteristics of a class. This ascription is based on the perception of a real characteristic of the analyst that includes him/her among the class of fathers, mothers, live beings, dead beings, and so on, so that the analyst can be identified with the elements of the class.[4] Projection is what enables analyst and patient to experience each other illusorily. But, as in the case of illusion, in which we can only become aware of our mistaken perception *a posteriori*, we can also only have the *experience* of having projected *a posteriori*—in other words, when for example, in the course of an interaction, the patient notices that he/she has included the analyst in a mental class of his/her own. Thus what is not self is experienced on the basis of categories originated in the self.

The first phase of mutative interpretation invokes the sense of reality from its symmetrical vertex, and the analyst reckons that he/she is being perceived as the archaic object, on the basis of a given aspect of his/her reality that lends itself to the illusion, and at the same time letting the patient know that the analyst is available for classification according to the patient's logic, without resorting to the application of the eye-for-an-eye/tooth-for-a-tooth retaliation. The fact that the unconscious can only know classes and not individuals makes it impossible for a person to be experienced unconsciously as an individual—in other words, as an object or subject that cannot be classified as the same as anyone else.

In the second instance, the sense of reality is invoked from the asymmetrical vertex. This enables the discrimination of the analyst in terms of the class in which he/she is included. Interpretation offers the possibility for the analyst to be perceived as belonging to other classes: for example, to the class of analysts who give interpretations. In its maximum expression, the asymmetrical components of sense of reality enable the other to be perceived as a singular object that cannot be classified as being similar to any other, a set defined by a single element—in other words, a subject similar to myself. This experience of the other allows me to look at myself from the eyes of the other, who is now a subject—that is, to be an object for the gaze of the other. This initiates the tension between recognizing and treating the other as subject or object (Benjamin, 1988).

The fact that a patient realizes that he/she is projecting is often associated with the fact that the analyst, no longer wishing to be treated like an object, might perform an act that, for the patient, symbolizes the analyst's condition as a free agent. In other words the analyst is not only an object created by the subject on the basis of a class existing in the patient's mind but also a subject. Usually, in these actions of the analyst an aggressive component is discernible. And this, according to Matte Blanco, is because asymmetry always entails the exercise of aggression, because it implies difference, severance, separation, and discontinuity within the symmetrical. I believe that the effect of mutative interpretation can be expanded to take into account the insight the patient feels when contrasting the experience of the analyst as object and as subject (Benjamin, 1988). This explains the curative effects of acts on the part of the analyst that, from a perspective that considers nothing but his/her function as an object for receiving the patient's projections, can be interpreted as loss of technical neutrality (Cassorla, 2004; Coltart, 1992; Ogden, 1994a; Symington, 1983).

The patient who accepts the analyst's condition of a subject—in other words, the validity of his subjective construction of the current situation—is open to the possibility of understanding that the real situation is capable of other subjective approximations that are equally valid in spite of being different from his/her own. This plausible conjecture of reality is maintained by someone who shares the condition of subject that interprets reality and for whom it is also possible to be an object. In this way, and as Merton Gill (1982) has stated, countertransference and transference can be considered plausible conjectures of a same shared reality, and so the patient's experiential record is extended in the measure that he/she is capable of understanding the existence of other plausible ways of conjecturing the situation that is currently being lived with the analyst.[5]

The sense of reality can be altered from the symmetrical or asymmetrical vertex. In the first case, there is not enough asymmetry to enable the patient to discriminate the analyst from the class into which the latter has been included. This is the case of psychotic transferences in which the analyst literally becomes mother or father. There is a lack of asymmetry, of temporo-spatial categories that prevent discrimination of internal and external object, or past object and present object, or object and subject, and of symbol and symbolized.

In the second case, the patient is unable to reach sufficient symmetry to be able to recognize an identity between the analyst and an internal or past object and does not attain an aspatial and atemporal mode of the experience. For example, the patient is unable to include the analyst in a more general class, as we saw in the example in which analysts and mothers become identical on the basis of a common characteristic, both nurture. This is the case of the anti-analysand described by McDougall (1990), for whom the analyst is always an analyst, an analyst, an analyst. Any transference interpretation is felt as an idea of the analyst that never gains emotional echo in the patient.

The Barangers (1961–62) refer in very similar terms to the alterations of the function of language in the analytic situation. Language should be able, on the one hand, to equate symbol with symbolized and act as a vehicle of symmetrical logic and, on the other, to be able to discriminate between them and be the carrier of asymmetrical logic. Inadequacies in any of these aspects constitute a great difficulty for the analyst's interpretation. For example, they state that in obsessive patients, words are unable to touch and awaken the patient's emotional life in the relationship with the analyst. The analyst is unable to act as bait. There is no equalization between symbol and symbolized. In the opposite case, the patient loses the capacity to differentiate between the word and what it designates. Interpretation is lived concretely. For example, the interpretation of erotic transference is understood as a seductive attempt on the part of the analyst. In both cases, the analyst stops acting as bait: in the first case because he/she is unable to arouse an illusion and in the second because illusion leads to hallucination.

The analyst's work is to find adequate words to cooperate with the patient's bilogic sense of reality. In their article "Process and non-process in analytic work", Madeleine Baranger, Willy Baranger, and Jorge Mom (1983) do not agree that the analyst should look for precision in his/her interpretations in terms of a scientific statement. Quite the opposite: the analyst should be able to use linguistic polysemy and—if we follow the intuition of Álvarez de Toledo (1953)—to add tone of voice to favour the analytic process. They propose a distinction of two moments in the interpretative act:

> the act of searching, similar to what children raised in the country do to catch crickets (they scratch the entrance of the insect's home with a straw, the curious cricket appears at the precise moment that it is caught). In our process, the entrapment would by the second moment of interpretation; an aspect of the unconscious that comes out and is captured by a new meaning. [Baranger, Baranger, & Mom, 1983, pp. 6–7]

This meaning is reached through dialogue. In this formulation, we see that the analyst's interpretation initially works as a bait to bring out the unconscious—which we could also call the projection of the patient, and then works on giving a meaning to what has emerged. The function of interpretation is similar to Strachey's mutative interpretation, as I have formulated it. Both aspects of the sense of reality are invoked in it.

Synthesis and discussion: the intersubjective construction of boundaries

From Matte Blanco's point of view, we could say that the background of the structure of the analytic relationship, the basic nucleus of the field, and the intersubjective field are comprehensible as descriptions of a level of the relationship that is structured around a specific logic and way of being, which both patient and analyst reach through their respective emotions. This basic level can correspond to what Matte Blanco has called the basic matrix of projection and introjection. Matte Blanco (1988) believes that "in the deep unconscious things—including those which regarded from outside appear as projection and introjection—do not occur, they simply are" (p. 194). This basic matrix of projection and introjection is a starting point for the emergence of introjective and projective processes, which require temporo-spatial categories to be mentally represented. In this "region" of the unconscious events do not exist, there is no inside and no outside, it is a simple manifestation of being. As Matte Blanco says, emotions are usually described in terms that underscore the lack of boundaries in their outlines, and this lack of precision is felt when the person is immersed in emotion. We speak of emotional climate, emotional atmospheres to account for an experience that is difficult in terms of delimitation: it can be inside or outside, or in both places, like the air that we breathe. In a similar way, Mitchell (2000) describes a level of the analytic relationship that he calls the level of affective permeability. He points out that affects are "contagious, and, on the deepest levels affective states are often transpersonal. . . . affects are evoked interpersonally through dense resonances between people, without regard for who, specifically, is feeling what" (p. 61). At this level, the concepts of time and space tend to disappear, as emotional experience tends to make us think along the lines of symmetrical logic. At this point of the relationship, there is a constant process of affective regulation that is predominantly unconscious and that does not recognize the other as someone with intentions, who is the agent of his/her own acts: the other is not conceived as subject or object. Language allows for a refining of affective regulation in the measure that affects can be fully symbolized. Early symbolization of affects can be concretized in images, which Elías Mallet da Rocha Barros (2000) has denominated "affective pictograms". This level of the intersubjective relationship can be defined as a field in which there is no full awareness of the other's subjectivity.

As Racker points out, the analyst's emotional disposition to allow penetration by the patient is extremely important at this level. This disposition allows the patient to make contact with emotions that have not been integrated into the self by means of the delimitation that the analyst might establish through interpretation, and to define what belongs to the analyst and what belongs to the patient. The analyst should be prepared to become infected with the emotions of the patient, trying to make sense of them later through words: in other words, the analyst should not fear and thus resist an emotional experience that would produce a symmetry with the patient. Fear of symmetrization, of loosening momentarily the boundaries of the self, can drive the analyst to establish an excessive asymmetry through a technique derived from a theory that might establish beforehand an indication of what is to be projected from the patient's mind.

Words take us to another level of intersubjective relationship: analytic dialogue, which can cover up or reveal the level of the intersubjective field. At this level, basic affective regulation processes can be signified. Language discrimination capacity allows for an initial delimitation of the emotional experience of patient and analyst alike and allows for the application of asymmetrical logic. It contributes to separating subject from object, to recognizing the other as a subject and clearly establishing the boundaries regarding who is who, and to establishing what is external and internal reality to each member of the analytic couple. In this way, projective identification is understood as a way of reaching, by means of the intersubjective dialogue, an *a posteriori* signification of interactions that contemplate intensive affective contagions of emotions that might be disruptive to the analyst. As the Barangers had done earlier, Jeremy Safran and Christopher Muran (2000) state that the concept can be used defensively to disregard the analyst's contribution. But it does not have to be used like this if it is understood as a conceptual framework that enables the analyst to give meaning to moments of anxiety during therapy, by reorienting him/her to look with curiosity into those same feelings, allowing for a second look at the events of the field (Baranger, Baranger, & Mom, 1983).

In any case, Safran and Muran continue by saying that the concept would appear to contain an element that can be used defensively by the analyst as it permits very quick inferences using his/her own experience to ascribe to the patient undesirable aspects that the latter wishes to get rid of. This contributes to avoiding looking into subtleties in the interaction involved in the process. To think of projective processes as attributions to the analyst on the basis of the patient's symmetrical aspect of sense of reality can help to focus on the analyst's own contribution. It can stimulate the analyst to look into which of his/her aspects the patient perceives or negates and that contribute to the patient's subjective constructions regarding the analyst. This also helps the patient to be less fearful of looking into his/her own contribution to the relationship.

If Matte Blanco provides a logical and ontological perspective for the comprehension of unconscious processes, the Río de la Plata writers provide a vincular understanding of the comprehension of the mind—a perspective that is notoriously absent in Matte Blanco's work. In this way, symmetry and asymmetry can also be taken to be dimensions of experience that are not independent from the quality of the emotional bond. The sense of reality will depend on the amount of symmetry or asymmetry that is possible according to the mutually regulated emotional state of each partner. This establishes a mutual determination between the level of the intersubjective field and the intersubjective dialogue. Greater emotional intensity equals greater difficulty in finding the asymmetrical component of sense of reality, and lesser emotional intensity equals greater difficulty in finding the symmetrical component of sense of reality. This affects both partners' ability to use language to balance both components of the sense of reality, in something resembling a mixture of scientific language and the language of myth and poetry.

These writers make a capital contribution when they say that language is, on the one hand, the medium used to transmit emotions and, on the other, that which allows a discrimination between what belongs to whom on the basis of a shared emotional experience, generated by the voice and by the words that shape language. In this way, language becomes something that, when placed simultaneously between analyst and patient, joins and separates them, facilitating the unique intimate relationship that exists in the analytic situation (Jordán-Moore, 1994).

They also make an enormous contribution when they emphasize the importance of reaching a temporality in which past, present, and future can be discriminated. This means turning time and space—categories that Matte Blanco sees as abstractions—into history. In this way, the dialectic between asymmetrical and symmetrical logic also means being able to place in a specific time and space those emotions that contain, in an atemporal and aspatial form, the relational history of each individual. The absence of space and time in the basic matrix of projection and introjection can be considered a different description—another way of naming the intersubjective field. The concept of a basic matrix underscores the fact that it is from this level of pure being that a negotiation is permanently taking place so as to delimit what is internal and what is external for each of the participants in the dialogue.

It is interesting to see how one of Winnicott's definitions of holding says that it is "not only the actual physical holding of the infant, but also the total environmental provision prior to the concept of *living with*. In other words, it refers to a three-dimensional or space relationship with time gradually added" (1960b, pp. 43–44). This would make time and space categories with which every human being constructs the world, but which are simultaneously constructed in the relational history of every human being. They are abstractions associated to the asymmetrical logic that require the exercise of aggression. The birth of space and time implies cutting, caesura, separation, and in this sense asymmetry is linked to aggression. This makes for the creation of a space, a distance between subject and object, between subject and subject. This is an aggression that is not necessarily destructive, but one that needs to be kept up in a relationship in order to create a vital space that will allow for the operation of projection.

Matte Blanco (1989) defines analytic work as going from symmetry to asymmetry through symmetry. I find this an excellent way of giving a logical definition of the two levels of the intersubjective relationship, in which the dialogue consists in the capacity to negotiate what makes us different, to establish what the internal and external world is for each member of the relationship, but starting from a permanent matrix in which we always experience ourselves-with-the-other as identical and which must be taken into account, even if we don't want or like it, because it is one of our ways of being. In this dialogue we need language as an intermediary object that joins and separates and that enables the construction of a personal history in which the abstractions of space and time are incarnated.

Finally, and in response to the question in the title of this paper: Is the dichotomy between internal and external reality real? The reader may already have understood that, like almost everything in life, the answer depends on the angle from which we consider the dichotomy. It is real from the asymmetrical mode of being point of view; it is not real from the symmetrical mode of being point of view. Perhaps for psychoanalysis atemporo-spatial reality vs. temporo-spatial reality would be a more real dichotomy. In the latter it is possible to speak of internal and external reality: categories that are not absolute but are being constantly written in a permanent intersubjective dialogue.

Notes

1. Levy-Bruhl's description of this kind of logic has many resonances with symmetrical logic as defined by Matte Blanco. It points also to a logic of the unconscious.

2. In this paper, affect and emotion are used as synonyms. Some writers use affect where it is an emotion for the subjective experience.

3. I am referring broadly to projective processes, including both projection and projective identification. Hinshelwood (1989) states that Klein uses the term "projection" to refer to: projection of an internal object, projection of an impulse, projection of an inner conflict, and projective identification (projection of a part of the self). At the same time, he states that the projection of the impulse, the object of the relationship, or of part of the self are indissolubly linked in the object relationship and cannot be fully distinguished.

4. Matte Blanco (1988) has described the possible similitude of this inclusion process in a class with Piaget's concept of assimilation. Nonetheless, he says that Piaget's assimilation would correspond to the equivalent class concept in which class elements have something in common and something that distinguishes them from each other. On the other hand, in the case of classes created in the unconscious, the equivalence of the elements is treated like an identity resulting from symmetrical logic. This leads to a lack of distinction of the elements of class (symmetrization)

5. It is important to refer to the etymology of the word "plausible": it comes from the Latin *plausibilis,* which means "something that deserves applause". So, if we consider transference to be a plausible conjecture, we are applauding the subjective vision of the other.

Commentary

Neville Symington

There are two comments that stand out in this informative chapter that gripped my attention. Juan Francisco Jordán-Moore refers to Matte Blanco, saying that the unconscious can recognize only classes, not individuals. I had not realized that Matte Blanco had said this, but I was very glad to know that he had. It is clinically a very important statement, because often when a patient is referring to someone, the analyst takes this as being a displacement from himself, whereas, following Matte Blanco, we would need to see the patient's statement as referring to a class to which the analyst, the individual referred to, and the patient all belong. In other words, in the unconscious there is an undifferentiated class and no persons at all. I came to realize this some years ago, and it has very considerably changed my way of working clinically. It has also led me to question what it is that enables that transition from the knowledge of a class to the knowledge of individual persons. How do I, as an analyst, proceed so as to facilitate that transition? The first thing is to realize that when the patient is talking about me as analyst or another individual, a class is being referred to. It is quite difficult to conceptualize oneself not as a person but as a part of an agglomerated class. This realization and subsequent conceptualization will itself alter the clinical transaction at the foundations. The second thing is that it will alert the analyst's attention to those changes that indicate the birth of a person arising out of the undifferentiated class and watch for symbols of this development.

The next statement is one that moved me profoundly, and, like any statement that shakes the foundations, it has still not clarified sufficiently in my mind for me to be able to comment on it succinctly. It is this statement of Matte Blanco's:

> In the deep unconscious things—including those which regarded from outside appear as projection and introjection—do not occur. They simply are. [1988, p. 194]

This reminds me of a comment made by Herbert Read:

> We speak commonly of "calling up" images and the metaphor suggests that there is a hidden depth from which the images emerge. [Read, 1943, p. 32]

It also made me think of that reality which has been referred to as the THAT by the seers of the Upanishads and as the infinite by Christian mystics such as Meister Eckhart and John of the Cross. Although their expression of this has varied, yet all these thinkers have stressed the utter simplicity of this reality and that out of it flows all the amazing diversity that surrounds us and is in us; that it is the source of activity whereas the activity itself is a manifestation of this origin but that the origin itself is utterly still. Bion used the term "O" for this. I think "O" stands for the Greek *Ontos,* which means Being or Reality, and this is the foundation of the personality—utterly simple and the source of activity but itself inactive. If this is right, then Matte Blanco and Bion both believe in this reality as being the deepest stratum in the personality. The clinical consequences of this are enormous. For instance guilt, in this perspective, is not the consequence of damage to the other, but arises from the smothering of this Reality in the personality, and all symbols are ultimately registrations of this Being that lies at the foundation of the intrapsychic and interpersonal. But I think there is another way of looking at this. I feel something when someone projects elements—*beta-elements* in Bion's formulation—at me or into me, but I may be registering a particular state. There may be truly no thing being projected. What we are talking of is a way of experiencing different states interpersonally and intrapsychically. But it is also this perspective that unifies the external and the internal. As Hippolyte Taine said, the internal perception and the external object are one event; though, because it is very difficult to "stand outside ourselves", it is seen as two, this is due to the limitation of our own minds. However, in the scholastic philosophical tradition a distinction was made between reasoning and an intellectual act. Reasoning is a process of comparing sensual imagery and thinking through to a mental concept using the initial perception as a spring-board, but the intellectual act grasps reality in itself, and it is this that can then be seen to encompass the internal and the external, the one and the many, the time-bound and the timeless.

These were the two most striking flashes of light in Dr Jordán-Moore's chapter. I go on now to make one or two critical points, but they are mostly, as I see it, inconsistencies and, as it were, more a matter for editorial improvement than any radical disagreement.

Freud did not discover internal reality. It had already been discovered when St. Augustine wrote his *Confessions* in the fourth century, but one only has to read that classic to see Augustine's familiarity with his inner world; in that book he recognizes jealousy even in a baby that is still at the breast. Then there have been many other thinkers in the religious tradition, such as Moses Maimonides, Moses de Leon, John of the Cross, Meister Eckhart, Fénelon, and then Blaise Pascal, whom Jordán-Moore quotes at the beginning of his article. But also in the secular tradition one can mention the Arabian philosopher Avicenna and then Descartes, Spinoza, Vico, Hamann, and Nietzsche, to mention just a few. I think Aldous Huxley was right when he said,

> One of the most extraordinary, because most gratuitous, pieces of twentieth-century vanity is the assumption that nobody knew anything about psychology before the days of Freud. But the real truth is that most modern psychologists understand human beings less well than did the ablest of their predecessors. [Huxley, 1980, p. 132]

Jordán-Moore says, "Nevertheless, we cannot but resort to the concepts of time and space to imagine this reality . . ."—but this is not right. The only way of conceptualizing this reality is to purify our thinking of time and space to the maximum extent possible. It is true that imagination is a faculty that manipulates the sensations that exist in time and space, but through an intellectual act it is possible to arrive at a mental concept of this reality. For instance, when Archimedes arrived at the mental concept of volume, his foreplay, as it were, was manipulating images through his imagination, but the mental concept of volume is itself devoid of sensational imagery. It is, of course, a concept in space, but it is possible to go further when the concept is devoid not only of imagery but of time and space also. For instance, Van Steenberghen argues this forcefully in his book *Ontology* (1952).

Jordán-Moore refers to Melanie Klein's description of the aggressive phantasy projected into the object in order to control and destroy it. This is as Melanie Klein described it, but I believe that the prime motive is not to control and destroy the object but to anaesthetize pain—in particular, the pain of knowing one's inner state of emptiness, chaos, and disarray. I believe that this needs to underpin Klein's description in order to understand the motive springs behind projective identification. It also gives as an underlying principle the individual's mode of managing pain: that pain is at the centre of all defensive operations. I believe that this perspective endows motivation with both a more accurate psychological description and, at the same time, a humane attitude to mental illness and psychiatric conditions.

I wanted to compliment Jordán-Moore on quoting Jiménez, who says that the idea that projective identification has an evacuative or communicative function has no *a priori* basis but only one that is *a posteriori*. I believe that many clinical errors are committed in the belief that there is an *a priori* meaning. This leads to error and also an unfortunate sentimentality.

I think that Jordán-Moore's article opens us to the deeper issues that psychoanalysis has always promised, and that this is a fruit of genuine psychoanalytic investigation.

7

Current psychoanalytic practice: psychic zones and the processes of unconscientization

Norberto C. Marucco

I would like to thank the IPA Publications Committee for giving me the opportunity of taking part in this publication, which means a recognition of Latin American psychoanalysis and thus contributes to its promotion. I will attempt to fulfil this important commitment by summing up here the ideas I have been developing throughout recent years—ideas that arose mainly from my own clinical work. The key concept is that of *psychic zones,* which refers to one way of understanding the psyche (its constitution and its forms of structuring, unconscientization,[1] and functioning) and approaching its psychopathological expressions as well as the resources of the technical work.

For the presentation of this theme, I have chosen to deal with the following aspects:

1. The patient today:
   a. present-day psychopathological problems;
   b. anxiety, drive force, and temporality;
2. *Psychic zones* and the processes of unconscientization;
3. What is unconscientized, and the standpoint of today's psychoanalyst.

The patient today

Present-day psychopathological problems

For a long time psychoanalysis has been limited almost exclusively to the treatment of what can be called the "classic neuroses", based on representation theory and the concept of transference neurosis—analysis that is, up to a certain point, "scientific", in the manner of Signorelli's elaboration in Freud and that, grounded on the field of representation, remained somewhat detached from other vicissitudes of the drive. Clinical work revealed the restrictions of this approach—so much so that at present the frontiers of psychoanalysis are defined by what lies outside or by what is "beyond" the concept of classic neuroses: that is, by those psychopathological expressions that surpass the mere return of the repressed and by the functioning of an unconscious that, shaped by repression, finds expression through its significant quality.[2]

With regard to psychopathology in current psychoanalysis, there are at least two clearly differentiated positions. One of these persists in defining psychopathology in terms of structures: neurotic, perverse, and psychotic (the "psychosomatic structure" may be included here); the other position (which is also mine) tends to understand psychopathology rather in terms of "ways of psychic functioning", which I have called "psychic zones"—a concept I develop further on. These "psychic zones" are determined by different ways of unconscientization and have particular forms of return of the unconscious and different expressions of anxiety.

The contemporary patient very often places us in a field that is "beyond what can be represented": a field of expressions related to the body, to narcissism, and to a kind of repetition compulsion that is a manifestation of the death drive. These expressions of psychopathology led me to think of the coexistence of "zones" or "areas" of psychic functioning, which are delineated according to a singular structuring of the psychic apparatus (Marucco, 2001) and which give rise to some configurations of the unconscious. These unconscientized zones present in the contemporary patient (with a predominance of some of them in different pathologies and to a clearly disproportionate extent in severely disturbed patients) dictate the analyst's standpoint and the conditions of the analytic field.

In my opinion, the contemporary patient is not a "new" patient whose pathology happens to be an original symptom elicited by his/

her peculiar relation to culture (a debatable subject, to be dealt with on a future occasion). Moreover, we can already find in the Rat Man (Freud, 1909d) and the Wolf Man (Freud, 1918) some hints that "foretell", in a way, for example, the splitting of the unconscious ego, and in Dora's homosexual passion (Freud, 1905 [1901]) we can read a narcissistic passion related to the unconscious of an "idealizing structure", which, as it was not taken into account, led to an analytic rupture. There are plenty of cases like these, not only among Freud's patients but among ours as well. However, the present frontiers of psychoanalysis are delineated by theoretical and clinical fundaments that, caught in a web of useless debates between presumably opposed viewpoints, have been arrested in their development for a very long time. This calls for a better "sharpening" of our conceptual tools to approach those zones of the unconscientized psyche that were, before, thought to be out of reach and also to attempt to discover other possible still unknown "areas of psychic functioning".

Anxiety, drive force, and temporality

At this point, I would like to discuss a particular type of anxiety that is often encountered in the contemporary patient: anxiety caused by the repetition compulsion, by life and death drives, by the vicissitudes of binding, and by the awareness of temporality.

Freud in "The 'Uncanny'" (1919h) states that in the unconscious mind there is a predominance of *repetition compulsion,* which governs the psychoanalysis of neurotic patients for a while. And in *Beyond the Pleasure Principle* (1920g) he contends that quite often this repetition compulsion becomes an obstacle when, at the end of the treatment, we struggle to achieve the patient's complete release (from the physician). And that the obscure anxiety experienced by those who are not familiar with psychoanalysis and who are afraid of awakening something that should be left dormant is in fact the emergence of this compulsion. Hence in all treatments this repetition compulsion arises sooner or later, especially at the end of the analysis—a point of unbinding from the analyst—when this obscure fear of the compulsion to repeat comes again. That is why, from my point of view, the repetition compulsion represents one of the great moments in Freud's discoveries—actually, a decisive one for psychoanalysis: because once repression is lifted, the compulsion to repeat—the Freudian *agieren* (Freud, 1914b), already discovered in 1914—emerges that throws light on the scene of the repressed desire, which cannot be remembered but appears in acts as it fails to find representation in words. These acts tend, like any repetition compelled by the life drive, to a new demand for signification, linkage, investment. Only when this binding occurs can a new temporality be reached and anxiety as a symptom dissolve, opening the way to the polymorphism of affects (pain, grief, pleasure, etc.).

There is another psychic functioning in which repetition compulsion and the death drive impose, to my mind, three different phases to anxiety: The first phase is a dead time for the analysis, when anxiety is overridden by repetition (André Green's *Murdering of Time,* 2001): an analytic impasse. In the clinical expression of this psychic functioning, today is the same as yesterday and as tomorrow. The second phase, the time of disinvestment, is laboriously established, and there is a progressive and gradual unbinding. We are approaching the "final time", when anxiety acquires a touch of "nothingness" [*nadificación*] in close proximity to anxieties of emptiness. This is, in fact, the reappearance of the old traumatic anxiety of helplessness after representation had been erased by an excess of repression [*zugrunde gehen*]. That is why I think it is "vital" (in the full meaning of the life drive) that the process of analysis should arrive at a third phase, to guide along a new pathway this repetition compulsion and its attendant fear of "nothingness" in the unbinding. This new moment is "marked" to a great extent by the analyst's stance and drive commitment (Marucco, 2003b). At this time anxiety of *the analyst's own sexual drive* may become invested and binding, activating in the patient the emergence of his life drive. Hence, there arises for the patient a new "drive" anxiety, which may turn into familiar expressions of this kind of anxiety but which also restores the pathway to dreaming and its wish-fulfilment and to the acknowledgement of the other's love and of love for the other.

This is the moment for psychoanalytic work to accomplish the psychic construction of this process—probably close to M. de M'Uzan's (1995) concept of *chimère*—which restores the anxiety that functions as the force of desire. From now on, this desire will steer the patient's life along pathways closer to love, work, and creativity. In Green's fruitful terms, this road is signposted by "the logic of hope".

Thus anxiety becomes a symptom of the life drive, which interrupts the inescapable dead time found in all "present-day neurotic pathologies".

Psychic zones and the processes of unconscientization

The concept of the unconscious involves the notion of psychic work—primary process, drives, the problem of representation, the question of the original and the secondary in psychoanalysis, and so on: a wide range of topics is immediately spawned. The unconscious requests—demands—the analyst's attention. Therefore, the analyst should first define his position when he attempts to explain, based on theory—from the *après coup* of the present moment—the existence of the unconscious or, in my words, *the dynamic of the processes of inconscientization* (the expression I use in this chapter because I think it is the most pertinent to convey my ideas).

Since I am emphasizing the dynamic of the processes of inconscientization, I shall not discuss here other subjects as important as the conception of the primary process that moulds the unconscious, nor the problematic of the original or of the unconscious as a psychic system or agency—that is, the problematic of the unconscious and the id (although at times I shall come close to them). In short, in this work about contemporary psychoanalytic practice my focus is on understanding *the unconscious* as a product of a modality of psychic functioning: *unconscientizing*.

My move away from regarding the unconscious as an agency or as a system, to explore instead the phenomena of unconscientization, has to do with my way of understanding Freud's works—because in my study of his texts and his thought I perceive the different modalities of unconscientization and their various types of expression in psychic functioning and in psychopathology, and also ways in which analytic practice should respond to the demands from each area.

Drawing on Freud's work and the contributions of post-Freudian writers, I shall attempt to describe what can be defined as *Freudian metapsychological organizations and their influence on the construction of the unconscious* (I use the term "psychic zone" to refer to each of these metapsychological organizations).

The approach I propose is based on what I consider the five basic Freudian pillars: five true "introductions"—as I prefer to call them—to fundamental metapsychological subjects that have had great repercussions on the understanding of the processes of unconscientization as well as on the installation of psychopathology. These five "introductions" determine the modality of the analytic treatment and of the resources of the clinical technique:

a. dreams;
b. narcissism;
c. death drive;
d. identifications;
e. fetishism.

These are fundamental concepts in Freud's works; not only are they landmarks in the evolution of metapsychology, but they also provide an explanation for the modalities of structuring the psychic apparatus. These different modalities determine "*zones*" or "*areas*" *of psychic functioning* according to each specific way of structuring. Freud discovered and described them throughout his works, although he did not define them as such. But he left clues for us to develop and define them more accurately now so as to facilitate the access to contemporary psychopathology. Psychopathological structures, with their clinical complexity, show us the manifestations of these "unconscientized zones", which coexist and overlap in the psychic apparatus. This does not mean viewing the psychic apparatus as a sort of map where the different regions are located, with clear-cut boundaries between them. Perhaps, as I have pointed out somewhere else, the most representative image of what I am trying to describe is found in Dali's painting "*Gala, naked, gazing at the sea*", in which, for the viewer standing at a distance of 20 meters, she is transformed into Abraham Lincoln's portrait ("*Homage to Rothko*").[3] The image is as a whole a unit, but from the *spectator's relative point of view* different structures are perceived, each with its *own logic* exposed to the senses in a particular way. In analysis this "point of view" is the patient–analyst couple interacting in the dynamic of the transference–countertransference. Each of these psychic zones, with its own specific way of structuring, functioning, and manifestation, also involves, in different and particular ways, the resources of silence, interpretation, construction, and the analyst's mind, and it leaves its mark on the conditions of the setting and on other aspects of psychoanalytic technique. According to this way of thinking, the setting is no longer a closed and, at times, dogmatic system but a field (Baranger & Baranger, 1969b) defined by the encounter, in an analytic situation propitious for the appearance of the various ways in which the psyche unconscientizes the psychic conflict.]

This is, briefly, the *updating* I propose to the understanding of and approach to contemporary analytic practice.

The *Interpretation of Dreams* (Freud, 1900a), conceptualizes a sexual and significant unconscious—outlined in this work on dreams and to be fully developed later in "The Unconscious" (Freud, 1915e). This idea, developed from Freud's so-called first topic, implied an unconscious formed by representations and one in which the drive force is obtained from the sexual drive affected by repression. This outlines a "zone" of the psychic apparatus characterized by manifestations of this sexual and significant *repressed unconscious,* and its pathological expressions are the "classic neuroses": hysteria, obsessional neurosis, phobic neuroses.

With the *Introduction to Narcissism* (1914c), Freud introduces us into "another psychoanalysis": basically that of the problematic of the ego in theory, in clinical work, and in the management of the treatment. Narcissism underlines one of the foundational moments in psychic structuring. Freud's description reconstructs the process that goes from auto-erotism to the conformation of narcissism—that is, this "new psychic act" by which the ego[4] is formed, which I call passive primary identification—(Marucco, 1978b), which Freud defines as preceding any object cathexis and Laplanche (1989) considers the enigmatic significant in the constitution of the unconscious and, perhaps, in the creation of the drive. This shows the importance of the object in the constitution of the psyche and consequently in the characteristics of pathology and the course of the analytic process. For the subject this object is of crucial importance, owing to the role it plays in the genesis of the ideal; thereby various paths are drawn, and so is fate: "the boy must . . ., the girl must . . ." as Freud puts it (1914c). Are these paths and this fate also found in the sphere of the repressed unconscious? Or are we in another area when we speak of "blindness", of the inexorability of fate? Perhaps we are here in another unconscientized zone: a narcissistic zone that mimics the history of the other's desire, in the manner of Chinese boxes—in other words, the importance of having the object and of frustration in face of the object or caused by it. Freud reminds us: out of frustration, an ideal is created. As a result love that had before been bestowed on the "true ego" is now devoted to the ideal, and a narcissistic ideal is installed, implying an intrapsychic structure I have named "idealizing structure" (Marucco, 1998b). This intrapsychic ideal, this idealizing structure, projected on an external object becomes the idealization of the object.

The introduction of narcissism throws light on the psychic zone in which the importance of the object is most significant and on the consequences the absence of the object entails in the forging of the ideal that attempts to reconstruct a mythic history of love independently of material reality. This mechanism results in the constitution of a defence against the power of the object. The processes of unconscientization that conform to the *idealizing structure* are a shelter from the power of the object but also a source of pathologies, when the projection of the intrapsychic ideal is placed on an external object that is endowed with too much power (addictions, depressions, some mass phenomena, etc.).[5]

We come now to the *introduction to the death drive* in Freud's works, which in my opinion, leads us along two different pathways: There is, on the one hand, *The Ego and the Id* (1923b) and the concept of repetition compulsion. The unconscious (that unconscious of the speech and the significant) is now also the unconscious of the trauma. When Freud in *Beyond the Pleasure Principle* (1920g) re-examines trauma, he turns the id of *The Ego and the Id* into a particularly rich clinical concept. The id (the unconscious) includes the unconscious, but it is something more, too. What is this "something more"? Up to now, the unconscious had been a *repressed* sexual unconscious, which found representations in words—we could have said, in the concept of the significant. Now, instead, *the id is an unconscious where the life drive and the death drive coexist* (the death drive expressed mainly as repetition compulsion). With the concept of the id, the analytic field includes histories of significants and histories of traumas. Psychic pathology, then, is not only how a desire is expressed, but also how pain is expressed: *the traumatic theory* is recovered again in 1920.

This "traumatic theory" is expressed on three levels of repetition: (a) the repetition of fragments and extensions of the Oedipus complex (corresponding to the unconscious of dreams—that is, the repressed, sexual, and significant unconscious of Freud's so-called first topic; (b) the repetition of the wounded narcissism that is "beyond the pleasure principle", one may say—beyond desire"—and that ultimately is a repetition of rebuff, of disappointment or what this conceals: *the unconscious of the idealizing structure;* (c) *the repetition of life experiences of primal time,* which are not bound in word representations. I called these memory traces "unmanageable" (Marucco, 1980), and I think that psychoanalytic work should aim at attaining their encounter with representation (Marucco, 1998c). The introduction of the death drive and with it the concept of repetition compulsion account for the existence of an area in the psychic apparatus that commands the repetition of these *unmanageable* traces of the primal time, which cannot be bound in the secondary process: point of expression of the preverbal traumas, of the violence of the object at the dawn of the psyche, and supreme expression of a cruel fate only to be avoided by the force of representation. Contemporary psychoanalysis explores the whole range of what can be represented, what cannot be represented, or what is not represented, related to the unconscious.[6]

Just as the introduction to narcissism and the death drive were useful to describe the area of the psychic apparatus that shows the importance of the object and that highlights in the analytic treatment the dialectic between drive and object, so the problematic of the ego and the superego introduced in *The Ego and the Id* deals more profoundly with the result of the dialectic between drive and object: *identification.*

Identification is, indeed, another great challenge for current psychoanalysis because of the difficulties that it presents. The "unconscious of the identifications" returns in general in the behaviour, in actions, but also in the attitude towards life, in the character. It is relevant to ask here why character was left "out" of analysis for such a long time. Different kinds of identification lead either to inclusion in culture or to the weakening of the drive.

The tension between ego and superego that is called the "unconscious sense of guilt" is expressed not only through the symptom of a loss of self-esteem (which is the main source of depressions and "void pathologies"), but also by the need to fall ill or to be punished. This sense of guilt, which is necessary for access to culture and at the same time is the origin of pathology, is one of the key subjects that need to be explored by current psychoanalysis.

Masochism poses no minor question. I am referring, specifically, to the primary masochism that dwells in the ego: a direct derivative of the death drive, which leads the ego to its destruction. Masochism of the ego and/or sadism of the superego: how to account for a drive that carries in itself the seeds of its own destruction? How to explain the confluence of this ego masochism with the effects of a superego, which, heir to an identification, also produce a fate of death? What is suicide? Is it an act precipitated by the drive or by a superego that strikes the ego with such merciless rage that it is pushed to its final destruction? To answer these questions, it is necessary to undertake a profound investigation of the "original" in the psyche and on the unconscious that lies beyond repression.

Lastly, the *introduction of fetishism* in the theory—as Pontalis (1977) called it—starts a new metapsychological development I have referred to as "the third Freudian topic" (Marucco, 1980), since it implies the appearance of a key defence: disavowal and a fundamental effect—ego splitting. We are now in a position to understand the psychic apparatus with an ego split by denial. To give a brief background to this subject: The structuring of the psychic apparatus depends on the interplay between the Oedipus complex and castration. In the development of his libidinal ties with father and mother, the child arrives at a time when he has to face, on one hand, the acknowledgement of his mother's castration and, on the other, his father's castration threat. If he acknowledges castration, his father's castration threat gains signification. Defence, then, must repress the drive, thereby constituting the repressed unconscious. The superego is the heir to the Oedipus complex. With "The Dissolution of the Oedipus Complex" (1924d), Freud crowned his phallic theory. The psychic apparatus completes its conformation with this dissolution. This ego ends up depending on its masters: the id, with its world of the drive force, and the superego, with its demands and external reality.[7]

However, three years later, with "Fetishism" (1927e), Freud apparently introduced the study of perversion. But he had already dealt with it much earlier: why did he feel the need to devote a paper to fetishism? Why, after the publication of "The Dissolution of the Oedipus Complex" and a final synthesis of the resolution of the Oedipus complex, does fetishism appear again? Freud returns to fetishism because he has found a mechanism that accounts not only for perversion itself, but also for a modality of structuring the apparatus based on *Verleugnung*.

As a result disavowal comes to play a fundamental part in the structuring of the psyche. Confronted with castration, a part of the ego will acknowledge it and will repress his Oedipus, giving rise to the repressed unconscious—the history of the dissolution of the Oedipus complex; but another part of the ego will disavow castration and in this way *give rise to an unrepressed unconscious, an unconscious produced by disavowal,* with a particular pathway of return. When the mother's castration is not acknowledged, the child creates in the place of the mother's penis (by displacement and transmutation of values) an object that becomes a condition for sexual pleasure: the fetish. This is perversion, and we are in the field of the pathology of disavowal. But if this transmutation of values and this displacement of the mother's penis is not about a concrete object but about something created by desire "at will", as Rosolato (1978) states (that shine on the nose, Freud, 1927e), then the "virtual fetish" (Marucco, 1997) is created: this immaterial, elusive other is the condition that is necessary to preserve the drive, since castration is thus avoided by displacement to an object that contains something of that primal, incestuous object but is not it. Octave Mannoni (1969) coined an enlightening phrase to describe in the patient's discourse the action of disavowal: "I know . . . but even so . . .". The "I know" denotes an acknowledgement of castration and the construction of the repressed unconscious, while the "but even so . . ." denotes the action of disavowal that *"unconscientizes" castration* and preserves the drive and its counterpart: phantasy. Hence the "virtual fetish" is a determining factor in the choice of the love object and in creativity. There is no possibility of creativity without this capacity for disavowing a certain part of reality that is at the same time accepted. This would imply creating an equivalence between castration and "reality" (Marucco, 2000).

Thus, the introduction of fetishism and the concept of disavowal that were the starting point for me to develop the concept of "virtual fetish" as the conditions of love and to specify the mode of functioning derived from denial and made possible by the "virtual fetish" (that possibility of acknowledging and in turn unacknowledging castration, respectively) describe the functioning of an unconscious zone of the psychic apparatus that has specific characteristics and clinical and psychopathological expressions.

The "virtual fetish" and disavowal are, then, structural, and both are conditions of the choice of the love object and survival of the drive and imply the possibility of creation. When the drive vanishes due to failure in constructing the "virtual fetish", which in a way ensures that something of the Oedipus drive will keep going in it, we run into normopathies, with the loss of the capacity for love. (This capacity for love meant for Freud one of the conditions of the analytic cure.)[8]

The unconscientized and the analyst's standpoints

I return here to my idea of "zones or areas of unconscious psychic functioning" but from the point of view of clinical work and the different positions the analyst should take to deal with the particular modes of psychopathological expression.

The analyst should sharpen his "analytic senses" in order to detect in the patient the various ways in which the unconscious is expressed in each of these "zones of psychic functioning" and, starting from there, find the most adequate therapeutic approach, adjusting his technical resources accordingly. Because of "timelessness" in the unconscious, most of the time we are likely to hear simultaneity and/ or juxtaposition in the expressions of the different zones. This renders the analytic work more complex. Consequently, the analyst should try to discern at each moment which unconscious psychic structure it is that is "speaking"—that is, the moment when it returns to the organized domain that was once left to become unconscientized—and from there be able to include it into a new temporality: that of the analytic process, that of life.

If I follow an order ("chronological" for the evolution of psychoanalytic theory) in the description of the different psychic zones, this is only for the purpose of organizing this presentation. Nevertheless, it is easy to verify that the progression of Freud's discoveries and the discoveries of those who followed him reveals, through this order, a gradually increasing degree of complexity, as regards both the constitution and organization of the psyche and its modalities of unconscientization and psychopathological manifestations.

The "zone of dreams"—probably just because it was the "first"—has been the most intensely examined by psychoanalytic theory, and thus it has yielded the best results (always in relative terms), the most satisfactory answers. The analyst's task focuses here mainly on the unveiling of the desire as it is expressed by the significants. And the analytic setting dictates that the patient should be lying on the couch . . ., his bodily movements inhibited . . ., the perceptive pole practically obliterated. It seems the right conditions for a chain of associations to develop in the manner of a dream (Green, 1990). Free-floating attention and interpretation determine in this zone the analyst's position, the analytic listening, to discover in the significant the nucleus of the repressed, condensed, or displaced unconscious and its modes of return: symptoms that become transference symptoms.

Free association is crucial, as it is a privileged tool to detect the sexual and significant unconscious. However, when we are dealing with other psychic zones where psychopathology is expressed by the act, is free association enough? Are we not in need of a "tool" that allows us to detect, for example, the expressions of the act? It should be remembered that the concept of the unconscious comprises what is repressed and something more than that. . . .

When the libido of the object is "wasted" in what Green (1990) called "erotic madness" (or "erotic psychosis") and Freud (1921c) described as falling in love, we are in this other zone: the narcissistic unconscious, which underlines the importance of the object in the constitution of the psyche and, therefore, in the characteristics of the pathology and in the course of the analytic process: Consequently, there is the zone of narcissism, of the creation of the ideal and the conformation of the *idealizing structure* (already mentioned above). When this "idealizing structure" is projected onto the analyst, an idealizing transference is set in train, which repeats a kind of "addictive love". The analyst is then included in a complex and particular network in which he is "assigned", "occupying" the place of the idealized object capable of determining the course of a life. How many changes can be attained in the circuit of repetition when the unconscious of this zone is detected, analysed, and dismantled, and how many blind paths can be created in an analysis in which this remains uncovered?

"Placed" here, the analyst should dismantle the power of idealization, retrieving as historic representation what had been transformed into psychic structure. To do so, he counts on *interpretation* and *constructions* to deal with the history of disillusion that took place and was denied, thus allowing its transformation into representation—that is, turning the unconscientized narcissistic child into an everlasting memory.

The analyst's position is challenged in a very special way when, as Eros loses the struggle for life, there arises in the present-day patient the action of the death drive expressed as an unconscious configured by a certain type of repetition and by effect of unlinking. So, when the analytic field ventures into this territory of the unconscious, special attention must be paid to "listening" to repetition and silence.

In these histories of traumas, it is not enough for the analyst to follow along the *vía de levare* [interpreting]; he/she needs also to take the *vía de porre*, which means giving signification to those traumas that keep repeating with diabolical insistence. Field of interpretation *and* of the construction of a history—histories of coming closer, of drifting apart, of distances. . . : this building of histories has at times been overdone in psychoanalysis, leaving transference dangerously out of the analytic field.

It is worth bearing in mind that when Freud described, in *Beyond the Pleasure Principle* (1920g), the repetition of pain, the repetition of trauma, what really amazed him *was* this—not always successful—attempt of the repetition of the trauma to be bound, so as to be able to enter the pleasure–displeasure series. It seems that in this sense for Freud the first principle was binding:[9] "*Without previous binding there would not be repetition but disorganization and fragmentation*" (Green, 2001). Therefore today the repetition compulsion is placed one step before pleasure, but with a nucleus that is *endlessly seeking linkage.* In this sense, repetition may be viewed as a possible demand from a blocked process of objectalization. The clinical expressions of this area of conscientization may be the impulse to act or psychosomatic manifestations. In clinical practice the analyst works with the patient in this search (for linkage and objectalization) in the *singularity of the analytic field* (Marucco, Korol, Marchionni, Rozitchner, & Vertzner de Marucco, 1995), including a much more complex idea of temporality. When an individual caught in the web of the repetition compulsion fails to reach binding, his time, to put it in Green's terms, is "murdered". This "murdering of time" poses a big challenge to present-day psychoanalysis, and in this regard the *analyst's unconscious libidinal force is fundamental* to provide linkage to this trauma, which has been kept subjected to compulsion to repetition.[10]

"Countertransference",[11]—or, more specifically, what the analyst's mind produces—is the privileged place from which to operate, both over the unbinding as well as over the memory traces that have failed to find representation in words. And the analyst will succeed in doing so if he/she resorts to his/her capacity for binding, together with a capacity for *reverie*—in Bion's words—for day-dreaming in this "zone" at the frontiers.

But how can we be sure that the words introduced by the analyst's mind are not coming from a problematic of his own? The analyst's analysis and his own self-analysis are indispensable to guard against the abuse that, as object, the latter may exercise over the patient. As regards this psychic zone, present-day analysis faces the challenge of transforming this fate, or at least part of it, into "a neurosis" that can be reached and modified by our analytic practice. This is what matters in this unconscientized zone: to counteract the paralysing effects of the bond with the object in order to recover the transforming, neogenetic (allow me the expression) force (Green, 1997) of the drive. This is, at least to my mind, what psychoanalysis should achieve in the unconscious of this psychic zone.

As to the unconscious sense of guilt as expression of the tension between ego and superego, there are plenty of data from clinical work that account for its presence and that, in extreme cases, can lead the individual to "live on his knees", asking for forgiveness, and apologizing even for being alive. This "condition" is wide-spread in culture. It may be found underlying the behaviour of submissive and obedient individuals who end up as active members of mass phenomena that eventually prove to be disastrous for society and culture. Freud asserts in a footnote about negative therapeutic reaction:

> If one can unmask this former object-cathexis behind the Ucs sense of guilt, the therapeutic success is often brilliant, but otherwise the outcome of one's efforts is by no means certain. It depends principally on the intensity of the sense of guilt; there is often no counteracting force of a similar order of strength which the treatment can oppose to it. Perhaps it may depend, too, on whether *the personality of the analyst allows of the patient's putting him in the place of his ego ideal and this involves a temptation for the analyst to play the part of prophet, saviour and redeemer to the patient.* Since the rules of analysis are diametrically opposed to the physician's making use of his personality in any such manner, it must be honestly confessed that here we have another limitation to the effective-

> ness of analysis; after all, analysis does not set out to make pathological reactions impossible, but give the patient's ego *freedom* to decide one way or other. [Freud, 1923b, p. 50; emphasis added]

This meaningful quotation warns us about the danger of suggestion (quite close, on the level of the clinical technique, to what has been placed in the sphere of some psychotherapies)—that is, of the other's power. I wonder whether there are exceptions to the prohibition of making use of the power of this suggestion—and if so, for how long? Is too long an analysis due to this power of suggestion? Freud put forward a clear and severe ethical warning: the analyst should refrain from becoming a "prophet" or "redeemer" and should give the patient the freedom to choose *even his/her illness.* Freud encourages us to go further on this. What does he have in mind when he says that, in spite of the risk of the analyst becoming "prophet" or "redeemer", it may also happen that the patient turns the analyst into his ego ideal and thus "escapes" from his own "destruction"? Can we always refuse such a risk? Or should we, on some occasions, decide on wearing those deceptive masks as prophets or redeemers, only to remove them later on, thus *leaving the individual free to choose his/her own path in life guided by his/her drives* instead of being compelled by the power of an object?

Echoes coming from the fierce struggle in the unconscious to extricate itself from the power of the object of the passive primary identification (Marucco, 1978b) reverberate in the negative therapeutic reactions (NTR)—that strange and paradoxical falling ill when the patient is, in fact, better. The patient improves in the treatment . . . however, instead of feeling well, he/she feels ill. What is the matter? Has psychoanalysis reached its ceiling?

Some agree with Freud in that at this point the analyst has to admit his limits. I myself think that it is precisely when we encounter this "falling ill when improving" that the analyst should do his best to grapple with this struggle between ego and superego—in this "*other unconscious*", in this other "psychic zone"—and work hard. This enemy puzzles us because it seems to rise from the depth of the analytic process itself and attack it and its representative, the analyst, directly. It is when *we give them hope and show our satisfaction with the results of the treatment* [emphasis added], that they show discontent and get much worse, Freud comments in *Ego and the Id* (1923b) amazed at these unexpected and apparently unaccountable reactions. But which gives hope? Is it the analysis or the analyst? Is it an imposition of the analyst's unconscientized wishes? If so, the negative therapeutic reaction could be at the service of unlinking from the other's desire and consequently be "positive" (Marucco, 1979) paving the way for the individual to reach disidentification, thus enabling him to unbind even from the analyst in the last stages of the analytic process. It is in this field—in the complexity of this "unconscious identification" with that other who constitutes and "alienates" and in the core of these "transference moments" (Marucco, 1978a)—that psychoanalysis will have to discover the pathways leading to a disidentification that regains for the subject the invigorating impulse of his own drive (Green, 1997). In present-day psychoanalysis some theories have come to propose identification with the analyst as a way of "correcting" pathological identifications; however, I believe that we should be extremely cautious about this matter. I would put it like this: the analyst should be neither so restrained as to represent for the patient a demand for disinvestment that can be dangerous for his/her psychic economy, nor favour an identification with the analyst that determines a new destiny that is so remote from the subject as the "life project" generated by his/her pathology.

Next I would like to deal with the processes of unconscientization that are produced by disavowal and the creation of the *"virtual fetish"* from the point of view of the clinical work and the analyst's position. Can the breach produced in the splitting of the ego by the mechanism of disavowal be closed? Should it be closed? Any attempt to close it would only mean moving it, to "correct" it in one sense or another—both potentially dangerous. If this crack in the splitting of the ego "moves" towards accepting castration (pushing out the area of disavowal), a progressive vanishing of the sexual drive may occur, generating the idealization of the object.[12]

If, instead, the crack "moves" towards the area of disavowal, then perversion may command the object relation even to the point of ignoring reality itself: delusion instead of creation.[13] An ideal outcome would be a creative balance between "I know" (acknowledgement of castration) and "but even so" (action of the unconscientized by disavowal that preserves the drive and its counterpart, phantasy). If the theory of the treatment favours excessively symbolic development (acknowledgement of castration), the creative space in the unconscious phantasy will be narrowed. Considering the problem in these terms, we can envisage a theory of sublimation related to the dialectic pair of the acknowledgement and non-acknowledgement of castration.

The *virtual fetish,* then, according to Freud, would imply the acceptance of castration and at the same time triumph over it. This little "detail" (*"the shine on the nose"*), which is not included in the stock-in-trade of post-modern sexual marketing, reflects a psychic structure that contains the potential for sexual satisfaction, the conditions of love and creation. As Assoun puts it: "psychoanalysis turns it into the 'instituting symptom' of the 'structural misunderstanding' that is castration. . . . The fetish is a *stigma indelebile* on account of which 'man' is subject to . . . splitting!" (1995, p. 154)

On the metapsychological level, the primacy of the phallus is thereby reaffirmed, while at the same time the "maternal" object retains its founding validity, and in the clinical situation (or in life) the unconscious of the sexual drive recovers its strength. Hence the *virtual fetish* must not only be respected and maintained but also be recreated in the unconscious of the analytic link. In our daily clinical work, we should be—active—observers of the encounter between the passion of the liberating drive and the presence of the object that demands idealization (castration?).

In short, any analysis that embarks upon the recognition of reality at any cost is likely to cause the curtailment of the force of the drive. The lack of drive is not only produced by the psychopathological history of the individual, but it can also be part of the history of the analytic process in which the effort to impose the recognition of reality at all costs has weakened the potency of the drive world in its two ways: creativity and satisfaction in the conditions of love.

If there is risk in overlooking the importance of the "but even so" in favour of the "I know", then the same is true with the opposite: that is, to encourage the "but even so" while failing to recognize the "I know". Analysis is best placed, in my opinion, in the adequate, laborious balance between the "I know" and the "but even so".

I believe it is time for me to stop. I have endeavoured to come out of "the blindness of the repressed unconscious" so as to think of different zones of unconscientization, its modes of functioning, and its psychopathological expression in the contemporary patient. I have also examined the analyst's various standpoints when confronted with these expressions of the unconscious in the contemporary patient. Nevertheless, I feel that there is still a long way to go. The end of this chapter is the beginning of an adventure—we may call it analytic fictions[14]—of uncertain outcome, but one that stimulates the encounter with my constantly elusive enigmas and the enigmas of our contemporary psychoanalytic practice.

Notes

To write this chapter, I have drawn on the ideas I have been developing for many years, especially in some of my latest works: "The Oedipus Complex, castration and the fetish" (1997), "Las neurosis hoy: En las vías de acceso a las 'zonas psíquicas'" [Neurosis nowadays: Some pathways to reach psychic zones] (1998b), " El placer en la realidad y en la fantasía" [Pleasure in fantasy and in reality] (2000), "Algunas puntuaciones psicoanalíticas desde mi práctica clínica" [Some psychoanalytic emphasis] (2001), "El analizado de hoy y lo inconciente" [Today's analysand and the unconscious] (2003b) and "La posición del analista [el otro] y la clínica actual" [The analyst's standpoint in current clinical work"] (2004). That is why I apologize to the reader for some inevitable reiterations.

1. By "unconscientization" (quite normal in Spanish), I mean the process by which something is rendered unconscious. The same holds true of the verb "unconscientize".

2. I would like to point out here that the concept of repression and repressed unconscious, which threw light on the field of psychoanalysis, also, similarly caused a blindness that delayed investigation into other ways of unconscientization, into the pathways of returning of these "other unconscious", and into the various ways in which the unconscious "works".

3. Salvador Dali, "Gala Contemplating the Mediterranean Sea which at Twenty Meters Becomes the Portrait of Abraham Lincoln: Homage to Rothko" (second version), 1976; on display at the Dali Teatre-Museu in Figueres, Spain.

4. The constitution of the ego is a substantial part of the theory. I have dealt with it at length especially in chapters 2 and 3 of my book *Cura analítica y transferencia* [Analytic treatment and transference] (1998a).

5. If a patient shows little tolerance of the absence of the object, it is because he was unable to construct the ideal to which to devote the love that had previously been bestowed by the object on the ego, thus rendering him subjected to it. At the other extreme of the pathology, when confronted with a rebuff—that is, an acknowledgment of castration—the individual enjoys a narcissistic union with the ideal, thus unlinking from the object. There is still another possibility: Freud describes a process by which this intrapsychic ideal is projected onto an external object. If this happens, a state of falling in love is produced: the individual hands his ego over to the power of the object.

6. Another disquieting question is associated with the death drive: if we consider that the sexual drive is stimulated from this excess of sexuality of the object, if life itself is born from the other's life, why not think that the death drive may also be connected with the death wish that springs from the

other because of his hatred, his hostility? It may be pertinent to point out here that this thought becomes much more complex in the analytic field and when the role of the analyst's desire in both the erotic and the thanatic forms is examined. To paraphrase Freud: the strongest army will obtain the final victory (1923b, 1937c): which will be the role of the analyst's libido directed towards his patient, his own drive force? No doubt, the analyst's desire is here quite meaningful, since he contributes his own drive commitment to produce change and transformation.

7. The ego harassed by these threats resorts to anxiety as a signal and starts from there the construction of an unconscious psychic structure, which I call a basic architecture of the psyche.

8. By "normopathies" I mean the various Freudian expressions that denote the different levels of repression, from the German term "*Untergang*" [repression] (1924d) to "*zugrunde gehen*" [destruction/annihilation] to conclude with *catastrophe* [catastrophe/demolition] (1925j), which aim at the cultural ideal of "erasing" in the unconscious the Oedipus complex. This would imply, to my mind, almost an abolition of the drive—or, to put it in another way, individuals who live deprived of drive-passion.

9. If it is agreed that previous to pleasure, or to nirvana, there is something we might call the "principle of linkage", this would provide a better understanding of concepts such as primary identification (which I called "passive") as preceding any libidinal bond of the object. C. and S. Botella (1997) probably refer to the same problematic with their "convergence–coherence principle" and Green (2001) with what he calls "time for binding".

10. I have discussed above the three types of anxiety engendered by repetition compulsion and prompted by the death drive.

11. I find the term "countertransference" extremely limited to convey my ideas concerning the analyst's unconscious. The term "analyst's mind" (Baranger, 1992) has a wider connotation, but it is still provisional in my conceptual system.

12. This means the reinstallation of the object in the pre-oedipal attachment, which, although it was necessary for the structural development of the subject, may prove to be iatrogenic in the treatment and "paralysing" in life, when it implies the reaffirmation of the power of this object. This power is disguised by "normopathies" that characterize some kinds of life.

13. Here I do not mean disavowal as structuring the psychic apparatus but its pathogenic effects. This is a very important and controversial subject in contemporary psychoanalytic literature.

14. Maud Mannoni (1980) concludes that any analyst who accompanies the present-day patient in his own process (thanks to the successive overcoming of what he does not know) is confronted, at a given point, with what has been hidden from him. But what is hidden from him as psychoanalyst has consequences (legible) on the patient's treatment. The analyst, urged by an inner demand, will accomplish a theoretical elaboration of what is hidden from him. In the same way as when madness destroys beliefs and this elicits truth, so the psychoanalytic "theory of fiction" may, at moments like this, produce truth. However, this may only happen provided the analyst is willing to give up the control of knowledge and with it that of illusory protection.

Commentary

Cesar Botella

Splitting and/or coherence?

Marucco's conception, as it will have been understood, corresponds perfectly to the Freudian spirit of post 1920, by virtue of two highly heuristic notions, namely, the *"zona inconcientizada"* [unconscientized zone] and the *"procesos de inconcientisación"* [processes of unconscientization]. To these may be added the notion of *"lo inconciente"* [the unconscious], which is not the Freudian *Ucs.* but a much larger domain resulting from an activity of psychic functioning, that of *"inconcientizar"* [unconscientizing], of which each "zona" imposes its own modality, its own processes of unconscientization. Marucco has thus come up with an original conception, such that Freud's work has to be reconsidered from this new perspective. It deserves a lengthy commentary, which is not possible within the limits of this current contribution. I therefore had to make a choice. Among the numerous points of view in his text, I have chosen to deal with the major difficulty of technique that haunts every analytic treatment—that is to say, how to cope with the emergence of "*a negative therapeutic reaction*" (NTR). Briefly, his position is as follows: the reactivation of the compulsion to repeat at the end of every analytic treatment is regarded as the inevitable consequence of the progressive disinvestment by the patient of the analyst and the analytic situation. The hypothesis he advances for resolving the NTR is based on the dynamic that he defines as the "unconscientized zone" of fetishism. It is based on the notion of "*virtual fetish*", which he has been developing for some years now. It is a daring hypothesis, if ever there was one—postulating that the mother's desire for a penis is displaced not onto a concrete object but onto something "virtual", "immaterial", which desire can create "at will". Marucco thus comes close here to the idea of Octave Mannoni, inspired by Lacan, concerning an attitude of the ego which accepts the reality of castration while denying it at the same time—an attitude Mannoni condenses into a striking formulation: *"I know, but even so"* (Mannoni, 1969)—on the one hand, *"I know"*, an acceptance and submission to the reality of the missing penis confirming the existence of castration, and, on the other, "*but even so*", which Marucco understands as "the action of disavowal that 'unconscientizes' castration and preserves the drive and its counterpart, phantasy". For by imposing the recognition of the reality of castration at any price, the analytic treatment runs the risk, according to Marucco, of provoking an impoverishment of drive functioning. Hence the affirmation: "The 'virtual fetish' and disavowal are, then, structural" . . . "a determining factor in the choice of the love object and in creativity. There is no possibility of creativity without this capacity for disavowing a certain part of reality that is at the same time accepted." Hence his conclusion at the end of his paper: "Analysis is best placed, in my opinion, in the adequate, laborious balance between the 'I know' and the 'but even so' . . .". This supposes that there exists in every psyche a splitting of the ego that I would qualify as supple, for neither of these two parts of the ego is unaware of the other at any moment; or as "functional splitting", to employ Gérard Bayle's (1996) formulation.

Marucco thus raises a major problem of analytic theory and technique. At the end of every analysis, when a NTR is always a possibility, there may be said to be an entanglement between loss of the object–analyst and a work of mourning, castration and its denial, and the fetish. This technical proposition is so innovatory that it merits both a time for reflection and time for practicing this new mode of listening with our patients with a view to envisaging their treatment in terms of this new conception of the link with reality. In the meantime, I will focus on the solution of the "virtual fetish", the intuition of which seems familiar to me, even if its conceptualization presents me with the problem of sharing a similar intuition while treating it with different conceptual tools. Here we are touching on one of the major problems of contemporary psychoanalysis. This is why exchanges are indispensable and why, if they are sufficient, we will eventually understand that the so-called Babel of contemporary psychoanalysis is ultimately less important than we think.

My conceptual tools will be based on the notions of trauma and "quality"; and, as I proceed, I will clarify the intuition that I think we share. I shall begin with three remarks.

The first is that Norberto Marucco is right to denounce the limits of an analytic theory that is limited to just one conception of psychoanalysis in Freud's work, framed solely in terms of representation. These limits must have been one of the reasons that led Freud to introduce the second topography in 1923 (*The Ego and the Id*) with a view to overcoming the theoretical shortcomings of what was referred to retrospectively as the first topography—that is to say, the papers on metapsychology of 1915 (1917d [1915]), governed by the idea of the repression of representations, which was seen as the principal foundation of psychic functioning. This theoretical change cannot be separated from the turning point of 1920, which saw the introduction of the death instinct. From then on, the pair repression/interpretation would only be one aspect of psychic functioning, a determining aspect certainly, but one that was included within the vast ensemble of the second topography with laws that were now more complex. This increased complexity arose from the psyche's need to combat the risks of disorganisation. The aim of this vital psychic work is to see to it that the processes of unbinding, which tend to be provoked by the constant activity of the death instinct, and the effects of the chaos of the unrepresented instinctual impulses, structurally constitutive of the id, are controlled and integrated within the representational networks of binding. In other words, with the introduction of the second topography, the principal function of the psyche became one of achieving a "work of binding", which Freud described as "one of the earliest and most significant functions of the mental apparatus" (Freud, 1920g). This was to be confirmed in 1923 with the introduction of the term Eros to refer to the sexual instincts, and it was supposed that Eros "by bringing about a more and more far-reaching combination of the particles into which living substance is dispersed, aims at complicating life and at the same time, of course, at preserving it" (Freud, 1923b). This resulted in a certain relativization in Freud's work of the pleasure principle as the principal law governing psychic life. Thus, in the "Revision of dream-theory", the first of the *New Introductory Lectures* (1933a, p. 29), the dream is no longer considered as a wish-fulfilment but as an "*attempt*" at fulfilment (the italics are Freud's). It thus took Freud 32 years, after *The Interpretation of Dreams* (1900a), to understand that, in the last instance, the fundamental function of the dream is that of exercising "*the earliest function*", that of "binding", of elaborating traumatic experiences, notably those of childhood. Elaborating, binding, representing, in order to avoid disorganization and chaos, is assumed to be the primary objective of psychic life. That the pleasure principle collaborates in this, that it is determining, no one doubts. The novelty, and I shall try to show this better further on, is that, for the Freud of post 1920, the pleasure principle was inseparable from and stood in a dialogical relationship, in Edgar Morin's sense, with binding, and as such was the best means of combating the death instinct. I shall come back to this later. To this one may add that the transition from the first to the second topography implies that the psyche must from thereon be thought of more in terms of process than solely in terms of its representational contents and of its systems. Similarly, the concepts of ego, id, and superego must be understood as referring to processes that are capable of permanent transformation, and must not be reduced to the idea of circumscribed and fixed agencies. Freud's thought thus opens itself up to the idea of a psyche whose foundation is no longer the classical one of networks of representations included within a hierarchy of topographies but that of a complex imbrication of processes varying according to the economo-dynamic conditions of the moment and in function of a dynamic defined by qualities—that is, those of representation, perception, hallucination, a dynamic to which I will also return later on. There are no new patients; there is a better understanding of psychic life.

The second remark is that convergence, the work of mourning and denial, of which Marucco speaks, was a theme Freud dealt with very early on. He had already alluded to it in a footnote in *The Interpretation of Dreams* (1900a, p. 254). A child, distraught by his father's sudden death, says: "*I know father's dead, but what I can't understand is why he doesn't come home to supper.*" It is true that Freud considered that, in children, the partial denial of reality was part of normal development. Equally, he thought that one could find similar manifestations in adults, even if only in dreams. He gives an example of this: "in the months following his father's death, he has repeatedly dreamt that *his father was alive once more and that he was talking to him in his usual way. But he felt it exceedingly painful that his father had really died, only without knowing it*" (1911b, p. 225). I shall come back to this.

The third remark I would like to make is that it is true that every individual passes through a stage of creating infantile sexual theories (Freud, 1908c, p. 205: the mother endowed with a penis, giving birth via the anus or the mouth, etc.) serving to deny the absence of the penis, the difference between the sexes. In short, whether it is in the child, faced with the reality of the absence of the penis, or the reality of a too painful object-loss, or whether it is in the adult, in both cases one finds a means of avoiding the suffering evoked by the formulation "I know, but even so".

However, why speak only of denial [*Verleugnung*]? Would it not be more exact to consider that "negation" [*Verneinung*] plays a part in this procedure?—negation, that is, in the sense that Freud gives it in his famous article of 1925 (Freud, 1925h, p. 235), which may be resumed by a sentence at the beginning of this text: "You ask who this person in the dream can be. It's not my mother." We emend this to: "So it *is* his mother." But perhaps it can be said that it is not really a question of denial or negation but of a procedure that involves both simultaneously. It would thus be necessary to reconsider the link with reality, the latter now being envisaged as having variable limits depending on the economic and dynamic circumstances, with trauma playing a determining role.

Trauma today

The notion of trauma must be considered in the context of its evolution. In Freud's work, at the outset, it was defined as an event that takes place at a given moment and is then repressed, the representational content of which being the reason for its painful effect. It is the cause of neurosis, and its return to consciousness represents the cure. But progressively, from 1920 onwards, trauma was to become in Freud's work a *"narcissistic scar"* (Freud, 1920g, p. 20). Then, at the end of his work, in *Moses and Monotheism: Three Essays* (1939a [1934–39], p. 75), he writes that *"the effect of traumas are of two kinds, positive and negative"*. As for the first, one finds the usual definition to the effect that the trauma can be located in time and is related to a precise event. However, in Freud's later thought, this "positive" trauma represents less an event that is suffered passively than an organization that the subject may have understood, or that he must have created, or at least organized, as a fact providing an causal explanation ordering his psychic life.

As far as "*negative reactions*" are concerned, they must be understood as the consequences of "something" that does not correspond to the notion of trauma in the usual sense of the term, and which in any case will never be found as a defined entity. We can gain a better understanding of the repercussions of this idea from the testamentary text *An Outline of Psychoanalysis,* written one year later (1940a [1938]). There, traumas are still more clearly envisaged as having no real temporal localization or determined factual content. They concern experiences, says Freud, prior to language, experiences of the *infans* who is still without a system of memory traces capable of recording them in the form of represented memories. As an extension of this, Winnicott, in a manuscript ("Fear of Breakdown") thought to have been written in 1963 and found after his death, had the genius to describe events that had taken place but which had not been experienced. Then, M. and W. Baranger, with J. Mom, described the "*trauma puro*" (Baranger, Baranger, & Mom, 1987). In the same vein, since 1983, we have been interested in the notion of "*negatives of trauma*" ("*négatifs du trauma*" : Botella, 1983, 1990), that is to say, irrespective of age or the level of psychic development, there is something that is "not yet experienced", a negativity that is inherent to every trauma and constitutive of it: "something that has been experienced in infancy and then forgotten returns—something that the child has seen or heard at time when he could still hardly speak . . ." (Freud, 1937d, p. 267). Masked by the manifest content, this *negative* is understood as constituting the background of all trauma, the consequence of a negativity of the relationship to the primary object (or to its current representative) insofar as the latter was unable to protect the subject, and is manifested indirectly through a feeling of emptiness, in the form of narcissistic despair without any representational content. For us, it is here that the explanation is to be found for NTRs, where the compulsion to repeat is the mark of the impossibility of carrying out a work of mourning vis-à-vis the treatment and the analyst owing to the negative transference of the "not yet experienced" dimension of the trauma onto the analytic situation and immobilizing it until it has been dealt with. Whether he likes it or not, the analyst makes himself an accomplice here by being unable, just as the parents were unable, to grasp and express this negative. As was the case in the past with the parents, the knot of the problem resides in the failure to "give the subject's experience intelligibility", in an insufficient "work of *répresentance*" (Green[11]) carried out in the analytic process, the responsibility for which lies with both the patient and the analyst.

The analysis of the Wolf Man, and the unilateral decision taken by Freud concerning the date for ending it, seem to confirm this. The account of this treatment reveals the two greatest technical errors of Freud that we know of, while at the same time bearing witness to his capacity for putting himself in question and for evolving. The first error was that the analysis was based on Freud's conviction, since the *Studies on Hysteria,* that the return of the memory was the equivalent of cure. Now, the discovery of the primal scene, a culminating moment in the treatment of the Wolf Man, only proved to be efficacious for a brief period of time, for the interpretation never represented for Sergei a true return of memory. Nor did he really have any conviction of its truth. This was a serious setback for Freud who had nonetheless written, just after the end of the treatment, "in the midsummer of 1914, . . . I believed that this cure was radical and permanent" (Freud, 1937c, p. 217). Freud thus had to resign himself to this failure and, on observing Sergei's successive relapses into illness, was obliged to change his technique from 1918 onward; especially as this moment coincided with the introduction of the death instinct (1920g), and then the notion of the id (1923b). In addition to this, at the same epoch and leading in the same direction, came the discovery of the traumatic neuroses as a result of the First World War. Here was a type of neurosis the pathological cause of which was to be found neither in infantile sexuality nor in a traumatic event of the past; nor did it originate in the *Ucs.* Freud was to conclude that its origin was of a quantitative order. This was a testing time for analytic theory; and it still remains a difficult theoretical and practical problem for psychoanalysts today—one with which Mordechai (Moty) Benyakar's writings are currently concerned.

With this new technical orientation, Freud searched for a solution in the balance of forces of instinctual functioning, in the economy of the quantitative, which is the reason why every analytic treatment necessarily has its limits. This is how Freud was to explain the treatment of the Wolf Man in 1937. Freud then cloaked himself in scientific modesty in the pessimism of "Analysis Terminable and Interminable" (1937c) with the notions of "*biological fact*" and *"bedrock"*. We see this as the second of Freud's errors concerning the treatment of Sergei.

But three months after this article, in "Constructions in Analysis" (1937d), the bases of Freud's technique were to evolve again. The accent was no longer placed on the quantitative but once again on the past, now envisaged differently. The conception of memory was widened. It was now no longer reduced to the notion of memory traces of represented memories. In a similar spirit, we ourselves (Botella & Botella, 1990) have described a *memory without recollections* to describe a memory, which, although it registers recollections, is not accessible to representations. We postulate that it is constituted by traumatic experiences from childhood, by what we have just called the *negatives of trauma*. It is our contention that it is possible to recover this other past by hallucinatory means, by the momentary occurrence of "true hallucinations . . . not psychotic", the unreal nature of which the patient is aware of. Sometimes this occurs in the regression of the session in an almost hallucinatory form, as a sort of flash; or in the totally hallucinatory form of the night dream, but more in its form than in its visual content. A profound change in the theory had occurred leading to a new analytic practice that would enable analysts to conduct analyses with more assurance, notably in the treatment of borderline states, and to find a more satisfactory way of dealing with the end of treatments and eventual NTRs.

The notion of psychic "quality"

It is thus in the hallucinatory realm that we hope to find a solution for the NTRs. Let us return to the problem of mourning, of loss and its denial. Certainly, in particularly painful states of mourning, for instance, in the case of a mother whose child has died, it frequently occurs that this mother, while recognizing her loss, has the feeling that the child is present, or even that she can hear or see the child, even though she knows perfectly well that this impression is hallucinatory in origin. If this hallucinatory impression is powerful, while remaining intrapsychic, endo-hallucinatory, the subject will not need to deny the loss in reality, or to claim a real presence. This is a mechanism that is part of normal mourning. Our memory and our recollections allow us to mourn by means of a procedure which is akin to magic and splitting, in that the person in mourning, thanks to the highly evocative capacity of the recollection, both recognizes the loss in reality and denies it at the same time—a sort of hallucinatory "but nonetheless" making it possible to keep the lost object psychically present. It could be said that the recollection is the equivalent of a magic technique, that a contradictory and complementary simultaneity constitutes the psychic processes of memory.

This *contradictory and complementary simultaneity,* which is always present, can be found at the very foundations of psychic processes. As with recollections, reality-testing can no longer be understood today as the mere neurophysiological result of the sense-organs. In *The Work of Psychic Figurability* (Botella, 2004), we described reality testing as a process in constant movement, where the distinction between internal and external is less a question of bodily limits and of the diktat of the sense-organs than of a psychic investment. Let us recall here that in "Negation" (1925h, p. 237), it is written: "What is unreal, merely a presentation and subjective, is *only internal*; what is real is also *outside*". Drawing inspiration from this, we have formulated reality testing in processual terms, not in function of a bodily outside–inside but in function of psychic qualities, in function of what is felt to be an internal representation or an external perception. Our formulation describing this process equally corresponds to a *contradictory and complementary simultaneity.* In our view, the object is "only inside—also outside" (Botella, 2004, p. 90). It is a transformational dynamic, based on the animistic foundations of the psyche, which allows for permanent readjustments in relation to losses endangering the sense of reality.

In short, this is why, in envisaging memory and reality-testing from the angle of *contradictory and complementary simultaneity,* Marucco's intuition concerning the idea of "virtual fetish", the *"ya lo sé . . . pero aún así"*, even if it comes from a different horizon, does not seem far removed from my own conception based on the notion of quality and on the possibility of transformation of a dynamic representation–perception–hallucination, creating flexible and uncertain psychic frontiers.

Freud was not far from grasping the importance of studying psychic life from the angle of the notion of "quality" when he gave chapter IV of *An Outline of Psycho-Analysis* (1940a [1938]) the title of

"Psychic Qualities". Although it had been more or less present in his work since the "Project" (1950 [1895]), this was the first time that the notion of "quality" had acquired such a rank. An inattentive reading of this chapter can lead one to think that it was simply a question of describing, once again, the three topographies, conscious, preconscious, and unconscious, considering them now as qualities. In fact, there was more to it than this. It seems to have been the means Freud found at the end of his life both of reinforcing the relativization of the topographical hierarchization, begun in the 1920s, and the idea, characteristic of the first topography, of psychic systems considered as more or less closed entities, and, on the other hand, of conceiving the psyche in the form of different processes depending on the different qualities that characterize each of them independent of any idea of temporal or spatial localization. These eventual changes of quality are to be metaphorized more as transformations than as a displacement of places; we are closer here to the chemical metaphor than to the temporo–spatial model of physics. In 1938, psychoanalysis was thus to be defined as "*the theory of the three qualities*" (Freud, 1940a [1938], p. 161). A theoretical opening thus becomes possible if, beyond Freud's explicit text concerning the conscious, the preconscious, and the unconscious, we understand three other qualities, namely, representation, perception, and hallucination, conceptualized as a dynamic process—that is to say, a dynamic process operating along the "*retrogredient*" and "*progredient*" paths described by Freud in *The Interpretation of Dreams*—terms that were respected by the French translation and poorly translated in English by "regressive" and "progressive" (Freud, 1900a, p. 547) where the essential meaning of the German term disappears, for the formulation "*regredienten Charakter*" employed by Freud does not correspond to "regressive" but simply to a different modality of functioning, that of nighttime, different from the "progredient" mode of daytime.

We have seen that the traumatic must be transformed into an intelligibility with a representable causality, by virtue of the creation of new bindings that did not exist before. It now becomes clear that the ideal conditions for this are more easily understandable in an analytic conception that takes account of "*the theory of three qualities*". In this context, one can see that in order to be caught and bound in the networks of representations, the traumatic perception must take the hallucinatory path. Hallucinatory repetition in nightmares involving traumatic perception is more than the consequence of a quantitative excess as Freud claims. It may be said to be the means for attaining the quality of representation and its integration in the networks of binding. This, in turn, implies a complex work. Here, two points need to be borne in mind: "*the dream-work is under some kind of necessity to combine all the sources . . . into a single unity in the dream itself*" (Freud, 1900a, p. 179). This was an idea that Freud was to generalize and clarify 12 years later in *Totem and Taboo* (1912–13, p. 95):

> There is an intellectual function in us which demands unity, connection and intelligibility from any material, whether of perception or thought, that comes within its grasp; and if, as a result of special circumstances, it is unable to establish a true connection, it does not hesitate to fabricate a false one. [Freud, 1912–13, p. 95]

For several years now we have considered this "permanent quest of binding" (Marucco) as a general psychic law to which we accord the rank of Principle of Convergence–Coherence (Botella, 1997). It is if the conditions of the setting allow for the existence of this "*regredient*" characteristic operating according to the model of the dream-work that one has a possibility of gaining access to the "*negative of the trauma*" and of "finding-creating" (Winnicott) an elaboration and a hallucinatory form of representation. There is no need then for "regression to the state of dependency", as advocated by Winnicott, in which the analyst *is* the mother of former times and becomes the mother in perception (Winnicott, 1958). Though it is not incompatible with this conception, we defend the idea of a *régression régrédiente* [regredient regression], which accedes to the quality *regrediency*. This is the name we give to what we consider to be a fourth quality, which may be said to possess both the characteristics of hallucination and representation. The path for gaining access to it is "*formal regression*" (Freud, 1900a, p. 548). The quality *regrediency* would make it possible to treat the psychic heterogeneous simultaneity in a singular way, giving it access by transformation of the *form*. One can see this transformation at work in the retrogressive work of the dream and during momentary hallucinatory episodes during the session, of which Freud speaks in "Constructions in Analysis" (Freud, 1937d). During analytic treatment there can occur certain moments of "*state of session*" (Botella, 2004, p. 80), a psychic state half way between waking functioning and the state of sleep, facilitating *hallucinatory regrediency,* a terrain on which new creative bindings can occur, giving the *negative of the trauma* access to the networks of bound representations. In other words, there is creativity (Freud constantly repeats that dreams are creative). Let us finish, then, by returning to the title of my contribution: "Splitting and/or coherence?" Two solutions for the NTR? Depending on the structure of the patient and that of the analyst?

It is time to conclude. We would like to thank Norberto Marucco for his approach to crucial problems of psychoanalysis, for his courage in proposing solutions that oblige us to call into question theoretical prejudices that obstruct the freedom of thought of the psychoanalytic practitioner. To conclude, I would say that, starting from the same intuition and awareness of the same problem, Marucco and I propose two different understandings and methods for avoiding and resolving NTRs. Perhaps between now and the panel on the "Evolution of Trauma" organized for the Rio Congress in 2005 we will both have been able to reflect further on the problem and will have developed our hypotheses so that it will be possible to continue the dialogue begun a few years ago at Montevideo during the Inter-regional Meeting in 1999.

Notes

Translated by Andrew Weller.

1. [*Translator's note*] *Répresentance:* "the multiple ways in which the basic forms of messages are represented, reproduced and transformed trying to articulate more or less compatible expressions, which in turn help their transmission from one type to another according to the tensions, censorship, achievements, emergencies that are taking place in the psychic apparatus" (Green, 2000a, p. 21).

8

Dreams and the unconscious in clinical practice

Alejandro Tamez-Morales

Summarizing Latin America's contribution on the topic of dreams is an enormous task. It would be very difficult to review everything written in our region on dreams in the confines of this chapter, so, with this in mind, I apologize beforehand to authors not quoted in this work.

This is a also a difficult theme, as Freud's (1900a) magnum opus was the *Interpretation of Dreams*, and this topic was a scientific obsession for our Viennese master; in the wake of his brilliance it is difficult to contribute and develop new ideas in this area.

There is no doubt that in his writings Freud not only gave us a method to decipher dreams, but also—in Chapter VII—founded the metapsychology needed to create a new science—in other words, he used dreams as a source of scientific creativity (Santamaría, 1990).

Therefore the task seems to be reduced—though by no means simplified—to only aspects of dream interpretation in clinical practice—in other words, how Latin American psychoanalysts of today work with the unconscious through the interpretation of dreams in analytic sessions.

First of all, I consider clinical psychoanalysis as the intention of a subject (the analyst) to analyse the unconscious of another (the analysand) through a special clinical methodology (free association), where diverse material (transference, resistances, dreams, etc.) is produced in reference to a special spatial relationship and through which one undertakes the analysis.

I consider the unconscious as that which we do not wish to know; therefore the patient is demanding something difficult of us, which makes our profession an impossible one.

On Latin American psychoanalytic theorization

If we speak about the contribution of Latin America to the interpretation of dreams, we must think, first of all, of Ángel Garma, a pioneer in psychoanalysis in Argentina. Born in Spain and trained in psychoanalysis in Germany under psychoanalytic filiation to Theodor Reik, he arrived in Buenos Aires and became an important member of the founding movement of the Argentine Psychoanalytic Association: this seed sprouted into the fastest-growing tree in the history of psychoanalysis, compared to any other city. This can only be achieved by being a "relatively good father–psychoanalyst".

Garma made several valuable contributions to psychoanalysis. Specifically, his research on dreams is perhaps the major contribution on the topic after Freud. He questioned the origin of dreams in a systematic way, considering traumatic events as the main contribution. Garma wrote in 1956: "We believe that the existence of a traumatic situation is a very important factor in the origin of dreams, possibly the most important factor of all" (p. 202). He added that the satisfaction of desires is secondary to the traumatic elements, stating: "the more or less intense satisfaction of desires conceals disagreeable situations to which the subject is subdued and that form the real foundation of the dream" (p. 204).

During his career, Garma maintained his central thesis: "Psychoanalytically the dream would have to be defined as an archaic thought, caused by the regression that comes both with sleeping and the attraction of repressed contents, which when acting traumatically cause hallucinatory experiences to the sleeper" (1968a, p. 24), later having to reformulate Freud's thesis based on the above regarding contact with reality (1968a, 1970). In 1968, he stated: "In my conceptualization, the Self judges as real or external that which he cannot reject through his counter-charges, while he judges as solely internal in origin that which he dominates—that is, it's an inverse concept from that pointed out by Freud. . . ." (1968b, p. 607). He mentioned the role that desires have in the genesis and in remembering dreams: "They are modifications that tend towards that which is pleasurable in the form of the satisfaction of desires that are frequently maniacal. These contents of the satisfaction of desires of all types have a very secondary importance in the genesis of dreams but intervene intensely in the fact that dreams are made conscious" (p. 607).

Garma (1974) divides dreams into three components: "(1) the dream screen . . ., (2) the primordial oneiric hallucination . . . the individual reliving his birth . . ., (3) the manifest hallucinatory content . . ." (pp. 143–144). He establishes that dreaming is a type of archaic but very extensive thought process in which there are judgements, reflections, criticisms, and similar processes to wide-awake and psychotic thinking.

When he turned 70 years of age, Ángel Garma was given a tribute in the APA psychoanalysis magazine (Zac de Goldstein, 1974), which presented a synthesis of his work and an interview by Raquel Zac de Goldstein, in which she reflected upon the origins of dreams in Garma's theorization and its relationship with masochism, saying:

> If the person who dreams does what he wants with his dreams—as Freud describes, if he manufactures them as he wants, then—Garma asks himself—why are dreams so timid in their realization of desires? And furthermore, Why are there so many indifferent and even disagreeable dreams? [pp. 849–850]
>
> . . . Masochism is what then makes, according to Garma, the Self deliver itself defenceless before the repetition of traumatic situations, achieving only a maniacal disguise of them as pleasurable. [p. 856]

In 1993 Garma received another tribute, and two Argentine colleagues wrote an overview of his contribution to the study of dreams, very commendable readings. Suárez (1993) points out to the clarity of Garma's writings, despite their depth, and Treszezamsky (1993) synthesizes Garma's central thesis in the following way: ". . . dreams are masked nightmares" (p. 487).

León Grinberg directed a study group on the manifest content of dreams and published his results in the APA psychoanalysis journal (1967). Based on Bion's theorization on his container/contained theory and on the "thinking thoughts machine", he suggested that we need a "dreaming dreams machine" and classified dreams as: (a) evacuative (that need an internal or external object as continent and happen in primitive patients), (b) mixed, (that need the continents but there is guilt and reparation), and (c) elaborative (with clear depressive elements).

Belonging to this group, an interesting article was also written by Isidoro Berenstein (1974) on the manifest content of dreams, analysing the dream of Irma. This author reached the following conclusion:

> [The manifest content] experiences a series of transformations, where the correlation and opposition enable successive passages until achieving the adequate significant through morphological, syntactic, semantic and logistic modifications. Dreams are a logical instrument that enables successive mediations and transformations between the contradictions of the present world and the child's world, unleashed by the diurnal remains. [p. 941]

Willy Baranger (1969) does not agree with the Grinberg group (Grinberg, 1967) in classifying dreams as evacuative because of the term's anal connotation, and he does not accept the idea of a "dreaming machine" because then we would have to talk about a differentiated machine for every psychic function.

Baranger suggests, based on Garma, that dreams are not the result of an individual process but are bipersonal—that is, in the dream's function we can find its communicative character, in psychoanalysis, to be heard by the analyst.

How are dreams interpreted

Garma (1956) does not advise the analysand to write down his dreams, because he can disturb dreaming with the new preoccupation. Besides, this technique does not improve interpretation. When interpreting remembered fragments, forgotten fragments generally turn up in time. Garma suggests that the analyst should not worry if the patient does not remember dreams: this is considered as any neurotic symptom and usually yields once the analytic process is put in motion. However, even though Freud's and Garma's recommendations of are similar in not showing any special interest in the oneiric production of our patients, I have proved with my colleagues and through my practice that we tend to listen in a special way to a patient when he is narrating a dream. This produces a certain type of unavoidable indoctrination, but it can be managed analytically if it perverts the process.

Even though there are writers who emphasize that the dream must not be taken as special material, I agree with Berenstein (1974) who advises that the analyst should ". . . take it as a differentiated story because of its autonomy, recognized both by the patient and by the analyst" (p. 916).

Within the interpretation technique, it is important to take into consideration the concretizing and dramatization of the dream (Garma, 1993), as well as the exaggerated valuation of a small detail. Further, according to Garma:

> The dream is divided into its different components, and the subject communicates his thoughts regarding each one of them. This way one gradually receives a series of associations that, little by little, are related among them, until they let the desires that originated the dream be glimpsed.
>
> We have seen until now that in order to interpret dreams, the psychoanalyst relies on what the subject exposes as associations. Also, he tries to find connections between the dream and everything else that the subject exposes during the psychoanalytic sessions, because sometimes in a thought in passing, without any apparent relationship to the dream, we can find the key to its understanding.
>
> To encourage the subject to further study his dreams and overcome the initial resistance, which is always present, one can sometimes suggest to the patient to draw them, in addition to giving a written description, but always after having associated the dream during the psychoanalytic session.
>
> In general, drawing dreams is of little value for the interpretation. However, in some cases it facilitates their understanding. Furthermore, for a didactic exposition of the psychoanalytic method of oneiric interpretation, drawn dreams are very useful. [Garma, 1943, pp. 454–455]

This Garmian statement of using drawings with didactic purposes is interesting. As child psychoanalysts, we use the drawings of dreams to facilitate communication with the patient. Particularly, I ask children to draw their dreams after they have narrated them in a session with good results.

We could add that the analyst needs to have a great deal of knowledge of the symbols used by the analysand and commonly used in the patient's environment—that is, I believe that the analyst must know the folklore of the analysand's habitat. Garma promoted the study of art and folklore through his studies on ornamental art (Treszezamsky, 1993).

Garma (1974) believed that through dreams one can discover foetal psychic phenomena. In his experience, dreams with manifest brilliant contents symbolize the dazzling experienced by all individuals during birth. Dreams of colours were awarded an excremental type interpretation, preferably anal. The loss of a train or any other vehicle of transportation means the loss of the possibility of vital realizations, and those of flying are interpreted as concrete, instinctive renunciations—in other words, "staying in mid-air".

With this last example we can see the influence of language and culture in modifying the interpretation. For example, in other geographical areas dreams of flying are interpreted as a tendency towards masturbation.

Baranger (1969) stresses the bipersonal character of the dream, as it does not only represent the past of the analysand, but it communicates something to the analyst. He advises against the danger of understanding the dream as the expression of a marvellous internal world of the patient, of transforming it into a "strange body", of creating a privileged material and creating an obstacle for the analysis by producing a fascinating link with the analyst. It helps us to avoid this resistance to understand the bipersonal communication of dreams—in other words, to understand the dream as part of the transference, as a communication of the dreamer with the analyst.

Berenstein (1974) suggests that all dreams can have one of three readings: (a) discursive, referring to the manifest content, (b) symbolic, alluding to the whole of latent phrases, and (c) structural, centred on the combination of oneiric units. Berenstein deals with this last part in a very interesting way through the analysis of Irma's injection dream. He lists the oneiric units by central themes. This can also be done in just one dream or in all the dreams of the patient and contribute to the understanding of the patient.

Particularly, I deal with dreams in the psychoanalytic clinical practice in several ways:

a. I do not ask anything about the dream; I let it pass by and let the patient continue his associations during the session, and I consider the whole session as a free association on the dream. When reviewing the session, I try to evaluate whether there was something that can be interpreted of the dream based on the confirmatory material of the complete session. I take the dream as the beginning of each session. Generally, I try to list and record in my memory how the patient began each session, and I confirm that the rest of the session offers the associations I need to understand what is being played in the transference–countertransference. The dream is also another medium that helps us to understand how the analytic process is developing.
b. I ask the patient to separate the dream and request associations on each part, following the classical Freudian technique.
c. I ask the patient to freely associate the totality of the dream and say what comes to his mind. Personally, I try not to ask the patient for interpretations to dreams, I only ask for thoughts and feelings. I ask what the dream makes him/her think of, whether it helps to understand something of him/herself or of what we are analysing. This last aspect is important so as to not receive a cliché answer from the patient on some method of intellectual interpretation of the dream, instead of giving the free associations on the dream and using these as a guide to its understanding.

Requesting dreams during evaluation

When a patient decides on coming to analysis, transferential paradigms are put into motion on what the patient imagines he or she is going to experience in the analysis. I routinely ask the patient during the evaluation, once it is well under way, for his/her dreams. Via this routine I investigate: (a) childhood dreams, (b) repetitive dreams, (c) nightmare-type dreams, and (d) dreams previous to the evaluation and/or during the evaluation.

These last dreams guide us on the first transferential paradigms and the context surrounding the evaluation. It also helps me to evaluate analysability criteria, because through the narrative we can understand the patient's capacity for reflection or mentalization.

What does the future analysand do with the dream; does he/she understand that it is the product of a past with an intense affective relationship with his parental imagos? Or does he only believe it is a senseless product of his tired mind during sleep?

Childhood dreams

There are dreams remembered from childhood. These have an effect that I would call of tertiary elaboration, as happens with any childhood memory. The primary is the known formation of the dream, with its respective disguise. The secondary is the deformation of the dream when being described *a posteriori,* with its forgetfulness curve and for the translation of visual images into words. The tertiary is the effect on the dream of having been thought during childhood and the consequential distortion due to the developmental stage of the infant at the time—that is, we remember a distorted past by the effect that it kindled in the immature mind of a child.

Either way, as Freud (1900a) pointed out, childhood dreams are very revealing, because they generally show very transparent aspects of childhood desires, without so much distortion.

Repeated dreams

It is common for our analysands to narrate dreams they have experienced repeatedly. Sometimes they do not experience them any longer, but they remember them well; at other times they continue having these dreams up to the present and during the analysis. It is common that even though it may not be exactly the same, there are certain elements that are repeated in every dream. I have even seen some patients who were unaware of the repetitive aspect of their dreams.

Grinberg mentions that every patient has certain constancy of some dream elements (quoted by Berenstein, 1974).

The following is the dream of a patient in analysis who frequently dreamt about a house that she could not enter: now, in analysis, there was a small change in the dream, a product of the analytic process:

It's a house that has, on the second floor, a secret room that I want to enter and can't; it has familiar furniture, and up to here is what I always dreamt. Yesterday, I dreamt that *I found a window through which I can look, but not enter.*

Nightmare-type dreams

It would seem that in this type of dream the subject did not finish the disguise of his dream; or, even though there is a disguise, it does not cover all it pretends to hide, and the dreamer perceives the sheep's skin as threatening, knows or feels that it hides the wolf underneath.

These types of dreams are frequent in all analysis, when we are disclosing new material, and it is not unusual that the dreamer has nightmares. They happen as if to advise the analysand: "Do not continue with this, or you will suffer terrible consequences!" It frequently happens that patients accuse us of making them more ill, and the nightmares become true resistances for the analysis.

A young woman in her twenties, with severe sexual inhibitions and a clinically depressed character, had the following nightmare: "*Bees at the school where I work stung me, they were in a place where I before had spilled soda and when I tried to clean up they stung me and many welts appeared on me.*" She makes mistakes, is self-critical, and tries to make reparation, but she ends up suffering a persecutory and prohibitive bee attack (mother).

The first dream in the analysis

It is common to discover that the first dream is a paradigmatic one of what was evaluated. Usually it is transparent, and one would like to interpret it completely. This interpretation is not recommended as a rule, because most of the time it later generates a greater resistance situation, to the extent that the patient ceases to dream and analyse. We could call such an interpretation as out of timing—in other words, very premature, as it does not follow the systematic work recommended by Freud, from the surface to the depth, like "the onion's layers".

Dreams of resistance

Resistance makes its appearance when dreams are not produced or are forgotten to such an extent that they cannot be brought to analysis. Also, dreaming can in itself become a great resistance: there are patients who cover their sessions with dreams. I remember a patient who brought some 4 or 5 dreams to each session and used dreaming as a way of not discovering himself to me: dreaming did not permit him to talk about himself. On some occasions, even though the dreams are produced as one would expect, one can see obstacles to the analysis in the dream's manifest content: for example, one can frequently observe in dreams the theme of resistance to paying (Garma, 1956). The subject or the analyst appears as economically interested. Also, the theme of the duration of the psychoanalysis appears frequently in dreams.

We can understand the dream as we do transference, as they can represent both the resistance and that which is resisted (Tamez, 1993). A patient with a severe childhood sexual trauma, who fought obsessively to isolate his own emotions, dreamt the following:

> *They were choking me with my own tie, and as I further untied the tie's knot, I felt I choked more.* I woke up with tachycardia.

It was evident through the manifest content that the patient did not allow himself to untie the knot prohibiting the emotional contents (from the body) to come out through his mouth, besides perceiving as a threat the invasion of his affections on his intellect. I analysed with the patient the need to resist the emergence of emotions. The same patient later dreamt that "he was *locked up in a prison of ice*".

Paradigmatic dreams

It often happens that analysing a dream has results that become central to the patient's analysis (Isaías, 1987). In general, they are accompanied by many emotions—anxiety, sadness, anger, surprise, and so on—but there is also a concordant countertransferential co-narrative (Racker, 1954). We may also be surprised by the dream and not only by it, but by what we interpret. In fact, the best interpretations we make for our analysands are those that surprise us after we have made them.

The following dream is of a young phobic with a history, during adolescence, of voyeurism, which caused a great deal of guilt. His paternal complex and castration are evident in the dream:

> *It was a dark night, and I was dressed as a nun from the time of the Crusades, in white, with an enormous cross on my chest. I was chained to my father; he was leading me by wiping me. He was dressed as a Roman gladiator from the time of Christ. Aggressive and angry, he was taking me to a place similar to where Christ was crucified. In fact, there was thunder in the sky, and it seemed that Christ was rising from the dead, because he descended from the clouds; he had a white dress. Then my father demanded that I ask forgiveness for all my sins, and I only looked at Christ with fear.*

From this dream a great deal of information could be analysed—as if the one dream synthesized the patient's central conflict. The father would have liked the patient to become a priest, to "cleanse" the sins of the family. Now his travel phobia does not let him leave the father's chains. The castration is presented by seeing himself as a nun, besides being prohibited, as a priest–nun, from being in a couple and having family. The analyst is the father who forces him to face his phallic mother–Christ.

A short time later, the instigating material of the oedipal guilt emerged:

> *I was with a couple of friends. They could not have any children, they were infertile; I was doing them the favour of helping them (he laughs)—that is, I had sexual intercourse with her, I got her pregnant. Later I saw her delivering on a hospital bed, and the room was like the cabin of an airplane, she had her legs spread open, and the baby was born, and it was myself as a baby. I saw the scene with great surprise and much anguish.*

Beside the narcissistic formulation of procreating himself, it is clear that the woman who gave birth to him is his mother. He has sex with his mother and is born on an airplane—that is, travelling represents his oedipal desires and rebellion before the paternal castration mandate.

After this analysis, the patient made his first attempts to conquer his fear to travel.

Transferential dreams

We are frequently dreamt of as barbers, stylists, tailors, servants, drivers, and, of course, doctors and people who help others (Garma, 1956). There may be sexual contents with the analyst to show submission or affection in the transference; we can be the father or the asexual priest.

Special aspects of every analyst are also used: in my case, for example, as I am a tall—almost 2 metres—white person, I am dreamt of as a giant, a Martian with many eyes, a polar bear, and so on.

A 16-year-old boy with outstanding intelligence and persecution in his relationship with his father stated the possibility of having his first sexual experience, with fears about my—paternal—prohibition. He had the following dream:

> *A two-metre-high Martian with three pair of eyes is following me; I escape and find a bear that is very furious and follows me: he claws at my legs, and I fear for my life.*

When he finished narrating the dream, the boy questioned the meaning of the dream; I called out: "Bear! Bear!"—with what the young boy recognizes as the folkloric expression that refers to the female vulva. He understands his fear of castration and paternal fear in the Martian that represents me as vigilant.

A young man in his twenties, with a severe characteropathy that maintained me in contact with his father due to his suicidal risk, dreamt:

> *We had agreed on meeting at a restaurant, you, a colleague of yours, and I, to talk about me. I was in a car with a chauffeur; you invited the chauffeur and two more colleagues whom you found at the restaurant. I got mad because there were too many people, and I got up and said to you: "You can stay here with your meeting."*

In candidates for the institute, and in colleagues in general, aspects of rivalry appear in dreams.

Besides, we must understand whether the transferential aspect presented by the patient in the dream has any material that may guide us about the affective aspects that are being involved—in other words, whether the transference is positive or negative.

Dreams of the analysis

Dreams of the analysis are related to transferential dreams. However, I distinguish between them for exposition reasons. Transferential dreams are, of course, part of the analysis as a whole, but there are dreams that refer more to the patient, or to the treatment itself, or to various circumstances of the treatment, such as its termination; I comment on these further on.

Dreaming about the treatment itself (Garma, 1956) produces contents such as radiology exams, acts of cleaning up, shaving, having a haircut, travelling by car, being naked in public, and so on.

Two colleagues, one Mexican (López, 1982, 1986) and another Brazilian (Andrade, 1994), have tried to validate the psychoanalytic process through the analysis of the patient's dreams.

Countertransferential dreams

It is a healthy practice to reflect on our own dreams in which our analysands appear. I am convinced that the analysis of the countertransference is crucial to understanding our patients, and at the same time it helps us to understand something about ourselves, without pretending to say that this can be used as an analysis of one's own analyst.

What I am saying agrees with Etchegoyen (1993) who, during his inaugural speech as President of the IPA in Amsterdam, stressed that the future of psychoanalysis is found in the analysis of the countertransference.

When reviewing a countertransferential dream, we must clarify whether it was the result of transferential aspects of the patient that found an echo or identified some complementary transferential aspects of the analyst (Racker, 1954), a situation that tends to pervert the analytic process and obscure its understanding.

On the other hand, the patient's transference can have an unconscious concordance with the unconscious thinking machine of the analyst and enable such a dream to further understanding of the analysand, surprising the analyst's own unconscious but enabling the analytic process to be clarified.

My dear friend Antonio Santamaría (1983), who is the most committed Mexican psychoanalyst to the study of dreams in my country, has a number of publications in the official magazine for the Mexican Psychoanalytic Association, and he has studied the nature of countertransference dreams. He distinguishes between those that occur during the analysis and those that occur once the analysis has terminated, considering the latter to be a creative elaboration of mourning on the part of the analyst.

Dreams of the termination of analysis

A distinguished lady finished her analysis in the fifth year. At the same time, she crowned the disappearance of her inhibitions by finishing her graduate studies in literature, all this in a positive transference:

> Last night I dreamt *I was flying in a plane, and there was a man on a balcony throwing a kiss at me, and I said to myself: "He can't see that I'm old", and also, that I shouldn't see him either; then the plane started to fly badly, and we landed at the Fine Arts museum.*

The patient says goodbye; I send her a kiss on her new journey, her desires make her sensualize the scene and she explains the impossibility of continuing our analytic relationship. She is old; she must also resign her desire of continuing in order to achieve emotional and professional growth. Some time later she dreams: "*I was inspecting my dresses in the closet, looking for those that were old and oxidized to throw them out with the rubbish, but then I gave them to the servant.*"

Again she presents me as the servant; she leaves me with what is internally destroyed in me, leaving me her negative parts so she can leave in a positive valence.

I present another dream of an hysterical patient towards the end of her analysis, in her sixth year:

> *Mother, father, and I were travelling by car very happily, and after coming down a slope there was a destroyed car, with two men; they seemed to be policemen. One was hurt and the other dead. I resuscitated the dead man: he didn't have a head, but he began reacting to my manoeuvres; I thought, now I can put the head back on and revive him.*

The dream establishes an internal reconciliation with the parental figures; the analysis/car encounters the need to rebuild the damaged superego and masculine (policemen) aspects of herself and manages to rebuild a less persecutory superego (Strachey, 1934). This dream, in my opinion and in that of the supervisor, announced the termination of her analysis. It could also be defined as a mixed dream according to Grinberg's classification (1967).

Trauma reparation dreams

These are dreams in which an event that was overwhelming for the subject is repeated. It can be reproduced with the same outcome as the original event or have a different one. What is more important here is that dreaming has the function of helping to resolve the trauma. The patient seeks to stop being frightened, to "digest" the conflictive event.

Typically, after a car accident, the subject will talk about what has happened to any trusted person he or she encounters. The patient also dreams about what has happened—as if the mind needed to re-accommodate this traumatic element within a past that establishes some distance. For this reason, repeating it in discourse and dreams enables the subject to convert it into history, establish a distance, lose the fear, and mourn for what is lost.

Conclusions

I have tried to present a review of Latin America's relevant contributions to work with dreams in psychoanalysis. In this process, I have established the way I work with dreams in my own experience as a psychoanalyst.

I maintain that the use of the interpretation of dreams to understand the analysand is an up-to-date approach and continues be an instrument of choice for all psychoanalysts.

Dream interpretation serves us to analyse the patients' motivation in coming to us or to understand the origin of their problems during childhood, or to understand the transference, or the resistance to analysis; to observe the analytic process, to reflect upon our countertransference, to infer the patient's central conflict, to visualize the termination of the analysis, and as a vehicle to resolve traumatic conflict.

Note

This chapter has been translated by Cristina Elenes.

Commentary

H. Shmuel Erlich

Ideologies separate us. Dreams and anguish bring us together.

Eugene Ionesco

Dreams and the unconscious are probably the two entities that unite psychoanalysts more than anything else. Wherever they are geographically, and no matter which theoretical framework they prefer, it is a foregone conclusion that a psychoanalyst will accord a place of prominence to dreams brought in the course of an analytic session and to their interpretation. Through the interpretation of dreams we are bound to recapitulate the stages of discovery and evolution of psychoanalysis, following in the giant footsteps of its founder. Thus dreams, and the engagement with them through daily practice and application, reaffirm the viability and accessibility of the Unconscious by the psychoanalytic method.

It was therefore with pleasure that I read our Latin American colleague's account of the place of dreams in his region's psychoanalytic practice. My immediate response, as I read Dr Tamez-Morales's contribution, was a feeling of identification and great familiarity—as if I chanced upon a close relative I had known about but had not met for a long time. The feeling of family, of belonging to the same group that practices similarly and thinks along like lines, was unmistakable. This is no small matter. As we all know, the hundred years since the publication of *The Interpretation of Dreams* (Freud, 1900a) and the inception of psychoanalysis have seen growing divergence, controversy, and disagreement among psychoanalysts in all matters of theory and practice, leading to a variety of working models and what might be described as a "confusion of tongues".

The divergence within psychoanalysis has not skipped over the place of the dream, the theory of its conception, construction, and presentation, and the technical stance from which one works with it (Loden, 2003). Indeed, for a while it even appeared as if the central and secure position occupied by dreams in clinical psychoanalysis had given way to other methods of deciphering and constructing the unconscious (e.g., Erikson, 1954). Nonetheless, the abiding sense of immediacy and intuitive conviction that accompanies dreams speaks to psychoanalysts directly and convincingly.

I will follow Alejandro Tamez-Morales's exposition and comment on some specific points of theory and then of practice.

Theory

Tamez-Morales first concentrates on Latin American developments in the theoretical sphere, beginning, naturally, with Garma. Some of the developments he describes I find to be parallel and complementary to those with which I am more familiar, while others are less so. Garma's approach to dreams emphasizes the role of a traumatic factor in the inception of the dream. In the passage quoted, Garma (1956) shifts the emphasis from the instinctual drive origins of the dream (Freud's "wish-fulfilment") to the experienced state of ego/self. Trauma and injury to the Self accordingly provide the background for the origin of the dream, with a masochistic surrender to their re-enactment in the form of the dream. This stance appears to anticipate self-psychological views (Ornstein, 1987) about the importance of self-states as the source of dreams. It also places considerable emphasis on "actual", perceived, or experienced early injuries to the Self. This view conforms to the one that many psychoanalysts would hold nowadays, under one kind of object relations theory or another. At the same time, it runs the risk of avoiding and not accessing independent portions of the analysand's developing psychic capacities (Loden, 2003).

Remaining at the theoretical level, I find of particular interest Baranger's (1969) notion that dreams are not merely the result of an individual process but are *bipersonal* and communicative—that is, intended to be heard by the analyst. This notion, with which I concur, expresses again an object-relations point of view that seems to anticipate by thirty years the intersubjective idea (Ogden, 1996, 1999) that the dream does not simply or merely belong to the dreamer, but takes on its meaning within the creative mutuality of the analytic space and an analytic third. There is, nonetheless, a subtle difference between Baranger's interpersonal, dyadic, uni-directional notion of the dream as a *communication* from patient to analyst and Ogden's view of the dream as a *creation* taking place within a space and context where ownership, as well as ultimate meaning, cannot be clearly assigned to one or other of the dyad, even though the dream is obviously brought into analysis by the analysand:

> As an experience generated in the (intersubjective) analytic dream space, a dream dreamt in the course of an analysis could be conceived of as a 'joint construction' . . . arising from the interplay of the unconscious of the analyst and the unconscious of the analysand. [Ogden, 1996, p. 892]

Taken together, these theoretical underpinnings suggest a strong Latin American theoretical preference for an object-relations point of view as the starting point for understanding and working with dreams. Such a preference is in accord with one of the foremost contemporary psychoanalytic trends all over the world. While I am in essential agreement with this approach, I would nonetheless argue that we need to balance this emphasis with elements of the classical Freudian approach to dreams, so as not to run the risk of throwing out the baby with the bathwater or of losing the unique and independent psychoanalytic understanding of the individual psyche as a mental system (apparatus) that has evolved over epochs to its present state.

Practice

Tamez-Morales has done a real service by devoting the major part of his contribution to how dreams are interpreted and dealt with in

Latin American practice. By furnishing a detailed picture of the actual use of dreams in clinical practice, he can provide a better and more reliable understanding of the place and function of dreams in analysis than through a theoretical presentation, though these are, of course, not entirely independent of each other. Some of these practices I regard as well-established working principles, others are innovative, and still others come as a surprise, and I would want to question them. Let me illustrate each of these.

An example of what I consider well-established, generally accepted current practice is the recommendation to regard everything—all that comes up during the particular session, as well as in other sessions, the history of the analysand and the analysis, etc.—as relevant dream-associations. I follow the same approach in my practice. In my view, the dream springs from deep primal layers of the mind, enhanced and filtered through numerous layers of experience, development, and psychic organization (De Monchaux, 1978; Erikson, 1954; Fonagy, 2000). The analyst, by virtue of becoming a new object for the patient in the transference, stimulates and attracts these layers of psychic experience, from the primitive to the recent and mature. The psychic material is organized around the experienced subject–object relatedness, coloured by affects, drives, pleasure–unpleasure, and experiential dimensions operating in the mind (Erlich, 2003; Kernberg, 1982; Stern, 1985). These experiential "bits" of relatedness give rise to the associative matrix (transference–countertransference) in which the analyst and analysand co-exist and intermesh. The dream that emerges from this matrix includes and symbolically always represents both analyst and analysand.

One described practice that I find innovative and useful is the use of dreams in the process of evaluation of patients for analysis. The idea of "evaluation" for psychoanalysis in itself may be regarded as outmoded in some quarters but, in my view, definitely has merit. Analysis is not a panacea, and to think of it as such is to tempt omnipotence. Questions of assessment and suitability are therefore relevant to psychoanalytic practice. To ask for dreams in general, and for certain kinds of dreams in particular, as Tamez-Morales suggests, can be of help not only in assessing the psychic capacities, potentials, and propensities of a prospective analysand, but at the same time as a way of introducing him or her into psychoanalysis. Dreams can thus serve as the royal road towards undertaking the exploration of the unconscious.

I find questionable the described practice of asking for a written account or drawing of dreams. The drawing of a dream, it is suggested, may have didactic value, though it is not therapeutically beneficial. The use of drawing with children's dreams is probably of a different order. But where adults are concerned, this practice reifies the dream as a pictorial image by having it drawn or as a textual product by asking for a written account. In both cases, it appears to detract from the elusive and unconscious position of the dream through an overemphasis on one specific aspect of it, be it textual, linguistic, or visual. While the latter are exceedingly important, the power and impact of the dream remains in the impossible, subversive, and enigmatic integration of all these elements into an overriding emergent quality. Breaking it down into its constituent parts renders it far too concrete and schematic. At the same time, it may also concretize and compromise the psychoanalytic process itself. What is at issue here is: What is the nature of the ultimate object of our interest, study, and understanding? Is it the oneiric dream specimen, its dynamic narrative, or the unconscious?

This question is as fundamental as it is difficult to decide, and it brings me to what I missed most in Tamez-Morales's discussion. A theory of dreams and the use of dreams in clinical practice are both intrinsically related to the unconscious. As I said above, the unconscious is perhaps what unites analysts most, and yet . . . analysts probably differ in their understanding and definition of the unconscious more than is usually expected or allowed. It is therefore extremely valuable to provide such a definition, especially in a chapter devoted to its understanding and usage. What we are given by Tamez-Morales is rather scant, however: he considers the unconscious "as that which we do not wish to know". Although this definition is both succinct and elegant, it leaves room for numerous questions and possible misunderstandings. If the unconscious is restricted to that which "we do not wish to know", it is limited to what is repressed and dissociated, possibly even consciously expelled from consciousness. While it is immediately connected to resistance ("therefore the patient is demanding something difficult of us, which makes our profession an impossible one"), it leaves out entirely the "unthought *unknown*" and unknowable. It seems to ignore somatic, biologically determined, archaic and primitive, yet nonetheless formative psychic experience. To the extent that this contribution represents and exemplifies Latin American thinking, it seems to limit itself to the descriptive unconscious and ignore or underemphasize the dynamic unconscious. This impression may, of course, be entirely wrong and misplaced, but it derives from my concern with the current diminution of the role of body and drives in the formation of the unconscious in general and of dreams in particular, and the sometimes exclusive emphasis on object relations and the "narrativization" of experience. This is especially pertinent in the case of dreams—the prime example of developmentally early, preverbal mentalization.

I would like to present a brief vignette with a dream that hopefully explicates what I just said. It supports Tamez-Morales' observation about the possible use of dreams in the service of resistance. My example is taken from the analysis of a man at the prime of his life, highly gifted, intelligent, verbal, and creative. He dreams a great deal, and many of the sessions begin with a dream, sometimes two. In the beginning of his analysis he suffered from a severely debilitating psychosomatic symptom that defied medical diagnosis. This symptom disappeared entirely after a few months of analysis without any direct interpretative work. He had been afraid of entering analysis, mainly out of fear that it would damage his creative powers. As analysis progressed, the anxiety subsided, and after several years he thought that analysis had definitely deepened and expanded his intellectual, imaginative, and creative capacities. In the course of the analysis, many of his neurotic conflicts surfaced and were analysed, but it became clear that along with them there was an abiding feeling of a different kind and order: an almost indescribable feeling of not being fully alive and connected with his prolific productions, the people around him, and, above all, with himself. This feeling defied analysis for a long time, until the following dream was brought by him. It was a simple dream, in contrast to his typically elaborate dreams that bore many rich associative links. In the dream *he says, very critically: "Words, words, words—so many words."* The impact of this dream was tremendous: it connected him all at once, like a flash of lightning, with the futility of his energetic efforts to find the "right" words, to put everything into a verbal cast, which undoubtedly had contributed a great deal towards the development of his impressive verbal skills. Moreover, it spoke eloquently about the existence of a level of innermost experience that needed no direct verbal elucidation, was probably incapable of it, and yet was nonetheless alive. This dream proved a turning point in the analysis and dramatically reduced his habitual tension and driven existence.

I could provide other dreams brought by this analysand, which were incomparably more detailed, dramatic, populated, and rich with associations. This dream, in comparison, is skeletal, meagre, and subversive. It uses words to undo and undermine the significance of words and verbalization, and this paradoxical undoing makes it all the more powerful. In no small measure its impact was also delivered through the tone and music of the utterance—a mixture of derision, disappointment, and sobering acceptance of an inherent limitation. It devalued verbal production while accepting the necessity of communicating. With this, it goes a long way beyond what can be said and expounded in so many words.

One of Freud's major insights into the nature of the unconscious is that it consists of representations of "*das Ding an Sich*" ["The thing in itself"], the most immediate acquisition of sense impressions, and that in order to become conscious, a representation needs to be joined to its verbal counterpart (Freud, 1915e). It is this primary and sensual unconscious that represents our deepest and truest psychic experience. It is also this unconscious that gives rise to dreams, visual traces being most powerful among our impressions, though not the only ones. We must bear in mind that the secondary revision of dreams and their transposition into the verbal and narrative mode is at a level removed from dream activity itself. The dream story and the telling of the dream are significant aspects of the totality of the dream, yet they are not to be confused with its unconscious formation, which they hide and mask even as they attempt to communicate it.

To conclude this all too brief delving into the unconscious as the matrix that gives rise to dreaming and dreams, I wish to underscore an additional factor: namely, the role of mourning in the process. The unavoidable gap between dreaming and recounting can be a major source of frustration due to the sense that true psychic reality is impossible to convey and communicate. It must always rely upon an illusion of sameness and wholeness. Yet the knowledge of the illusory and playful new reality thus achieved is difficult to bear and accept without adequate mourning over its imperfection. Some of our patients find this mourning difficult and downright unacceptable, and our work with them and their dreams must involve such a mourning process.

9

Child and adolescent psychoanalysis in Latin America

Virginia Ungar

Child and adolescent psychoanalysis has had a considerable development in Latin America, compared to other places in the world, both in the theoretical–clinical profundity of its contributions and in the degree of expansion in its practice. This fact has always aroused the interest of scholars in social studies, as psychoanalysis is, indeed, a sophisticated theory and practice. In this sense, one of the striking factors is that at the time of the emergence of psychoanalytic practice with children, the place where we live was very distant from the key centres.

Although this chapter covers child and adolescent psychoanalysis in Latin America, it refers in greater detail to the situation in Argentina, as that is where I live and work. Regarding the other Latin American countries, where the study and practice of child analysis also has great significance in their society and culture, I shall contribute the details I have managed to gather thanks to the generous help of colleagues who provided them, knowing that due to lack of space or adequate information, highly prominent people as well as very important contributions are certain to be left out.

Argentina

If we approach the question of child and adolescent analysis regarding its all-pervading influence in our present culture, I believe that if a survey were to be carried out in any primary or secondary school in one of Argentina's major cities, more than half of the children and young people present in a hypothetical classroom would be able to define what a therapist does. Either they themselves or a little brother, cousin, or friend are sure to have been in contact with some sort of psychological consultation, assessment, or treatment.

There are many reasons for this. An in-depth study involving different disciplines, such as social psychology, anthropology, sociology, and history, in addition to psychoanalysis could perhaps account for the roots of this phenomenon.

It is my own point of view—which in no way attempts to embark upon such a study—that if we consider the historical and sociocultural context in which the practice and teaching of psychoanalysis in Argentina emerged towards the end of the 1930s, I believe a major reason lies in the composition of our population. At the time, Buenos Aires had six million inhabitants, the majority of them immigrants and their descendants. Most of these immigrants were of Spanish or Italian origin, and in these families the children sharing in family life at all times has been, and still is, a constant feature. The presence of children, not only during daytime but also at night at family gatherings and in public places, at shows and in restaurants has always been notable. In modern times, the central function of the family has been bringing up children, and so at these latitudes the child's place at the centre of the family structure has facilitated the unprecedented take-off of analytic treatment.

The immigrants—or the majority of them—who came from a Europe decimated by war saw their initial hopes of finding Paradise Lost in Argentina dashed. Using the theory of narcissism, it is then easy to understand how they naturally came to project their ideal onto their children. Parents would sacrifice any immediate personal fulfilment, devoting all their personal and economic efforts to educating their children well, and these children were, in their turn, predestined to carry forward the torch of progress.

If we put this feature together with the all-pervading influence of psychoanalysis in our culture, the favourable intersection that furthered the expansion of child analysis in Argentina—indeed, in all of Latin America—may perhaps become clear.

Although it could certainly be said that there is not "one" child and adolescent psychoanalysis but, rather, many different practices on the part of various circles linked—or not—to training institutions, this chapter focuses on the child and adolescent analysis that was channelled into the psychoanalytic movement within the canon of the International Psychoanalytic Association. It is not my intention to rule out or to denigrate the importance of the fruitful work, also based on a psychoanalytic background, that is carried out and published outside the institutions linked to the IPA. However, as it is not a sphere I know in depth or one within which I work, I would not be able to deal with them in a fair and equal way.

In any case, child analysis in Argentina goes back to the time of a group of pioneers who were also university professors, and it is to that history we shall now be heading.

At the end of the 1930s, a group of young doctors gathered around Enrique Pichon Rivière and Arnaldo Rascovsky to begin to study Freudian work in depth and to try to apply the knowledge acquired in their practice.

With the arrival of Ángel Garma and Céles Ernesto Cárcamo—trained in Berlin and Paris, respectively—the opportunities for prospective analysts to begin analytic treatment opened up. Halfway through 1942, Marie Langer arrived, having carried out her analytic training in Vienna.

Thus the stage was set for the creation of a psychoanalytic society. This was how the Argentine Psychoanalytic Association (APA) was founded in December 1942, its founding members being Ángel Garma, Céles Ernesto Cárcamo, Guillermo Ferrari Hardoy, Arnaldo Rascovsky, Enrique Pichon Rivière, and Marie Langer (Aberastury, Cesio, & Aberastury, 1967).

In the meantime, in war-torn Europe, the "Controversial Discussions" were taking place in London, continuing a debate started in 1927 on the occasion of the symposium on child analysis between Anna Freud and Melanie Klein. I do not think it is excessive to maintain that the seeds of the Controversies lie in the passionate discussion between the two "mothers" of child analysis, regarding the possibility of a young child developing a transference relationship with his/her analyst. This discussion was based on the differences between the two analysts regarding their conception of the early psychic development—the model of the mind.

During the years that followed, another group of analysts, Heinrich Racker and Arminda Aberastury among them, started their analytic training in Buenos Aires. Racker, in fact, was continuing his analytic training begun in Vienna, completing it in 1946. Arminda Aberastury was named Associate Member in 1948, with the presentation of "Psicoanálisis de un niño esquizofrénico" [Psychoanalysis of a schizophrenic boy] and "Fobia a los globos en una niña de once meses" [Phobia of balloons in an 11-month-old girl] (Aberastury, 1950), titles that already show the author's interest in child psychoanalysis.

In those years, Melanie Klein's ideas predominated in an almost hegemonic way in our circle. At any rate, each of the abovementioned psychoanalysts adopted some aspect of Kleinian theory and, from there onwards, developed it further according to their own interests, derived from clinical work with patients. I believe that this ability for each analyst to follow her/his own theoretical path without remaining linked to a dogmatic adhesion to British ideas has been a distinctive feature of the thought of this region.

To my mind, a vision of child analysis in Latin America could not but begin with a look at the genealogy. In order to examine this field, a study of its origins—the founding moment—is important. It is in this sense that the figure of Arminda Aberastury grows even more as a true pioneer of child analysis. I sincerely believe that, apart from the factors mentioned earlier related to the enormous importance and significance that child analysis has had and still has in the region, it is the enthusiasm, courage, the unrelenting search, the great capacity for observation, and great creativity of the first child analysts that have left a mark and opened up a path, which has then been followed by a great many analysts who have regarded them as their teachers.

Aberastury's figure embodies the traits of a true pioneer—one who leaves a mark. She began her explorations in a psychiatric circle by bringing the "Las Mercedes" mental institution within a psychoanalytic purview, and with this enquiry she founded a practice in which the child and her/his symptoms acquire human status. The first patient Arminda started treating with an analytic outlook, in 1937, was an 8-year-old girl, whom she saw daily in the waiting-room, as the girl used to accompany her mother while the latter came for psychiatric treatment with Pichon Rivière. The girl had been diagnosed as an oligophrenic, and at first Aberastury, on noticing in her a look that was as intelligent as it was anxious, decided to treat her with a pedagogical approach, until she came to read Anna Freud's 1927 book on child psychoanalysis. Subsequently it came to be known that the girl went on to have a normal development, becoming a teacher in her adult life (Susana Lustig de Ferrer, personal communication, 2004).

Arminda Aberastury, who was born in Buenos Aires in 1910 and died in the same city in 1971, had attended the teaching course in pedagogy at the School of Philosophy and Literature, as at that time the School of Psychology did not yet exist. As she herself comments (Aberastury, 1974), she had worked for years on baby wards until 1937, when she met the abovementioned girl.

In 1933 Aberastury had met Enrique Pichon Rivière, whom she married four years later. In 1942 she started her training analysis with Ángel Garma, and in the same year she became acquainted with Melanie Klein's work and, in that way, with the play technique that Klein had created.

Aberastury became a great proselytizer of Kleinian work, translating, with the help of Elizabeth Goode de Garma, Klein's *The Psycho-Analysis of Children* (Klein, 1932). During the same time she began to correspond with Melanie Klein; this grew into a frequent exchange of letters, which they kept up for more than a decade, until 1958. In 1952 Aberastury travelled to London, where she met Klein in person. From 1947 on, Elizabeth Goode de Garma—called "Betty" by those close to her—had been working with Aberastury, who considered her to be her closest collaborator at the time, both of them sharing clinical experiences and training tasks. Betty Garma travelled to London in 1948 and presented before Melanie Klein and a group of analysts the analytic case of a 21-month-old boy (Goode de Garma, 1992), which allowed her to corroborate Kleinian theories and opened up the possibility of treating such young children, as well as leading to a discussion of the technical problems that enriched the experience. In the same year, 1948, the first course on child psychoanalysis was offered at the APA; at first this course was compulsory for all analysts in training. In 1957 the first APA symposium on child psychoanalysis took place.

In chapter IV of her book *Teoría y técnica del psicoanálisis de niños* [Theory and technique of the analysis of children], Aberastury

(1974) mentions that in 1959 Elfriede S. Lustig de Ferrer, during the Paediatrics Congress in the city of Mar del Plata, organized a round-table discussion about child psychoanalysis in which psychoanalysts, paediatricians, and an odonto-paediatrician took part. The author stresses that during this stage Susana Lustig de Ferrer was her closest collaborator, just as Betty Garma had been earlier.

Arminda Aberastury taught for 25 years at the APA's Institute of Psychoanalysis, but her contributions extended far beyond this, including several conferences, publications, and lectures at universities, both in Argentina and abroad. There is no doubt that she made invaluable contributions to psychoanalysis, not least her 1962 book *Teoría y técnica del psicoanálisis de niños* [Theory and technique in child psychoanalysis] (1962), which is, in my opinion, unrivalled to this day, and in which she engages in clinical, technical, and theoretical considerations. The great importance she accords to the assessment period, to the interviews with parents, and to the playing interviews, in which she detects the phantasy of illness as well as the phantasy of recovery, which is of great value regarding the prognosis, is evident in the book. The playing interview is Arminda Aberastury's creation, and it has become a mandatory element in consultation with children in Argentina.

In the book *El juego de construír casas: Su interpretación y valor diagnóstico* [The game of building houses: Its interpretation and diagnostic value] (1961), Aberastury presents a game that allows the inference of the unconscious phantasy regarding the physical self-image. In *El niño y sus juegos* [The child and his play] (1968), beautifully illustrated with pictures, she shows the evolutionary sequence of the child's play, from the use of the rattle to the adult's play. Among her publications there are also two books devoted to adolescence: *Adolescencia* [Adolescence] (Aberastury, Lustig de Ferrer, et al., 1970) and *Adolescencia normal* [Normal adolescence] (Aberastury, Knobel, et al., 1970).

Now, to be fair to Aberastury, we must say that her influence has gone beyond the limits of psychoanalytic consulting-rooms, as she was able to apply psychoanalytic knowledge and experience to other fields, such as orientation to parents and her work with odonto-paediatricians, paediatricians and educators.

As far as individual development of Kleinian ideas on the part of the writers from Río de la Plata is concerned, one of its exponents is

Arminda Aberastury herself: she contributed to the theories about early psychic development, proposing the existence of a previous genital phase, which would belong to a time of life prior to the first year of age (Aberastury, 1964). She actually modified the outline of the development of infantile sexuality already posited by Freud by establishing a genital phase previous to the anal phase. Following Kleinian tradition, Aberastury found the empirical grounds for her theoretical work in her analytic work with child and adult patients, in supervisions, as well as in child observation and in her work with parents.

Aberastury studied the significance of the appearance of teeth as an instrument that carries out the cannibalistic fantasies that appear regularly in the second half of the first year of life, and she suggested that the emergence of teeth, which takes place at that time of life, modifies anxieties in a qualitative and quantitative way, because what had, until then, been a phantasy about the possible destruction of the object and of the ego becomes the daily verification of having an instrument capable of destroying. This proof of reality provided by the capability of the tooth takes depressive anxieties to a maximum and unchains mourning mechanisms and the subsequent search for another sort of union, this time with the father.

From Aberastury's work onwards, a large number of analysts have carried the pioneer's torch, continuing the analytic work with children and starting to include other psychoanalytic schools in addition to the Kleinian. In this sense, the work of D. W. Winnicott, whose papers were first published in APA's Journal in 1959, was taken up by a whole generation of analysts and was included both in written productions and contributions to national and international congresses and in the clinical work in the consulting-room. *Playing and Reality*, Winnicott's book published in 1971, became an essential reference text for anyone who was working as a child analyst.

Contributions from the field of communication theory and from other kinds of therapy, such as couple, bonding, and family therapies, also began to appear in the writings and presentations of various writers.

It was during the 1970s that the theoretical school of French psychoanalysis also first made itself heard in scientific discussions. The presence of S. Leclaire in 1974 and of André Green in 1977 (Rozenbaum de Schvartzman, 2004), opened up a path to other ways of considering both theoretical and clinical work, a situation that continued with the visits of Piera Aulagnier and Joyce McDougall in the 1980s.

Regarding child analysis, F. Dolto and M. Mannoni's ideas had an impact on the ways in which the child is considered in the context of its social and family structure.

Returning to the history of child and adolescent analysis in Argentina, in 1974 the Child and Adolescent Department was created at the APA, owing to the driving force of a group of child analysts led by Susana Lustig de Ferrer and including Elizabeth Goode de Garma, Eduardo Salas, Carlos Robles Gorriti, Isidoro Gurman, and others. This Department bears the name of "Arminda Aberastury", in a well-deserved tribute to the person who introduced and popularized child analysis. According to what E. Lustig de Ferrer (Rozenbaum de Schvartzman, 2004) tells us, the idea of forming the department emerged from the need to create training authorities in child and adolescent psychoanalysis; this led, in 1976, to the creation of the specialization course, which offers the opportunity of obtaining a specialist degree.

From 1979 on, annual symposia on child and adolescent psychoanalysis have been held in the APA.

In 1997, at the Barcelona International Congress of Psychoanalysis, the IPA's first Committee on Child and Adolescent Psychoanalysis (COCAP)[1] was created, with the aim of combining criteria and promoting the analysts' training in the speciality. It was first chaired by Anne Marie Sandler, the co-chair for Latin America being Susana Lustig De Ferrer; I served as the member for Argentina. Among the first analysts who were accredited by the IPA as child and adolescent analysts, there are today 120 members of the APA who have already received training on the specialization course, which has existed since 1976.

It is necessary to remember that the 1970s unfolded in an atmosphere of great tension in Argentina, and there is no doubt that this had an impact on the psychoanalytic circle. All Latin America was affected by political and economic instability, at a time when the world was being shaken by events such as the Paris Student Uprising of May 1968. These were times of action in Argentina (Arbiser, 2003) during which a great number of prestigious analysts left the APA; in 1971, after the International Psychoanalytic Congress in Vienna, they set up the Document and Platform Movements.

In 1976, with the *coup d'état,* began the most tragic period in Argentine history. Psychoanalysis, its practice and teaching, began to be harassed, while to the rhythm of growing inflation psychotherapy practices alternative to psychoanalysis appeared hand in hand with an economic policy that stimulated "consumerism" and with a social situation that generated an extremely high level of unease.

At the heart of the official psychoanalytic institution, the debates and differences regarding the conception of psychoanalysis and analytic training produced a significant split, which gave way to the creation of the Buenos Aires Psychoanalytic Association, recognized as the IPA's Provisional Society in 1977 at the Jerusalem Congress and as a Component Society in 1979 at the New York City Congress.

Among the group of founding members of the Buenos Aires Psychoanalytic Association, there were three experienced and well-known child analysts who had trained in the APA, supervising, studying, and working close to Arminda Aberastury. They were Elena Evelson, Delia Faigón, and Ana Kaplan. During a second period, the new association was joined by a larger group of analysts, among whom there were also experienced child and adolescent analysts, including Rebeca Grinberg, Asbed Aryan, Raúl Levin, José Valeros, Miguel Siniavsky, Alicia Sirota, Mary Kuitka, Elsa Labos, Silvio Zirlinger, and Samuel Zysman, to name just a few.

Shortly after the creation of the Buenos Aires Psychoanalytic Association, a group of members and candidates started to meet with the aim of exchanging clinical experiences and theoretical ideas with regard to child and adolescent analysis. Thus was organized a group that met regularly, where child themes and clinical cases alternated with those on adolescents on a weekly basis.

In 1985, the group became the Child and Adolescent Area, working in the same way and attended regularly by 20 people. The Area began to engage in other activities, which attracted the presence of resident psychologists and psychiatrists, and at the same time Area members started to be regularly invited to conduct teaching and supervision activities at various Mental Health Institutions.

In 1988, the then president, Reggy Serebriany, appointed three members of the Institution—Alicia Sirota, Raúl Levin, and Asbed Aryan—to form a commission for the study of a training project on child and adolescent psychoanalysis. This group worked with the advice of an education expert to opt for the creation of a department.

On 12 March 1991, under the presidency of Guillermo Ferschtut, the creation of a Child and Adolescent Department was approved at the Members' Assembly, the first directors being Alicia Sirota and Raúl Levin. Among the department's aims were "[to] co-ordinate, promote and centralize at the Buenos Aires Psychoanalytic Association the activities related to child and adolescent psychoanalysis in their different varieties: clinical, training, educational, scientific, bibliographical, historical, etc." (Levin, 2002). From the very moment of its creation a weekly day-time meeting schedule was established, during which courses, conferences, and the presentation of clinical materials were to be carried out. In addition to candidates and members of the Institution, colleagues from other institutions take part in these activities as well.

The department has also stimulated the organization of different activities, among which are those in the Buenos Aires Psychoanalytic Association that have already been mentioned, as well as courses and supervisions at hospitals and primary prevention activities in the community. Since June 1993, biannual symposia have been held, to which Argentine colleagues have contributed greatly and which have been attended by analysts from different parts of South America.

In 2000, COCAP approved a training programme on child and adolescent psychoanalysis that began in August 2004. Between 2000 and March 2003, 115 members of the Institution were recognized as child and adolescent analysts, according to the Grandfather Clause.

It is necessary to point out that the other Argentine Psychoanalytic Associations, such as those in Rosario, Córdoba, and Mendoza, as well as the Argentine Society of Psychoanalysis, all have child and adolescent analysts recognized by the IPA, and they regularly develop activities linked to these themes.

Having outlined the development of child and adolescent analysis in Argentina, which to a certain extent can be considered the birthplace of this movement, I shall now try to offer a profile regarding the evolution and current situation in other Latin American countries. To do so, I have relied on the contributions from colleagues who have given me the appropriate information.

Chile

The Chilean Psychoanalytic Association was founded in August 1949, recognized by the IPA, Allende Navarro being its first President.

During the 1950s at the University Psychiatric Clinic, the first group interested in child psychoanalysis was set up. It consisted of Ximena Artaza, Ruth Riesenberg, and Enrique Rosenblatt, and it was directed by Erika Guzmán. The first papers on the subject presented at the Association emerged from this group.

During the 1960s, a group of child and adolescent psychiatrists and psychologists from the Calvo Mackenna Hospital's Unit of Infantile Psychiatry—which was directed by Guillermo Altamirano, psychiatrist and, later, psychoanalyst—trained to be child and adolescent therapists with a psycho-dynamic orientation. The early members of this group were Isolda Armijo, Eliana Corona, and Mario Gomberoff. Some of them started to practise child and adolescent psychoanalysis. The group continued to grow and included supervisors such as Luciana Bonn de Matte, Mario Gomberoff, and Erika Guzmán.

Starting from these experiences, study groups on the theory and technique of child analysis were set up. They were periodically visited by foreign analysts, who provided their knowledge and experience in this field; among them, Ruth Riesenberg from England, Aurora Perez from Argentina, and Paulina Kernberg from the States stand out.

In 1995 Mario Gomberoff and the psychologist Liliana Pualuan created the first child and adolescent psychoanalyst training programme, which has been working steadily to the present day. Halfway through the year 2000 the IPA officially recognized the Child and Adolescent Department of the Chilean Psychoanalytic Association.

Peru

The history of the development of child and adolescent psychoanalysis in Peru goes back to the beginning of the 1970s, when the first pioneers arrived in the country.

Saúl Peña K. arrived in Lima, having trained at the British Society within the framework of the Independent School. Having been in analysis with Paula Heimann and qualified as a child and adolescent analyst, he was supervised by Donald Winnicott, Marion Milner, and Massoud Khan and attended the theoretical–clinical seminar Anna Freud used to give on Wednesdays at the Hampstead Clinic. Peña brought together a group of child and adolescent therapists, who entered into continuous supervision with him.

Rafael Ernesto López, who had trained in Canada, also arrived in Peru, where he carried out psychoanalytic training and worked in therapeutic communities with adolescents suffering from addiction problems.

Later, Max Hernández and Moisés Lemlij, who had also trained at the British Society, gave seminars on technique, theory of development, and psychopathology, all within the area of child and adolescent analysis.

This is the basic training received by the four analysts who were recognized as child and adolescent analysts on the basis of the Grandfather Clause, owing to COCAP's negotiations with the IPA—Elena Piazzon, Roberto Scerpella, Rosario Zuzunaga, and Sara M. Flores. The year 1996 saw the arrival of María Paz de la Puente, who had trained at the Argentine Psychoanalytic Association.

Venezuela

During the 1960s and 1970s, Hernán Quijada and Hugo Dominguez, who had trained at the Argentine Psychoanalytic Association, began to introduce the psychoanalytic treatment of children and adolescents in Venezuela, along with Miriam López and Guillermo Teruel, who had trained in London at the British Society, and Jesus Fuenmayor, who trained under the supervision of Manuel Kizer and Julio Aray—both of whom had trained at the Argentine Psychoanalytic Association—and Antonio García Fernández, who had trained in Chile. Periodically they were visited, for study groups, conferences, and supervisions, mainly by analysts coming from Argentina.

Hernán Quijada founded the Behaviour Council Clinic, where many psychiatrists worked; some of them—Fernando Acuña, Jesus Fuenmayor, and Serapio Marcano, for example—are today child and adolescent analysts.

By that time, some psychoanalysts who had worked with children and adolescents in Argentina and Mexico—Manuel Kizer, Julio Aray, Juan Antonio Olivares, and Antonio Briceño Monzant—had also arrived in Venezuela. Serapio Marcano founded an Interdisciplinary Centre for the Study of Adolescence and formed, along with other similar Pan American groups, the Pan American Forum for the Study of Adolescence. He also introduced, at the Central University of Venezuela [UCV], the first psychoanalytically oriented courses on child and adolescent psychology and psychopathology in the School of Psychology.

The National Institute of Infantile Psychiatry was founded in the 1960s. Many analysts worked there, Alicia Lusse, Dolores Torres, Ana Teresa Torres, and Norma Saade, among them. María Cristina Ashworth also worked at the Child Foundation during the 1980s.

At the Caracas Psychoanalytic Society the first director of the Child and Adolescent Department was Esther Aznar, and the present director is Elvira Larrovere.

In the Venezuelan Psychoanalytic Association there are 13 child and adolescent analysts recognized by the IPA according to the Grandfather Clause. A two-year course on child and adolescent psychotherapy and a semester course on child psychoanalysis are taught, the latter directed by Miriam López.

Colombia

The Colombian Psychoanalytic Society was approved by the IPA in 1961, having functioned for many years as the Colombian Group of Psychoanalytic Studies. Its founding members were José Francisco Socarrás, who trained in Paris, where he carried out the first studies on child psychoanalysis with Serge Lebovici, Arturo Lizarazo, who trained in Chile, and Hernán Quijada, a Venezuelan who settled in Colombia and who had also carried out psychoanalysis studies in France, working with hospitalized children. Lizarazo's first disciples were Tufik Meluk and Gustavo Ángel Villegas, who was one of the most important pioneers in the teaching of child psychoanalysis in Colombia and was the first president of the Colombian Psychoanalytic Society in 1961.

At a later date Carlos Plata arrived from Buenos Aires, having finished his training in the APA in 1952 and having had analysis with Arnaldo Rascovsky. Plata introduced Kleinian theory in Colombia, contributing new ideas and a fresh impetus to the psychoanalytic technique.

Among the members of the Society's second and third years were Guillermo Ballesteros, José Joaquín Gutiérrez, and Inga Villareal, who later became interested in child psychoanalysis and who were pioneering teachers and training analysts of the generations that followed. Guillermo Ballesteros had attended seminars at the British Institute of Psychoanalysis in 1966 and supervised with Bick and Joseph; at present he is a professor at the Institute of the Colombian Psychoanalytic Society. Inga Villarreal has been one of the most outstanding personalities in the field of child and adolescent analysis; in her capacity as the Society's training analyst she has contributed to the training and supervision of those candidates interested in child and adolescent analysis and she is considered a pioneer in the planning of the Institute's child and adolescent curriculum as well as the various programmes and seminars on this subject.

Eduardo Gómez Escallón has been a full member since 1978 and a training analyst since 1984; during his professional practice he has excelled in the development of a valuable contribution in the area of child and adolescent psychoanalysis. Within his teaching activities he has trained several generations of psychoanalysts interested in this field by means of theoretical and clinical seminars and personal as well as group supervisions.

The Child and Adolescent Department was created in April 2001. The Board of Directors appointed Martha Maldonado Archila as Coordinator and Clara Maya Gallego as Secretary.

The Colombian Psychoanalytic Society has 14 members recognized by the IPA according to the Grandfather Clause. At present, the first post-graduate course on child and adolescent psychoanalysis in Colombia is due to start in 2005. In addition, a non-formal seminar on child and adolescent psychoanalysis was started by the Colombian Freudian Psychoanalytic (Provisional) Society in 2002.

Brazil

Outlining the profile of development of child and adolescent psychoanalysis in Brazil leads us to focus on three areas: São Paulo, Porto Alegre, and Rio de Janeiro. From these we can examine the evolution of this subject into the rest of the societies and study groups, which at present add up to 14.

The Brazilian Psychoanalytic Society of São Paulo was founded in 1944, the Rio de Janeiro Psychoanalytic Society in 1953, the Brazilian Psychoanalytic Society of Rio de Janeiro in 1957 (Ferreira Abrao, 1999) and the Porto Alegre Psychoanalytical Society in 1961, all four being recognized by the IPA, and, in time, each of them becoming Component Societies. The main focus of the psychoanalytic production goes on to be generated within these four institutions.

The first analysts who introduced child and adolescent psychoanalysis largely trained abroad. At the beginning of the 1950s, Lygia Alcántara de Amaral from São Paulo and Maria Manhaes from Rio de Janeiro both had contact with analysts from the English School in London, working at the Tavistock Clinic as well as at the British Society.

At the same time, Decio Soares de Souza left Porto Alegre and lived in London from 1951 to 1954, being recognized there as a child and adult analyst by the British Psychoanalytical Society and thus becoming the first child analyst in Brazil to be recognized by the IPA. On his return he settled in Rio de Janeiro and joined a group that would later become the Brazilian Psychoanalytic Society of Rio de Janeiro. He was very influential, the vast majority of the child analysts who were working during the 1950s and the 1960s having trained with him.

Manoel Thomaz Moreira Lyra was also a pioneer figure in child analysis. Having trained in London, he went back to Brazil in 1958, there becoming a member of the same Society as Souza.

Another analyst who sought training in London was Virginia Leone Bicudo, but when she left the country, she was already a psychoanalyst trained at the São Paulo Society.

Husband and wife Zaira and Mario Martins also left the region of Rio Grande do Sul in 1944, heading for Buenos Aires in search of analytic training at the APA, where Zaira came into contact with Arminda Aberastury. They returned to Porto Alegre in 1948, where Zaira Martins became a pioneer in child analysis.

In 1964 Arminda Aberastury began to travel on a monthly basis to Rio de Janeiro, becoming a stimulus to the growing interest in the training on this subject. In 1972 a regular course on child analysis started in São Paulo—organized by Amélia Vasconcellos, and with the Argentine analysts Eduardo Kalina and Arminda Aberastury. After Arminda's death, her place was taken by Mauricio Knobel. They would also welcome the visit of other Argentine analysts such as Susana Lustig de Ferrer, Eduardo Salas, Isidoro Berenstein, Betty Garma, and Rebeca Grinberg. The child analysts who followed the pioneers came from this initial group, and they included Neyla Franca, Marisa Melega, and Sergio Trunst, among others.

Also in 1972, the Porto Alegre Psychoanalytical Society (Silveira Araujo, 1988) was regularly visited by Arminda Aberastury and Elizabeth Goode de Garma. At that time, Zaira Martins was supervising three candidates who would later become the child analysts who made child and adolescent training official: Marlene Silveira Araujo, Rute S. de Maltz, and Nara Caron, the latter two being the ones who introduced infant observation. In March 1997 the training course on child and adolescent psychoanalysis started, and it currently has several groups of graduates. In July 2000 the training programme was approved by the IPA through COCAP.

In 1976 until 1981, a course on child psychoanalysis was offered at the Brazilian Psychoanalytic Society of São Paulo, promoted from the Institute by Amelia Vasconcellos with the attendance of the Uruguayan psychoanalysts Vida and Luis Prego Silva. In 1978 the course was offered in more structured conditions and lasted for three years. In 1988 the Paulist Society made the specialization in child psychoanalysis official.

In 1997, with the creation of COCAP, Nilde Parada Franch, an experienced child and adolescent analyst and a professor at the Society, was appointed a member of the Latin American Sub-Committee of IPA's abovementioned Committee. In the same year the child and adolescent course was integrated into the Psychoanalytic Training Institute, and in 2000 the Programme was approved by the IPA. In 1975 the Institute's Officials from the Brazilian Psychoanalytic Society of Rio de Janeiro recognized a group of professionals with experience in the field as child psychoanalysts, and the training course on child analysis was also made official. Likewise, in October 2001, Marlene Silveira Araujo, of the Porto Alegre Psychoanalytical Society, was appointed a member of COCAP.

The outlook regarding child analysis in Brazil is highly promising. At present (2004), there are 14 associations, including provisional and component societies and study groups recognized by the IPA. Even those societies that have not yet made their training programmes official are developing many activities to do with child and adolescent analysis. They organize symposia, they invite analysts from their own country as well as from abroad, and they give courses and work in a permanent exchange with the community. An example of this is the Childhood and Adolescence Nucleus of the Brazilian Psychoanalytical Society of Porto Alegre, which, along with the Society's Board of Officials, has presented a project to the IPA's Programme, "Development of Psychoanalytical Practice and Training: Facing the Crisis in Psychoanalysis". The project, entitled "The Expansion of Child and Adolescent Psychoanalysis", is aimed at spreading child psychoanalysis in the society, in the school community, and in the community in general, and it maintains a website specializing in school themes. The project has been fully approved by the IPA.

Uruguay

Uruguay is a country with a strong tradition in the practice, theoretical depth, and research in the field of child and adolescent analysis. To start at the beginning, the Uruguayan Psychoanalytic Association was founded in 1955, and was then recognized as an IPA Component Society in 1961, at the Edinburgh International Congress. This was the culmination of a long process that had begun in 1954 with the presence of Madeleine and Willy Baranger, who devoted themselves fully to the training activity. This history has also got a pre-history, as most of the founding members had come from the Psychiatry Department of the Paediatric Hospital "Dr Pedro Visca", where the psychological aspects of ill children had been studied since 1948.

Among these founding members with experience in work with children were Luis Enrique Prego Silva, Vida Maberino de Prego Silva, Mercedes and Héctor Garbarino, Gloria Mieres, Celia Porro, Marta Nieto, and Isabel Plosa.

Child analysis has always had a preferential place in the training of all analysts belonging to the Uruguayan Institute. The first child supervisions were given by Madeleine Baranger and Arminda Aberastury, who was in close contact with the Association from 1956 to 1963.

Another antecedent is the work carried out by Héctor Garbarino and Mercedes Freire at the Fund of Family Benefits of the Work Ministry, in a clinic devoted to work with children. Working alongside the Garbarinos from 1954 to 1973 were Maren Viñar and Gloria Mieres, who wrote several papers—the product of their research carried out there. The so called "Mercedes Group", which emerged from the Uruguayan Psychoanalytic Association, founded in 1974, was an antecedent of the present "Children's Lab". In the initial group, in addition to those mentioned earlier, Myrta Casas de Pereda, R. Bernardi, J. C. Plá, Luisa de Urtubey, Silvia Sapriza, and Daniel Gil, among others, also took part.

At the "Children's Lab", which holds weekly meetings, a subject is chosen, and it is developed throughout the year. Papers published at both national and international congresses have emerged from this task.

In 1982 the "Adolescents' Lab" was created, and, similarly to the "Children's Lab", it has weekly meetings in which a chosen subject is developed throughout the year. This subject becomes the axis of an annual clinical meeting that is attended by analysts from other Latin American Psychoanalytic Societies, such as those in Argentina, Brazil, and Chile.

Both labs have been created with the purpose of exchanging experiences and ideas, promoting the interest in child and adolescent psychoanalysis, investigating subjects related to it, and organizing the members' attendance to national and international Congresses. It serves an important role at the Institute regarding training, as it allows members and candidates to interchange clinical experiences and theoretical ideas.

Since the year 2000, 31 members from the Uruguayan Psychoanalytic Association have been recognized by the IPA as child and adolescent psychoanalysts, according to the Grandfather Clause. Uruguay had, in Carmen Médici de Steiner, its first representative in COCAP; currently Maren U. de Viñar fills that role. A training programme was also approved, taking effect from March 2003.

Mexico

Psychoanalysis emerged in Mexico in the 1930s (López & León de López, 1992), by means of publications, departments, and seminars. A number of professionals interested in psychoanalytic training decided to go abroad in order to obtain it; they started returning in the mid- to late 1950s (Pérez de Plá, 1994). Alfredo Namnum and Ramón Parres arrived from the States, Rafael Barajas from France, José Luis González, Avelino Gonzáles, José Remus, and Estela Remus from Buenos Aires. Estela Remus brought ideas and experiences about analytic practice with children that she had acquired in contact with Arminda Aberastury. In 1957 the Mexican Psychoanalytic Association (Cesio, 2000) was recognized by the IPA.

Victor Manuel Aíza, who had trained in child psychiatry in the States, was one of the first to be interested in child practice and in the teaching of theories connected with child development at the Mexican Psychoanalytic Association. In the adolescence field, Héctor Prado Huante, Marco Antonio Dupont, and Armando Barriguete were prominent figures.

During the 1960s and 1970s a group of psychodynamically oriented child psychiatrists arrived back in Mexico, having trained in the United States. Rodolfo Ortega Borbón, Sergio Toscano, Eduardo Dallal y Castillo, and Marcelo Salles all carried out their psychoanalytic training at the Mexican Psychoanalytic Association. Likewise, at the beginning of the 1970s the Centre of Juvenile Integration started its work; at the end of the decade it was directed by Pablo Cuevas Corona, a psychiatrist and psychoanalyst who had graduated from the Mexican Psychoanalytic Association.

An important fact is that in 1972 the course on child psychiatry and adolescence was organized at the Autonomous University of Mexico, coordinated and organized by Manuel Isaías López. The teachers on the course had a clear psychoanalytic orientation (Salles, 2002), thus opening up the possibility of joining a group of child psychiatrists, trained abroad and in Mexico, in a structured course that was offered at an institution with great academic prestige.

Halfway through the 1970s, a group of exiled South American psychoanalysts arrived, among them child analysts such as Silvia Bleichmar and Diego García Reynoso. Esperanza Pérez de Plá, having trained in Uruguay, became a member of the Mexican Psychoanalytic association and later was part of the first generation of child analysts who took the First Course on Infantile Psychoanalysis at the Mexican Psychoanalytic Association, which opened in May 1981, under the auspices of the Institute and directed at the time by Antonio Santamaría. Victor Aíza was appointed coordinator of the Area of Child Psychoanalysis (Santamaría, 1984).

It was in 1993 that the project of the course on child psychoanalysis—presented by Manuel Isaías López—was picked up and was put into practice in February of the same year. In July 2002 the training programme on child and adolescent psychoanalysis was approved by the IPA, along with the recognition of 22 analysts as specialists in child and adolescent psychoanalysis by means of the Grandfather Clause.

Mexico has had a member on the Committee on Child and Adolescent Psychoanalysis (COCAP) since its beginning in 1997; the first representative was Eduardo Dallal y Castillo and the present one is Manuel Isaías López.

Conclusions

The historical outline we have sketched appears to me to be necessary: new generations of child and adolescent analysts need to know their origins, need to trace the genealogy in order to be able to grasp the enormous drive the pioneers have given to this field. Child psychoanalysis has had to wait several decades since the famous debate between Melanie Klein and Anna Freud, who, in spite of having conflicting theoretical and clinical opinions, always claimed a space for the field of analytic practice with children and adolescents. As we have seen, it was not until 1997 that the Committee on Child and Adolescent Psychoanalysis was created at the IPA. However, as we have been able to show in this brief outline, child and adolescent psychoanalysis has not ceased to grow and develop in Latin America, and I emphasize the fact that a decisive element in this has been the enthusiasm, conviction, creativity, and courage of these early pioneers.

In each country we have seen how they have differentiated child analysis from organicist psychiatry, started to use the analytic method with very young children, and introduced psychoanalytic ideas at universities, in hospital departments, as well as in the paediatric and educational communities. A distinctive feature—arising, more precisely, from Río de la Plata—is that the pioneers developed the theory individually, according to their interests, derived from the clinical work with their patients. In the beginning they took up Kleinian ideas and adapted it to their own work, moving away from whichever form of dogmatism. This is how Arminda Aberastury presented her theory of the *previous genital phase,* Arnaldo Rascovsky (1960) advanced his theories on *foetal mental states* and, later on, *filicide,* and José Bleger (1967) developed his ideas on the early psychic development, presenting the *glischrocaric position,* which would come before the Kleinian paranoid-schizoid position.

The times of a certain dogmatism would, of course, come later, owing perhaps to the need for consolidation. However, the theoretical perspective kept widening. The strong influence of Lacan's thought would soon appear in Buenos Aires, which also made an impact on the field of child analysis. It is necessary to stress that here the influence of French thought undoubtedly has been, and is, represented by Lacan's disciples, such as Françoise Dolto, Maud Mannoni and Piera Aulagnier, who have made their own paths. With them a different dimension of the origins of the psyche was introduced, one more distant from the Kleinian notion of a psychic apparatus that is in existence from the beginning and with a strong biological influence, to include the mark of the desire of the Other.

The effects that these ideas have undoubtedly had on child and adolescent analysts have to do with a further inclusion of parents in child analysis—not always their physical presence, but taking into account the great relevance of the framework of parental fantasies and desires in the approach to the symptoms that appear in childhood.

It is true as well that in Argentina couple and family psychoanalysis has had a theoretical expansion and a deepening of great relevance, especially the contributions made by Janine Puget and Isidoro Berenstein, whose ideas have also extended beyond Argentina's frontiers to spread to other Latin American psychoanalytic centres.

By taking into account this present theoretical map, we can approach the present prevailing conditions regarding child and adolescent practice.

The analyst who today treats young people in his consulting-room knows that we are witness to an accelerated transformation of institutions. In this sense, many of our consultations have to do with young people coming from new family configurations. It is also true that we live in a time of crises and changes: the value of money, the poor result of saving, or the notion of democracy—to take just a few of the points that could be considered as essential in the raising of children at the time child and adolescent analytic practice was emerging in Latin America—are no longer certainties.

Who could today support the notion of saving when there are families that have seen their scant reserves gathered through daily effort disappear as a result of local and world movements of economic policy, which have reduced their personal assets to zero? Not to mention the concept of democracy, of the value of voting at the time of choosing leaders in our long-suffering Latin America, which has seen from one minute to the next the fall of governments and the establishment of totalitarian regimes with human costs we can barely imagine.

The outside world is threatening to the child and to the youth, not only because it is new and unknown: it is literally threatening. They can suffer various degrees of violence, ranging from dying at the railway station where they wait for the train that will take them to school or to university to being mugged, kidnapped, or raped. And the world is also threatening for those young people with unemployed fathers, with drug-addicted sisters or brothers, living in a country with extremely high poverty or with corrupt systems that look unchangeable.

In any case, my personal opinion is that we, as psychoanalysts, should try to avoid taking a normative position that idealizes or condemns the models of the time. Rather, I believe, we should reflect on what is going on and try to understand so as to be always attentive to the emergence of *new* things.

It is also true that the practice of analysis is under the pressure of socio-economic conditions that affect Latin American people's attention to their health. Today, quick results are demanded, and in certain circumstances this forces the work in the consulting-room to adjust to the available conditions.

I am convinced that the psychoanalysis–psychotherapy controversy can be settled by maintaining that the most effective psychotherapy is that which is based on psychoanalysis, and that in order to work with psychotherapy it is necessary to have had psychoanalytic training (Ungar, 2001). This leads to the acquisition of the *analytic attitude*—a quality of the personality that will always be present in a trained therapist, whether leading a psychoanalytic treatment or a psychoanalytic psychotherapy or working in a consultation session.

Even when the conditions for the analytic work are difficult—or perhaps because of it—child and adolescent psychoanalysis has continued making progress and expanding in a constant and sustained way. In our region it has pervaded the ways of thinking and working in different areas, such as medicine, the judicial ambit, education, communication sciences—in fact, culture as a whole. It is still a field for questioning, challenges, and creativity. It is in the hands of young analysts to maintain the creative inspiration our teachers have left us.

Notes

1. COCAP: At present, Peter Blos is the Chair, and I have succeeded Susana Lustig de Ferrer in the position of Co-Chair for Latin America.

2. The Grandfather Clause has allowed the recognition of a large number of the IPA's members—who had received training in the speciality before the existence of programmes in each local psychoanalytic society—as child and adolescent analysts.

3. I am particularly grateful to María Cristina Ashworth, Ana Rosa Chait de Trachtenberg, Sara Flores, Ana Kaplan, Raúl Levin, Susana Lustig de Ferrer, Carmen Médici de Steiner, Martha Maldonado, Nilde Parada Franch, Liliana Pualuan de Gomberoff, Ana Rozenbaum de Schvartzman, Marlene Silveira Araujo, and Maren Viñar for all the help they offered in contributing with the required information.

Commentary

Florence Guignard

Due to her personal qualities and her professional commitment in psychoanalysis, both with adults and with children and adolescent patients, Virginia Ungar has become the Chair of Latin American Societies' members in COCAP (Committee on Child and Adolescent Psychoanalysis), created by the IPA during the Barcelona International Congress in 1997.

As the representative of the two French Societies of Psychoanalysis in COCAP, I am particularly happy to comment on her beautiful and fascinating chapter about the present situation of child and adolescent psychoanalysis in Latin America.

The author's altogether precise and vivid descriptions allow the reader to understand better the exceptional ground on which, at the end of the 1930s, adult and child analysis grew together in an constant and fruitful interaction.

These days, she writes, "more than half of the children and young people . . . would be able to define what a therapist does. Either they themselves or a little brother, cousin, or friend are sure to have been in contact with some sort of psychological consultation, assessment, or treatment."

We know that immigration brings about a traumatic break that places any individual in a very specific situation of ambivalence both towards her/his origins and towards her/his children. These latter are intensely cathected as being in charge of the immigrants' narcissism and ego ideal, since their parents had to abandon their land and culture to survive and have a new start in life.

Many Latin American researchers in the human sciences became interested in the exceptional conjuncture that allowed psychoanalysis to grow to such a great extent, so far from its European origins. Indeed, most of the Latin American universities developed a considerable amount of research in social psychology, as well as in anthropology and history. This, according to Virginia Ungar, is the result of the fantastic creativity of several generations of practitioners in different fields, since the 1930s.

Buenos Aires is given as an example *princeps* by the author. In the 1930s, most of the six millions of inhabitants of this city consisted of European immigrants, mainly Italians and Spanish, who traditionally have their children participating to every moment of family and social life.

With Nazism and Fascism rising in Europe, a new generation of European immigrants arrived in Latin America in the 1940s. Among them were several psychoanalysts, trained in Berlin (Ángel Garma), Paris (Céles Ernesto Cárcamo), and Vienna (Marie Langer, Heinrich Racker).

The first Psychoanalytic Society (APA) was founded in 1942 by these immigrants, and by several other local practitioners who had been trained by them. In this psychoanalytic generation, we find great names, such as Arnaldo Rascovsky, Enrique Pichon Rivière, and Arminda Aberastury. Aberastury has been a real pioneer in the field of child analysis, and we can regret that her main book, *Theory and Technique in Child Analysis,* has not yet been translated into French, as it is a true book of reference. Among the very many great figures of psychoanalysis of that time, I would take this opportunity to voice my regret also that the work of José Bleger, namely *Symbiosis and Ambiguity*, has inexplicably been out of print in French for many years, regardless of the fundamental elements dealt with about the setting, the kind of material that is contained in the frame of a psychoanalytic treatment, and the way to bring it into the analytic dialogue.

Virginia Ungar describes how, since 1954, Argentine psychoanalysts trained many Uruguayan practitioners as well. Child analysis was deeply rooted in training by Arminda Aberastury, and Madeleine and Willy Baranger—who were of French origin—played a role of paramount importance in this training.

When I came to Uruguay, I found there one of the most active Societies in Latin America, with a broad interest in foreign authors through an intense activity of translation and invitations to foreign colleagues. Together, the first two generations of Argentine and Uruguayan psychoanalysts, nurtured by the Controversies between Anna Freud and Melanie Klein, developed a tremendous freedom of thinking and creativity, always within the framework of psychoanalytic technique and method.

Through a close connection between practitioners in analysis and both paediatricians and educators, psychoanalysis reached several generations of patients and their families simultaneously. Baby observation completed the panel of possibilities, for the analysts, to broaden their field of research about their daily practice and the training of candidates.

As a result of such a state of mind, psychoanalytic training in two of the Argentine IPA Societies as well as in the Uruguayan Society of Psychoanalysis has developed training in child and adolescent psychoanalysis.

In 1976, the military putsch that brought dictators to lead Argentina, Uruguay, and other Latin American countries for so many years reduced considerably the number of psychoanalysts who remained there, and it became difficult to keep up the mentality of the brilliant pioneers. Soon afterward—1977–1979—a schism occurred in the APA, and a second Argentine Society of Psychoanalysis—APdeBA—was created.

Other influences came to boost a new start in both societies—namely, the translation of the work of D. W. Winnicott and the theory of communication of the Palo Alto School.

In the 1970s, a new link was also established with French analysis: the works of Serge Leclaire, André Green, Piera Aulagnier, Joyce McDougall, as well as Françoise Dolto and Maud Mannoni became significantly influential in the training of young analysts. Today, the French influence at the university is almost exclusively Lacanian.

In Brazil, the first Society was created in 1944, followed by Rio de Janeiro in 1953 and 1957, Porto Alegre in 1961, and others later on.

In the 1990s, due to kind invitations of Brazilian colleagues, I went twice to work in this beautiful and huge country, in São Paulo, in Porto Alegre, and in several places in the *Nordeste*. Everywhere, I could appreciate the interest in child and adolescent psychoanalysis. In São Paulo, I was impressed by the thoughtful structure of the training in the field, and in Porto Alegre, I heard much about the great efforts made in the past to visit patients at home when these were too poor and too far away to join a psychiatric unit. Unfortunately, economic recession put an end to this clever and generous initiative, but I think there is much to learn for each one of us from this particular connection with the population, typical of the spirit of Latin American pioneers. I also had the honour to see my first book, on Dr Elías Mallet da Rocha Barros' proposition, translated into Brazilian Portuguese by Imago (Rio) and the pleasure to see it sold in many places.[1]

Virginia Ungar also describes the important development of child and adolescent psychoanalysis in Chile (from 1960 onwards), Peru (from the 1970s onwards), and Venezuela (from 1970 onwards), and she mentions special developments of this discipline in two countries: in Colombia, where, since 1961, child analysis has been implanted by a student of Serge Lebovici, José Francisco Socarrás; and in Mexico, where such a practice started in the 1930s, was interrupted during World War II, and was re-started in the 1950s by psychoanalysts trained abroad, mainly in North America. But the spirit of Latin American pioneers came to help again in the 1970s, as after the military putsch in their country, Uruguayan refugees emigrated to Mexico, thus "*making the best of a bad job*", as W. R. Bion would say.

Conclusions

Today, hundreds of Latin American psychoanalysts have been accredited as child and adolescent analysts through Virginia Ungar's contribution. This means that, thanks to her patient and painstaking work with the different Societies, COCAP has studied how each of them has organized the training in child analysis, compared to the criteria used for the adult setting in each Society.

She confirms that the pioneers' mentality is still vivid and brings its vitality to the entire field of psychoanalysis. In many places, a special department for child analysis has been functioning for more than 25 years, with a qualification at every level, including trainees and training analysts in a general movement. One day per week is dedicated to lectures and clinical and theoretical seminars in the general training.

The links with the outside world are still maintained, as they were by the pioneers, and these are increasing in a way adapted to the current changes of society in general.

I would like to stress the fact that Latin American Societies have also woven strong links with both the Italian Societies, in which people like Antonino Ferro, Giuseppe Di Chiara, and many others are engaged in the same occupations.

I do hope that my own country, France, will soon catch up on the tremendous delay we suffer from in the organization of an official training in child and adolescent psychoanalysis within our IPA Societies. In creating, ten years ago, with Annie Anzieu of the Association Psychanalytique de France, a European Society for child and adolescent psychoanalysis, and in cooperating with the efforts of Björn Salomonsson within the European Psychoanalytic Federation, some of us are working hard against the old, relentlessly returning point of view that "any trained psychoanalyst is able to work with children and adolescents".

Note

1. *O infantil aô vivo* (Rio de Janeiro: Imago, 1997).

REFERENCES

Aberastury, A. (1950). Fobia a los globos en una niña de once meses. *Revista de Psicoanálisis, 7* (4).

Aberastury, A. (1958). Dentition, walking and speech in relation to the depressive position. *International Journal of Psychoanalysis, 39* (2/3): 167–171.

Aberastury, A. (1961). *El juego de construír casas. Su interpretación y valor diagnóstico.* Buenos Aires: Paidós.

Aberastury, A. (1962). *Teoría y técnica del psicoanálisis de niños.* Buenos Aires: Paidós, 1974.

Aberastury, A. (1964). La fase genital previa. *Revista de Psicoanálisis, 21* (3).

Aberastury, A. (1968). *El niño y sus juegos.* Buenos Aires: Paidós.

Aberastury, A., Cesio, F., & Aberastury, M. (1967). *Historia, enseñanza y ejercicio legal del psicoanálisis.* Buenos Aires: Bibliográfica Omega.

Aberastury, A., Knobel, M., Dornbusch, A., Goldestein, N., Rosenthal, G., & Salas, E. J. (1970). *Adolescencia normal.* Buenos Aires: Paidós.

Aberastury, A., Lustig de Ferrer, E. S., Zac de Goldstein, R., de Jarast, S. G., Kalina, E., Knobel, M., Rivelis de Paz, L., & Rolla, E. (1970). *Adolescencia.* Buenos Aires: Kargieman.

Ahumada, J. L. (1999). *Descubrimiento y refutaciones. La lógica de la indagación psicoanalítica.* Madrid: Biblioteca Nueva.

Aisemberg, E. (1998–99). Más allá de la representación: Los afectos. *Revista de Psicoanálisis (Número Especial Internacional), 6*: 197–214.

Albrecht Schwaber, E. (1995). Towards a definition of the term and concept of interaction. *International Journal of Psychoanalysis, 76.*

Albrecht Schwaber, E. (1997). Letter to the Editor. *International Journal of Psychoanalysis, 78* (1): 158.

Albrecht Schwaber, E. (1998). "Traveling affectively alone": A personal derailment in analytic listening. *Journal of the American Psychoanalytic Association, 46* (4): 1046–1065.

Allende Navarro, F. (1926). El valor de la psicoanálisis en policlínica. Contribución a la psicología clínica. In: E. Casaula, J. Coloma, & J. F. Jordán (Eds.), *Cuarenta años de psicoanálisis en Chile. Biografía de una sociedad científica.* Santiago de Chile: Ananké, 1991.

Álvarez de Toledo, L. (1954). El análisis del "asociar", del "interpretar" y de "las palabras". *Revista de Psicoanálisis, 2*: 267–313. [Also in: *Revista Latinoamericana de Psicoanálisis, FEPAL 1* (1994): 87–108; also published as: The analysis of "associating", "interpreting" and "words". *International Journal of Psychoanalysis, 77* (1996): 291–317.]

Amati-Mehler, J., Canestri, J., & Argentieri, S. (1990). *The Babel of the Unconscious.* Madison, CT: International Universities Press, 1993.

Andrade, A. M. (1994). Validaçâo do processo clínico analítico: o papel dos sonhos. *Revista Brasileira de Psicanálise, 28* (3).

Andrade de Azevedo, A. M., Stucchi Vannucchi, A. M., & Hadaza Sandler, E. (2004). "Yes, tenemos bananas!!?" Paper presented at IJPA Conference, Marcas identificatorias del psicoanálisis en América Latina, Rio de Janeiro, June.

Anscombre, J. C., & Ducrot, O. (1988). *La argumentación en la lengua.* Madrid: Gredos, 1994.

Anzieu, D. (1981). La función semiótica para Piaget y para el psicoanalista. In: *Psicoanálisis y lenguaje, del cuerpo a la palabra.* Buenos Aires: Kapelusz, 1981.

Apel, K. O. (1994). *Le logos propre au langage humain.* Combas: Ed. de l'Eclat.

Arbiser, S. (2003). Psicoanálisis en Argentina. *Revista Uruguaya de Psicoanálisis, 97.*

Arbiser, S. (2004). *Psicoanálisis en Argentina* (in press).

Aron, L. (1996). *A Meeting of Minds: Mutuality in Psychoanalysis.* Hillsdale, NJ: Analytic Press.

Arrué, O. (1991). Orígenes e identidad del movimiento psicoanalítico chileno. In: E. Casaula, J. Coloma, & J. F. Jordán (Eds.), *Cuarenta años de psicoanálisis en Chile. Biografía de una sociedad científica.* Santiago de Chile: Ananké, 1991.

Assoun, P.-L. (1995). *El fetichismo.* Buenos Aires: Ediciones Nueva Visión.

Austin, J. (1957). *How To Do Things with Words.* Oxford: Clarendon Press, 1962.

Authier-Revuz, J. (1974). Hétérogéneités énonciatives. *Langages, 78*: 98–111.

Authier-Revuz, J. (1984). Hétérogénéité montrée et hétérogénéité constitutive: Eléments pour une approche de l'autre dans le discours. *DRLAV (Paris), 26.*

Bach, E. (1989). *Informal Lectures on Formal Semantics.* New York: State University of New York.

Bakhtin, M. (1984). *Problems of Dostoevsky's Poetics.* Minneapolis, MN: University of Minnesota, 1993.

Balán, J. (1991). *Cuéntame tu vida.* Buenos Aires: Planeta.

Baranger, M. (1992). La mente del analista, de la escucha a la interpretación. *Revista de Psicoanálisis, 49* (2): 225. [Also published as: The mind of the analyst: From listening to interpretation. (Pre-published Papers, 38th IPA Congress, Amsterdam.) *International Journal of Psychoanalysis, 74* (1993): 15–24.]

Baranger, M. (1993). The mind of the analyst: From listening to interpretation. *International Journal of Psychoanalysis, 74*: 15–24.

Baranger, M., & Baranger, W. (1961–62). La situación analítica como campo dinámico. *Revista Uruguaya de Psicoanálisis, 4* (1): 3–54. [Also in: W. Baranger & M. Baranger, *Problemas del campo psicoanalítico.* Buenos Aires: Kargieman, 1993.]

Baranger, M., Baranger, W., & Mom, J. (1982). Proceso y no proceso en el trabajo analítico. *Revista de Psicoanálisis, 39*: 527–549. [Also published as: Process and non-process in analytic work. *International Journal of Psychoanalysis, 64* (1983): 1–15.]

Baranger, M., Baranger, W., & Mom, J. (1983). Process and non-process in analytic work. *International Journal of Psychoanalysis, 64*: 1–15.

Baranger, M., Baranger, W., & Mom, J. (1987). El trauma psíquico infantil, de nosotros a Freud; trauma puro, retroactividad y reconstrucción. *Revista de Psicoanálisis, 44* (4): 771. [Also published as: The infantile psychic trauma from us to Freud: Pure trauma retroactivity and reconstruction. *International Journal of Psychoanalysis, 69* (1988): 113–129.]

Baranger, W. (1969). El sueño como medio de comunicación. In: W. Baranger & M. Baranger, *Problemas del campo psicoanalítico.* Buenos Aires: Kargieman.

Baranger, W. (1979). "Proceso en espiral" y "campo dinámico". *Revista Uruguaya de Psicoanálisis, 59*: 17–32.

Baranger, W. (1992). "The Affects in the Countertransference". Panel, Los afectos en la contratransferencia, at 14th Congreso Psicoanalítico de America Latina, Buenos Aires.

Baranger, W., & Baranger, M. (1961–62). La situación analítica como campo dinámico. *Revista Uruguaya de Psicoanálisis, 4* (1).

Baranger, W., & Baranger, M. (1969a). La situación analítica como campo dinámico. In: *Problemas del campo psicoanalítico.* Buenos Aires: Kargieman.

Baranger, W., & Baranger, M. (1969b). *Problemas del campo psicoanalítico.* Buenos Aires: Kargieman.

Baranger, W., Baranger, M., & Mom, J. (1978). Patología de la transferencia y contratransferencia en el psicoanálisis actual. El campo perverso. *Revista de Psicoanálisis, 35* (5).

Baranger, W., Goldstein, N., & Goldstein, R. (1989). Acerca de la desidentificación. *Revista de Psicoanálisis, 46* (6): 895.

Barros, E. M. (2000). Affect and pictographic image. *International Journal of Psychoanalysis, 81*: 1087–1099.

Bayle, G. (1996). Les clivages. (Paper presented to the Congrès de Psychanalyse de Langue Française.) *Revue Française de Psychanalyse (Special Congress Issue), 60.*

Benjamin, J. (1988). *The Bonds of Love: Psychoanalysis, Feminism and the Problem of Domination.* New York: Pantheon Books.

Benveniste, E. (1966). *Problemas de lingüística general.* Mexico: Siglo XXI, 1988.

Berenstein, I. (1974). Sobre el contenido manifiesto de los sueños. *Revista de Psicoanálisis, 31* (4): 915–952.

Berenstein, I. (1975a). La estructura semiótica del sujeto y del objeto en psicoanálisis. In: *El lenguaje, Vol. 3.* Buenos Aires: Imago.

Berenstein, I. (1975b). *El complejo de Edipo. Estructura y significación.* Buenos Aires: Paidós.

Berenstein, I., & Puget, J. (1997). *Lo vincular. Clínica y técnica psicoanalítica.* Buenos Aires: Paidós.

Bernardi, B. de L. (1993). El sustrato compartido de la interpretación: imágenes, afectos y palabras en la experiencia analítica. *Revista de Psicoanálisis, 50* (4/5).

Bernardi, B. de L. (2000). The countertransference: A Latin American view. *International Journal of Psychoanalysis, 81* (1).

Bernardi, R. (2002). The need of true controversies in psychoanalysis: The debates about M. Klein and J. Lacan in the Río de la Plata. *International Journal of Psychoanalysis, 83*: 851–873.

Bernardi, R. (2004). El porvenir de un diálogo. *Revista de Psicoanálisis, 61* (1): 113–128.

Bernardi, R., & de León, B. (1993). Does our self analysis take into consideration our assumptions? In: J. Barron (Ed.), *Self-Analysis, Critical Inquiries, Personal Visions* (pp. 29–46). London: Analytic Press.

Besserman Vianna, H. (1994). *Não conte a ninguém.* Rio de Janeiro: Imago Ed. [Also published as: *N'en parlez à personne.* Paris: L'Harmattan, 1997; and as: *No se lo cuente a nadie. Política del psicoanálisis frente a la dictadura y la tortura.* Buenos Aires: Polemos, 1998.]

Bezoari, M., & Ferro, A. (1990). Elementos de un modelo del campo psicoanalítico. Los agregados funcionales. *Revista de Psicoanálisis, 47* (5/6): 852.

Bezoari, M., & Ferro, A. (1991). From a play between "parts" to transformations in the couple: Psychoanalysis in a bipersonal field. In: L. Nissim Momigliano & A. Robutti (Eds.), *Shared Experience: The Psychoanalytic Dialogue.* London: Karnac, 1992.

Bianchedi, E. (2004). "Evolucion en Y de Bion." Paper presented at Conference, Bion 2004, São Paulo, Brazil, 15 July, sponsored by the Sociedad e Brasileira de Psicanályse de São Paulo.

Bion, W. R. (1952). Group dynamics: A review. *International Journal of Psychoanalysis. 33*: 235–247. [Also in: *New Directions in Psycho-Analysis*. London: Tavistock, 1955; and in: *Experiences in Groups*. London: Tavistock, 1961.]

Bion, W. R. (1956). Development of schizophrenic thought. *International Journal of Psychoanalysis, 37*. [Also in: *Second Thoughts*. London: Heinemann Medical, 1967.]

Bion, W. R. (1957). On arrogance. *International Journal of Psychoanalysis, 39* (1958). [Also in: *Second Thoughts*. London: Heinemann Medical, 1967; reprinted London: Karnac, 1987, 1990, 1993.]

Bion, W. R. (1959). Attacks on linking. *International Journal of Psychoanalysis,40*. [Also in: *Second Thoughts*. London: Heinemann Medical, 1967; reprinted London: Karnac, 1987, 1990, 1993.]

Bion, W. R. (1961). *Experiences in Groups*. London: Tavistock.

Bion, W. R. (1962a). *Learning from Experience*. London: Heinemann Medical [reprinted London: Karnac, 1984].

Bion, W. R. (1962b). A theory of thinking. *International Journal of Psychoanalysis, 53*. [Also in: *Second Thoughts*. London: Heinemann Medical, 1967; reprinted London: Karnac, 1987, 1990, 1993.]

Bion, W. R. (1963). *Elements of Psychoanalysis*. London: Heinemann Medical [reprinted London: Karnac, 1984].

Bion, W. R. (1965). *Transformations*. London: Heinemann Medical [reprinted London: Karnac, 1984].

Bion, W. R. (1967). Notes on the theory of schizophrenia. In: *Second Thoughts*. London: Heinemann Medical, 1967 [reprinted London: Karnac, 1987, 1990, 1993].

Bion, W. R. (1970). *Attention and Interpretation*. London: Heinemann Medical [reprinted London: Karnac, 1984].

Bion, W. R. (1973). *Conferências Brasileiras I*. Rio de Janeiro: Imago Ed. [Also in: *Brazilian Lectures*. London: Karnac, 1990.]

Bion, W. R. (1977). *Two Papers: The Grid and Caesura*. London: Karnac, 1989.

Bion, W. R. (1978). *Four Discussions with W. R. Bion*. Strath Tay: Clunie Press.

Bion, W. R. (1991). *A Memoir of the Future*. London: Karnac.

Bion, W. R. (1992). *Cogitations*. London: Karnac.

Bishop, D. (1997). *Uncommon Understanding: Development and Disorders of Language Comprehension in Children*. Hove: Psychology Press.

Bleger, J. (1967). *Simbiosis y ambigüedad. Estudio psicoanalítico*. Buenos Aires: Paidós.

Bleichmar, H. (1983). *El narcisismo. Estudio sobre la enunciación y la gramática inconsciente*. Buenos Aires: Nueva Visión.

Bleichmar, H. (1997). *Avances en psicoterapia psicoanalítica*. Barcelona: Paidós.

Bleichmar, H. (2001). El cambio terapéutico a la luz de los conocimientos actuales sobre la memoria y los múltiples procesamientos inconscientes. *Revista de Psicoanálisis (Aperturas psicoanalíticas), 9.*

Bollas, C. (1976). Le langage secret de la mère et de l'enfant. *Du Secret. Nouvelle Revue de Psychanalyse, 14:* 246.

Bollas, C. (1979). The transformational object. *International Journal of Psychoanalysis, 60* (1).

Botella, C., & Botella, S. (1983). Notes cliniques sur la figurabilité et l'interprétation. *Revue Française de Psychanalyse, 3.*

Botella, C., & Botella, S. (1990). La problématique de la régression formelle de la pensée et l'hallucinatoire. *Monographies de la Revue Française de Psychanalyse.* Colloque de l'UNESCO, *Psychanalyse: Questions pour demain,* 1989.

Botella, C., & Botella, S. (1997). *Más allá de la representación.* Valencia: Promolibro.

Botella, C., & Botella, S. (2004). *The Work of Psychic Figurability,* trans. A. Weller. London: Brunner-Routledge. [Originally published as *La figurabilité psychique.* Paris-Genève: Delachaux et Niestlé, 2001; also published as: *La figurabilidad psíquica.* Buenos Aires: Amorrortu Ed., 2003.]

Cabanne, J., & Suàrez, E. E. (2000). Transtorno bipolar: Interacción psiquiátrico-psicoanalítica. In: *Los duelos y sus destinos. Depresiones hoy (Actas del Primer Congreso Uruguayo de Psicoanálisis), Vol. 2* (pp. 112–123). Montevideo: Impresora Gráfica.

Canestri, J. (1994). Transformations. *International Journal of Psychoanalysis, 75* (5/6): 1080.

Canestri, J. (1999). Alcune note e un esempio su attività linguistica e psicoanalisi. *Psicoanalisi, 3* (1): 68–82.

Canestri, J. (2000). Notes on linguistic activity and psychoanalysis. In: *Changing Ideas in a Changing World: The Revolution in Psychoanalysis.* London & New York: Karnac.

Canestri, J. (2002a). On the contribution of the most recent research on language applied to psychoanalytic practice, with regard to regional differences. In: *International Symposium: Psychoanalysis as an Empirical, Interdisciplinary Science.* Vienna: Austrian Academy of Sciences (in press in German and English).

Canestri, J. (2002b). Trois, le nombre magique: Green avec Peirce. In: *Penser les limites. Ëcrits en l'honneur d'André Green.* Paris: Delachaux et Niestlé.

Cárcamo, C. E. (1992). *Escritos.* Buenos Aires: Kargieman.

Carruthers, P. (2002). *The Cognitive Functions of Language in Behavioral and Brain Sciences.* Cambridge: Cambridge University Press.

Carruthers, P. (2003). On Fodor's Problem. *Mind and Language, 18* (5): 502–523.

Carruthers, P., & Boucher, J. (Eds.) (1998). *Language and Thought: Interdisciplinary Themes.* Cambridge: Cambridge University Press.

Casas de Pereda, M. (1999). *En el camino de la simbolización. Producción del sujeto Psíquico.* Buenos Aires: Paidós.

Casaula, E., Coloma, J., & Jordán, J. F. (Eds.) (1991). *Cuarenta años de psicoanálisis en Chile. Biografía de una sociedad científica.* Santiago de Chile: Ananké.

Cassorla, R. M. (2004). "Del baluarte al 'enactment': el 'no-sueño' en el teatro del análisis." [From the bastion to enactment: The "non-dream" in the theatre of analysis]. Paper presented at IJPA Conference, Marcas identificatorias del psicoanálisis en América Latina, Rio de Janeiro, June.

Cesio, F. R. (1956). Un caso de "reacción terapéutica negativa". *Revista de Psicoanálisis, 13*: 522–526.

Cesio, F. R. (2000). *La gesta psicoanalítica en América Latina.* Buenos Aires: La Peste.

Chomsky, N. (1957). *Syntactic Structures.* The Hague: Mouton, 1965.

Chomsky, N. (1965). *Aspects of the Theory of Syntax.* Cambridge, MA: MIT Press.

Chomsky, N. (1984). *Modular Approaches to the Study of the Mind.* San Diego, CA: San Diego State University Press.

Colson, D. (1995). An analyst's multiple losses: Countertransference and other reactions. *Contemporary Psychoanalysis, 31*: 459.

Coltart, N. (1992). *Slouching towards Bethlehem . . . And Other Psychoanalytic Explorations.* London: Free Association Books.

Cooper, A. M. (1986). Some limitations on therapeutic effectiveness: The "burnout syndrome" in psychoanalysis. *Psychoanalytic Quarterly, 55* (4): 576–598.

Corrao, F. (1986). Il concetto di campo come modello teorico. *Gruppo e Funzione Analitica, 7*: 9–21.

Culioli, A. (1990). *Pour une linguistique de l'énontiation. Operations et représentations, Vol. 1.* Paris: Ophrys.

Culioli, A. (2002). *Variations sur la linguistique.* Paris: Klincksieck.

D'Alvia, R. (2003). "Realidades-traumas-cuerpos en nuestra cultura." Paper presented at IJPA Conference, Marcas identificatorias del psicoanálisis en América Latina, Rio de Janeiro, June 2004.

Danon-Boileau, L. (1987). *Le sujet de l'énonciation. Psychanalyse et linguistique.* Paris: Ophrys.

Davidson, D. (1984). *Inquiries into Truth and Interpretation.* Oxford: Oxford University Press.

de León, B. (1993). El sustrato compartido de la interpretación. Imágenes, afectos y palabras en la experiencia analítica. (Presented at the 38th IPA Congress, Amsterdam.) *Revista de Psicoanálisis, 50* (4/5): 809–826.

de León, B. (2000). The countertransference: A Latin American view. *International Journal of Psychoanalysis, 81*: 331–351.

de León, B. (2004). "Affects and Words in Interpretative Modes of Transference." Paper presented at the 43rd IPA Congress, New Orleans.

de León, B., & Bernardi, R. (2000). *Contratransferencia.* Buenos Aires: Ed. Polemos.

Del Valle, E. (1998–99). Lo irrepresentable. *Revista de Psicoanálisis (Número Especial Internacional), 6.*

Del Valle, E. (2003). Símbolos en M. Klein y en algunos autores representativos de la Escuela Inglesa. *Revista de Psicoanálisis, 60:* 1.

De Monchaux, C. (1978). Dreaming and the organizing function of the ego. *International Journal of Psychoanalysis, 59:* 443–453.

De Saussure, F. (1916). *Curso de Lingüística General.* Buenos Aires: Losada, 1945.

Detienne, M. (1981). *Les Maîtres de Vérité dans la Grêce archaïque.* Paris: Editions de la Découverte; Rio de Janeiro: Jorge Zahar Ed., 1988.

de Urtubey, L. (1994). Le travail de contre-transfert. *Revue Française de Psychanalyse, 58:* 1271–1388.

Deutsch, H. (1926). Occult processes occurring during psychoanalysis. In: G. Devereux (Ed.), *Psychoanalysis and the Occult* (pp. 133–146). New York: International Universities Press.

Dewald, P. A. (1982). Serious illness in the analyst: Transference, countertransference and reality responses. *Journal of the American Psychoanalytic Association, 30* (2): 347–363.

Dolto, F. (1989). *Palabras para adolescentes.* Buenos Aires: Atlántida. [First published as: *Paroles pour Adolescents,* with C. Percheminier & C. Dolto-Tolitch. Paris: Hatier, 1988; new edition: Paris: Gallimard, 1999.]

Duarte, A. L. de (2000). Más allá de la información dada: Cómo construimos nuestras hipótesis Clínicas. *Revista de la Sociedad Argentina de Psicoanálisis, 3.*

Ducrot, O. (1984). *El decir y lo dicho.* Barcelona: Paidós, 1986.

Dunn, I. (1995). Intersubjectivity: A critical review. *International Journal of Psychoanalysis, 76* (4).

Dupont, M. A. (1997). *Los fundadores.* Mexico: Tesis Económicas Profesionales.

Eckhart, Meister (1260–1327). *Traités et Sermons,* trans. F. A. & J. M., intro. M. de Gandillac. Paris: Aubier-Montaigne, 1942.

Erikson, E. H. (1954). The dream specimen of psychoanalysis. *Journal of the American Psychoanalytic Association, 2:* 5–55.

Erlich, H. S. (2003). Experience—what is it? *International Journal of Psychoanalysis, 84:* 1125–1147.

Etchegoyen, R. H. (1986). *The Fundamentals of Psychoanalyic Technique.* London, Karnac, 1991. [Also published as: *Los fundamentos de la técnica psicoanalítica.* Buenos Aires: Amorrortu Ed., 1986.]

Etchegoyen, R. H. (1993). Inaugural speech as President of the IPA. Presented at the 38th IPA Congress, Amsterdam.

Etchegoyen, R. H., & Zysman, S. (2004). "Melanie Klein en Buenos Aires. Comienzos y desarrollos." Paper presented at IJPA Conference, Marcas identificatorias del psicoanálisis en América Latina, Rio de Janeiro, June.

Fenichel, O. (1945). *The Psychoanalytic Theory of the Neuroses.* New York:

Norton. [Also published as: *Teoría psicoanalítica de las neurosis.* Buenos Aires: Paidós, 1957.]

Ferenczi, S. (1919). On the technique of psychoanalysis. *Further Contributions to the Theory and Technique of Psychoanalysis* (pp. 177–189). New York: Basic Books, 1952.

Ferenczi, S. (1920). The further development of an active therapy in psychoanalysis. *Further Contributions to the Theory and Technique of Psychoanalysis* (pp. 177–189). New York: Basic Books, 1952.

Ferreira Abrao, J. L. (1999). "Um percurso pela historia da sicanalise de Criancas no Brasil." Doctoral dissertation, Universidade Estadual Paulista de Assis.

Ferro, A. (1992). *The Bipersonal Field: Experiences in Child Analysis.* London: New Library/Routledge, 1999.

Ferro, A. (2001). *La sesión analítica.* Buenos Aires: Lumen. [Also published as: *In the Analyst's Consulting Room.* London & New York: Routledge Brunner, 2002.]

Ferro, A. (2002a). Desde la tiranía del Superyó a la democracia de los afectos. *Revista de Psicoanálisis, 59* (4): 861.

Ferro A. (2002b). *Seeds of Illness and Seeds of Recovery: The Genesis of Suffering and the Role of Psychoanalysis.* London & New York: Routledge, New Library of Psychoanalysis, 20.

Fiorini, H. (1995). Los procesos terciarios, arquitecturas del movimiento. *El Psiquismo Creador* (Chap. 6). Buenos Aires: Paidós.

Fischbein, J. (1999). Más allá de la representación: El acto. *Revista de Psicoanálisis, 56* (2): 261–282.

Fischbein, J. (2000). La clínica psicoanalítica y las enfermedades somáticas. *Psicoanálisis: Revista de APdeBA, 22* (1).

Fodor, J. (1983). *The Modularity of Mind.* Cambridge, MA: MIT Press.

Fonagy, I. (1970–71). Dire l'indicible. Messages du style verbal. *Revue Française de Psychanalyse, 2* (1988).

Fonagy, P. (2000). Dreams of borderline patients. In: R. J. Perelberg (Ed.), *Dreaming and Thinking.* London: Institute of Psychoanalysis.

Fonagy, P., Gergely, G., Jurist, E. L., & Target, M. (2002). *Affect Regulation, Mentalization, and the Development of the Self.* New York: Other Press.

Freud, A. (1927). *Psicoanálisis del niño.* Buenos Aires: Hormé, 1986.

Freud, S. (1890). Psychical (or mental) treatment. *S.E, 7.*

Freud, S. (1900a). *The Interpretation of Dreams. S.E., 4/5.* [*Die Traumdeutung. G.W.*, 2/3.]

Freud, S. (1901b). *The Psychopathology of Everyday Life. S.E., 6.*

Freud, S. (1905c). *Jokes and their Relation to the Unconscious. S.E., 8.*

Freud, S. (1905e [1901]). Fragment of an analysis of a case of hysteria. *S.E., 7.*

Freud S. (1908c). On the sexual theories of children, *S.E., 9.*

Freud, S. (1909b). Analysis of a phobia in a five-year-old boy. *S.E., 10.*

Freud, S. (1909d). Notes upon a case of obsessional neurosis. *S.E., 10.*

Freud, S. (1910d). The future prospects of psycho-analytic therapy. *S.E., 11* (pp. 139–152).
Freud S. (1911b). Formulations on the two principles of mental functioning. *S.E., 12.*
Freud, S. (1911–15 [1914]). Papers on technique. *S.E., 12.*
Freud, S. (1912b). The dynamics of transference. *S.E., 12.*
Freud, S. (1912e). Recommendations to physicians practising psycho-analysis. *S.E., 12* (pp. 109–120).
Freud S. (1912–13). *Totem and Taboo. S.E. 13.*
Freud, S. (1914c). On narcissism: An introduction. *S.E., 14.*
Freud, S. (1914d). On the history of the psycho-analytical movement. *S.E., 14.*
Freud, S. (1915a). Observations on transference-love (Further recommendations on the technique of psycho-analysis. III). *S.E., 12* (pp. 157–173).
Freud, S. (1915e). The unconscious, *S.E., 14* (pp. 166–204).
Freud, S. (1916–17). *Introductory Lectures on Psycho-Analysis, S.E., 15* (Lectures 6 and 7).
Freud, S. (1917d [1915]). A metapsychological approach to the theory of dreams. *S.E., 14.*
Freud, S. (1917e [1915]). Mourning and melancholia. *S.E., 14.*
Freud, S. (1918b [1914]). From the history of an infantile neurosis. *S.E., 17.*
Freud, S. (1919h). The "uncanny". *S.E., 17.*
Freud, S. (1920a). The psychogenesis of a case of homosexuality in a woman. *S.E., 18.*
Freud, S. (1920g). *Beyond the Pleasure Principle, S.E., 18.*
Freud, S. (1921c). *Group Psychology and the Analysis of the Ego. S.E., 18.*
Freud, S. (1922a). Dreams and telepathy. *S.E., 18.*
Freud, S. (1923b). *The Ego and the Id, S.E., 19.*
Freud, S. (1923c [1922]). Remarks on the theory and practice of dream-interpretation. *S.E., 19.*
Freud, S. (1924d). The dissolution of the Oedipus complex. *S.E., 19.*
Freud, S. (1924e). The loss of reality in neurosis and psychosis. *S.E., 19.*
Freud, S. (1924f [1923]). A short account of psycho-analysis. *S.E., 19.*
Freud, S. (1925i). Some additional notes on dream-interpretation as a whole. *S.E., 19.*
Freud S. (1925h), Negation, *S.E. 19.*
Freud, S. (1925j). Some psychical consequences of the anatomical distinction between the sexes. *S.E., 19.*
Freud, S. (1927c). *The Future of an Illusion. S.E., 21.*
Freud, S. (1927e). Fetishism. *S.E., 21.*
Freud, S. (1933a). *New Introductory Lectures on Psycho-Analysis. S.E.*, 22.
Freud, S. (1937c). Analysis terminable and interminable. *S.E., 23.*
Freud S. (1937d). Constructions in analysis. *S.E., 23.*
Freud S. (1939a [1934–38]). *Moses and Monotheism. S.E., 23.*

Freud S. (1940a [1938]). *An Outline of Psycho-Analysis. S.E., 23.*
Freud, S. (1941d [1921]). Psychoanalysis and telepathy. *S.E., 18.*
Freud, S. (1950 [1895]). A project for a scientific psychology. *S.E., 1.*
Gabbard, G. O. (1997). A reconsideration of objectivity in the analyst. *International Journal of Psychoanalysis, 78* (1).
Gabbard, G. (2003). Miscarriages of psychoanalytic treatment with suicidal patients. *International Journal of Psychoanalysis, 84*: 249–262.
Garbarino, H. (1990). Un nuevo modelo de la mente. *Revista Latinoamericana de Psicoanálisis, FEPAL, 1* (1994): 87–108.
García, G. L. (1980). *Oscar Masotta y el psicoanálisis del castellano.* Barcelona: Argonauta.
Garma, Á. (1931). La realidad exterior y los instintos en la esquizofrenia. In: *Libro Anual de Psicoanálisis.* Lima: Editorial Montevideo, 1990.
Garma, Á. (1943). El método psicoanalítico de interpretación de los sueños. Introducción a la psicología onírica. *Revista de Psicoanálisis, 50* (1993): 447–470.
Garma, Á. (1968a). El pensar amplio de los sueños. *Revista de Psicoanálisis, 25* (1): 9–26.
Garma, Á. (1968b). Traumas o satisfacciones de deseos en la génesis de los sueños. *Revista de Psicoanálisis, 25* (3/4): 589–615.
Garma, Á. (1970a). Génesis y contenido primordial de la alucinación onírica. *Revista de Psicoanálisis,* 25 (3): 489–552.
Garma, Á. (1970b). *Nuevas aportaciones al psicoanálisis de los sueños.* Buenos Aires: Paidós.
Garma, Á. (1974). Mis investigaciones psicoanalíticas originales en el transcurso de cuarenta y cinco años. *Revista de Psicoanálisis, 31* (1/2): 141–175.
Garma, Á. (1993). El método psicoanalítico de interpretación de los sueños. *Revista de Psicoanálisis, 50* (2): 447–470.
Garma, B. (1992). *Niños en análisis. Clínica psicoanalítica.* Buenos Aires: Kargieman.
Garza Guerrero, C. (2002). Organisational and educational internal impediments of psychoanlysis: Contemporary challenges. *International Journal of Psychoanalysis, 83*: 1407–1433.
Gibeault, A. (2001). Du processus analytique en psychanalyse et en psychothérapie: de l'interpersonnel à l'intrapsychique. *Revue Française de Psychanalyse* (*Courants de la psychanalyse contemporaine), 65*: 49.
Gill, M. (1982). *Analysis of Transference.* New York: International Universities Press.
Goode de Garma, E. (1992). Psicoanálisis de un niño de 21 meses. In: B. Garma, *Niños en análisis. Clínica psicoanalítica.* Buenos Aires: Kargieman.
Green, A. (1973). *Le discours vivant.* Paris: Presses Universitaires de France; Rio de Janeiro: Livraria Francisco Alves Ed., 1982.
Green, A. (1975). The analyst, symbolization and absence in the analytic setting. *International Journal of Psychoanalysis, 56*: 1–22. [Also in: *On Private*

Madness. London: Hogarth, 1986; reprinted London: Karnac, 1997. Also as: L'analyste, la symbolisation et l'absence dans le cadre analytique. In: *La folie privée.* Paris: Gallimard, 1990.]

Green, A. (1976). El concepto de lo fronterizo. In: *De locuras privadas.* Buenos Aires: Amorrortu, 1990. [Le concept de limite. In: *La folie privée.* Paris: Gallimard, 1990. The borderline concept. In: *On Private Madness.* London: Hogarth, 1986; reprinted London: Karnac, 1997.]

Green, A. (1984). *El lenguaje en el psicoanálisis.* Buenos Aires: Amorrortu, 1995. [Le langage dans la psychanalyse. In: *Langages,* Paris: Les Belles Lettres, 1984.]

Green, A. (1988). *Narcisismo de vida, Narcisismo de morte.* São Paulo: Editora Escuta. [*Narcissisme de vie narcissisme de mort.* Paris: Minuit, 1983. *Life Narcissim, Death Narcissism.* London: Free Association Books, 2001.]

Green, A. (1989). La tiercéité. In: *La pensée clinique.* Paris: Ed. Odile Jacob, 2002.

Green, A. (1990). *La nueva clínica psicoanalítica y la teoría de Freud.* Buenos Aires: Amorrortu Ed.

Green, A. (1995a). *La causalité psychique: Entre nature et culture.* Paris: Ed. Odile Jacob.

Green, A. (1995b). *Propédeutique. La métapsychologie revisitée.* Seyssel, France: Champ Vallon. [*La metapsicología revisitada.* Buenos Aires: Eudeba, 1996.]

Green, A. (1997). *Las cadenas de Eros.* Buenos Aires: Amorrortu Ed. [*The Chains of Eros: The Actuality of the Sexual in Psychoanalysis.* New York: Other Press, 1999.]

Green, A. (1998). Sobre a discriminação e a indiscriminação afeto-representação. *Revista Brasileira de Psicanálise, 32.*

Green, A. (1999a). Coloquio en APA. *Revista de psicoanálisis, 56* (2).

Green, A. (1999b). Genèse et situation des états-limites. In: *Les états-limites.* Paris: Presse Universitaires de France.

Green, A. (2000a). *André Green at the Squiggle Foundation,* ed. J. Abram. London: Karnac.

Green, A. (2000b). Le cadre analytique: Son intériorisation chez l'analyste et son application dans la pratique. In: *L'avenir d'une désillusion.* Paris: Presse Universitaires de France.

Green, A. (2001). *El tiempo fragmentado.* Buenos Aires: Amorrortu Ed. [*Le temps eclaté.* Paris: Presses Universitaires de France, 2000.]

Green, A. (2002). *Idées directrices pour une psychanalyse contemporaine.* Paris: Presse Universitaires de France.

Greimas, A. (1966). *Semántica estructural.* Madrid: Gredos, 1971.

Greve Schlegel, G. (1910). "Sobre psicología y psicoterapia de ciertos estados angustiosos." Paper presented at the International American Congress of Medicine and Hygiene, Buenos Aires.

Grice, H. (1957). Meaning: Philosophical review. In: P. F. Strawson (Ed.), *Philosophical Logic.* Oxford: Oxford University Press, 1971.

Grice, H. (1967). "Logic and Conversation." Unpublished manuscript of the William James Lectures, Harvard University.

Grice, H. (1981). Presupposition and conversational implicature. In: *Radical Pragmatics*. New York: Academic Press.

Grinberg, L. (1956). Sobre algunos problemas de técnica psicoanalítica determinados por la identificación y contraidentificación proyectivas. *Revista de Psicoanálisis, 13*: 507–511.

Grinberg, L. (1958). Aspectos mágicos en la transferencia y en la contratransferencia. Sus implicaciones técnicas. Identificación y "contraidentificación" proyectivas. *Revista de Psicoanálisis, 15*: 341–368.

Grinberg, L. (1963). Psicopatología de la identificación y contraidentificación proyectivas y de la contratransferencia. *Revista de Psicoanálisis, 20*: 113–123.

Grinberg, L. (1964). *Culpa y depresión. Estudio psicoanalítico.* Buenos Aires: Paidós. [*Guilt and Depression*, trans. C. Trollope. London: Karnac, 1992.]

Grinberg, L. (1967). Función del soñar y clasificación clínica de los sueños en el proceso analítico. *Revista de Psicoanálisis, 24:* 171–186.

Grinberg, L. (1982). "Los afectos en la contratransferencia. Más allá de la contraidentificación proyectiva." (Introduction to the panel, Los afectos en la contratransferencia, 16th Congreso Latinoamericano de Psicoanálisis.) *FEPAL, Garamond, Actas*: 205–209.

Grinberg, L., & Grinberg, R. (1960). Los sueños del día lunes. *Revista de Psicoanálisis, 17*: 164–170.

Grinberg, L., & Grinberg, R. (1984). *Psicoanálisis de la migración y el exilio.* Madrid: Alianza Editorial. [*Psychoanalytic Perspectives on Migration and Exile* (transl. N. Festinger). New Haven, CT: Yale University Press,1989.]

Grotstein, J. (Ed.) (1981). *Do I Dare Disturb the Universe? A Memorial to Wilfred R. Bion.* Beverly Hills, CA: Caesura Press [revised edition London: Karnac, 1983].

Grotstein, J. (2000). *Who Is the Dreamer Who Dreams the Dream? A Study of Psychic Presences.* Hillsdale, NJ: Analytic Press.

Grotstein, J. (2004a). "The Light Militia of the Lower Sky": The deeper nature of dreaming and phantasying. *Psychoanalytic Dialogues, 14*: 99–118.

Grotstein, J. (2004b). The "Seventh Servant": The implications of a truth drive in Bion's theory of "O". *International Journal of Psychoanalysis, 85*: 1081–1101.

Guignard, F. (1996). *Au Vif de l'Infantile. Réflexions sur la situation analytique.* Champs psychanalytiques. Lausanne: Delachaux & Niestlé. [2nd edition, 2002. Also published as: *O infantil ao vivo. Reflexões sobre a situação analítica*, trans. M. Pedreira, Rio de Janeiro: Imago, 1997; as: *Nel vivo dell'infantile. Riflessioni sulla situazione analitica*, ed. A. Ferro, trans. A. Lastrico. Milan: Franco Angeli, 1999; and as: *En el núcleo vivo de lo infantil, reflexiones sobre la situación analítica*, trans. P. G. Nacher, Madrid: Biblioteca Nueva, 2003.]

Guignard F. (1997). *Épître à l'objet.* Coll. Épîtres. Paris, P.U.F. [Also published as: *Pulsioni e vicissitudini dell'oggetto,* trans. N. I. Ferro. Milan: Borla, 2000; and as: *Epistola al objeto,* trans. P. G. Nacher & A. G. Martinez. Valencia: Promolibro, 2001.]

Guillaumin, J. (1996). *L'objet.* Bordeaux: L'Esprit du Temps.

Hanly, C. M. (1995). On facts and ideas in psychoanalysis. *International Journal of Psychoanalysis, 76* (5).

Hartmann, H. (1939). *Ego Psychology and the Problem of Adaptation.* New York: International Universities Press.

Heidegger, M. (1951–52). *Was heisst Denken?* [*O que significa pensar?*] Petrópolis: Vozes Ed. [Also published as: *What is Called Thinking?,* trans. F. D. Wieck & J. G. Gray. New York: Harper & Row, 1968.]

Heimann, P. (1950). On counter-transference. *International Journal of Psychoanalysis, 31*: 81–84. [Also in: *Revista Uruguaya de Psicoanálisis, 4* (1961–62):137–149.]

Heimann, P. (1959). Countertransference. *British Journal of Medical Psychology, 33* (1960, No. 9): 9–15.

Heisenberg, W. (1969). *The Part and the Whole.* Munich. [Also published as: *A Parte e o Todo.* Rio de Janeiro: Contraponto Ed., 1996.]

Hermann, F. (1992). La Rani de Chittor. Le Visage. In: *De la trahison.* Paris: Presse Universitaires de France, 1999.

Hernández, M. (1992). *Memoria del bien perdido.* Lima: Peruvian Library of Psychoanalysis.

Hinshelwood, R. (1989). *A Dictionary of Kleinian Thought.* London: Free Association Press. [Also published as: *Diccionario del pensamiento kleiniano.* Buenos Aires: Amorrortu Ed., 1992.]

Hinzner, H., & Noemí, C. (1986). Versión psicoanalítica de la realidad externa. *Revista Chilena de Psicoanálisis, 5*: 35–43.

Hunter, V. (1994). *Psychoanalists Talk.* New York: Guilford Press.

Huxley, A. (1980). *The Perennial Philosophy.* London: Chatto & Windus.

Isaacs, S. (1952). The nature and function of phantasy. In: M. Klein, P. Heimann, S. Isaacs, & J. Riviere (Eds.), *Developments in Psycho-Analysis.* London: Hogarth Press [reprinted London: Karnac, 1989].

Isaías, M. (1987). El sueño y la fantasía masturbatoria central. *Cuadernos de Psicoanálisis, 20*: 28–34.

Jacobs, T. (1986). On countertransference enactments. *Journal of the American Psychoanalytic Association, 34*: 289–307.

Jakobson, R. (1963). Functions of language. In: J. P. B. Allen & S. Pit Corder (Eds.), *The Edinburgh Course in Applied Linguistics.* Oxford: Oxford University Press, 1973.

Jiménez, J. P. (1992). La contribución del analista en los procesos de identificación proyectiva. *Revista Chilena de Psicoanálisis, 9*: 54–66.

Jones, E. (1919). The theory of symbolism. *Papers on Psychoanalysis.* London: Balliere, Tindall & Cox, 1938.

Jordán, J. F. (1992). The transference: Distortion or plausible conjecture? *International Journal of Psychoanalysis, 73*: 729–738.

Jordán-Moore, J. F. (1994). Intimacy and science: The publication of clinical facts in psychoanalysis. *International Journal of Psychoanalysis, 75*: 1251–1266.

Kancyper, L. (1983). "El baluarte en el sujeto y en el campo intersubjetivo en un caso clínico." Paper presented at the Argentine Psychoanalytic Association, April 14.

Kancyper, L. (1985). Adolescencia y a posteriori. *Revista de Psicoanálisis, 42* (3): 535.

Kancyper, L. (1989). *Jorge Luis Borges o el laberinto de Narciso.* Buenos Aires: Paidos.

Kancyper, L. (1990a). Adolescencia y desidentificación. *Revista de Psicoanálisis, 47* (4): 750.

Kancyper, L. (1990b). Narcisismo y pigmalionismo. *Revista de Psicoanálisis, 48* (1991, No. 5/6): 1003.

Kancyper, L. (1991). Remordimiento y resentimiento en el complejo fraterno. (Paper presented at the 37th IPA Congress, Buenos Aires.) *Revista de Psicoanálisis, 48* (1): 120.

Kancyper, L. (1992). "Resentimiento y odio en la confrontación generacional." Paper presented at the 20th International Congress and 30th Symposium, APA.

Kancyper, L. (1994a). *Angustia y poder en la confrontación generacional.* Córdoba: FEPAL.

Kancyper, L. (1994b). "Eros y Ananké en la confrontación generacional." Paper presented at the 4th APA Conference on Family and Couple Psychoanalysis.

Kancyper, L. (1995). "Complejo de Edipo y complejo fraterno." Paper presented at the 39th IPA Congress, San Francisco.

Kancyper, L. (Ed.) (1998). *Volviendo a pensar con Willy y Medeleine Baranger.* Buenos Aires: Lumen, 1999.

Kancyper, L. (2000). *La confrontación generacional.* Buenos Aires: Lumen, 2003. [Also published as: *Il confronto generazionale.* Milan: F. Angeli, 2000, p. 101.]

Kerbrat-Orecchioni, C. (1991). Hétérogénéité énonciative et conversation. *Le sens et ses hétérogénéités.* Paris: Éditions du CNRS.

Kerbrat-Orecchioni, C. (1996). *La enunciación. De la subjetividad en el lenguaje.* Buenos Aires: Edicial, 1997.

Kernberg, O. (1965). Notes on countertransference. *Journal of the American Psychoanalytic Association, 13*: 38–56. [Also published as: Notas sobre la contratransferencia. *Revista Asociación Argentina de Psicoterapia para Graduados,* 20 (1994): 11–28.]

Kernberg, O. (1982). Self, ego, affects and drives. *Journal of the American Psychoanalytic Association, 30*: 893–917.

Kernberg, O. (1986). Institutional problems of psychoanalytic education. *Journal of the American Psychoanalytic Association, 34*: 799–834.

Kernberg, O. (1987). An ego psychology–object relations theory approach to the transference. *Psychoanalytic Quarterly, 56*: 197–221.

Kernberg, O. (2004a). *Aggressivity, Narcissism and Self-Destructiveness in the Psychotherapeutic Relationship* (pp. 167–183). New Haven, CT: Yale University Press.

Kernberg, O. (2004b). *Contemporary Controversies in Psychoanalytic Theories, Techniques, and Applications* (pp. 232–245). New Haven, CT: Yale University Press.

Klein, M. (1929). Infantile anxiety situations reflected in a work of art and in the creative impulse. In: *Love, Guilt and Reparation and Other Works.* London: Hogarth Press, 1975 [reprinted London: Karnac, 1975].

Klein, M. (1932). *The Psycho-Analysis of Children. The Writings of Melanie Klein, Vol. 2.* London: Hogarth Press, 1975 [reprinted London: Karnac, 1975].

Klein, M. (1935). A contribution to the psychogenesis of manic-depressive states. *International Journal of Psychoanalysis, 16*: 145–174. In: *Love, Guilt and Reparation and Other Works.* London: Hogarth Press, 1975 [reprinted London: Karnac, 1975].

Klein, M. (1946). Notes on some schizoid mechanisms. In: *Envy and Gratitude and Other Works.* London: Hogarth Press, 1975 [reprinted London: Karnac, 1975].

Klein, M. (1957). Envy and gratitude. In: *Envy and Gratitude and Other Works.* London: Tavistock, 1975 [reprinted London: Karnac, 1975; Rio de Janeiro: Imago Ed., 1974].

Klimovsky, G. (2004). *Epistemología y psicoanálisis.* Buenos Aires: Ediciones Biebel.

Kristeva, J. (1993). *Les nouvelles maladies de l'âme.* Paris: Fayard.

Kristeva, J. (1999). La transubstantiation de Proust. *Marcel Proust visiteur des psychanalystes. Revue Française de Psychanalyse, 63.*

Labov, W., & Fanshell, D. (1977). *Therapeutic Discourse: Psychotherapy as Conversation.* New York: Academic Press.

Lacan, J. (1953). Fonction et champ de la parole et du langage en psychanalyse. In: *Écrits.* Paris: Éditions du Seuil, 1966. [Also published as: The function and field of speech and language in psychoanalysis. In: *Écrits.* London: Tavistock, 1977.]

Lacan, J. (1957). Agency of the letter in the unconscious. In: *Écrits.* London: Tavistock, 1977.

Lacan, J. (1966). *Écrits.* Paris: Éditions du Seuil.

Ladrière, J. (1970). *L'Articulation du Sens. Discours scientifique et parole de la foi.* Paris: Aubier-Montaigne.

Langer, M. (1951). *Maternidad y sexo.* Buenos Aires: Paidós. [*Motherhood and Sexuality.* London: Guilford, 1992.]

Langer, M. (Ed.) (1972). *Cuestionamos. Documentos de crítica a la ubicación actual del psicoanálisis.* Buenos Aires: Granica Ed.

Langer, M., & Bauleo, A. (1987). *Cuestionamos.* Buenos Aires: Búsqueda. [Also published as: *Cuestionamos: Politics, Power, and Opposition in Argentina.* London: Free Association Books, 1992.]

Langer, M., del Palacio, J., & Guinsberg, E. (1983). *Memoria, historia y diálogo psicoanalítico.* Mexico: Folios Ediciones.

Langer, S. (1953). *An Introduction to Symbolic Logic.* New York: Dover.

Laplanche, J. (1970–73). *La angustia. Problemáticas I.* Buenos Aires: Amorrortu, 1981.

Laplanche, J. (1989). *Nuevos fundamentos para el psicoanálisis.* Buenos Aires: Amorrortu Ed. [*Nouveaux fondements pour la psychanalyse. La séduction originaire.* Paris: PUF, 1987.]

Laplanche, J. (1996). *La prioridad del otro en psicoanálisis.* Buenos Aires: Amorrortu Ed.

Laplanche, J., & Pontalis, J.-B. (1967). *The Language of Psychoanalysis.* London: Hogarth Press, 1973 [reprinted London: Karnac, 1988]. [First published as: *Vocabulaire de la psychanalyse.* Paris: Presses Universitaires de France; also published as: *Diccionario de psicoanálisis.* Barcelona: Labor, 1971.]

Lavandera, B., et al. (1987). Análisis sociolingüístico del discurso político (II). In: *Cuadernos de Lingüística.* Buenos Aires: Facultad de Filosofía y Letras, University of Buenos Aires.

Lemlij, M. (Ed.) (1991). *El múltiple interés del psicoanálisis—77 años después.* Lima: Peruvian Library of Psychoanalysis.

Levin, R. (2002). Una postal del Departamento de Niñez y Adolescencia de APdeBA. *Devenir (Claustro de candidatos de ApdeBA, Buenos Aires), 11* (2).

Lévi-Strauss, C. (1958). *Anthropologie structurale.* Paris: Plon.

Liberman, D. (1962). *La comunicación en terapéutica psicoanalítica.* Buenos Aires: EUDEBA, 1966.

Liberman, D. (1970–72). *Lingüística, interacción comunicativa y proceso psicoanalítico, Vols. 1–3.* Buenos Aires: Galerna, Nueva Visión, 1976.

Liberman, D. (1976). Changes in the theory and practice of psychoanalysis. *International Journal of Psychoanalysis, 57*: 101–107.

Lieven, E. (1978). Turn-taking and pragmatics: Two issues in early child language. In: R. N. Campbell & P. Smith (Eds.), *Recent Advances in the Psychology of Language: Language Development and Mother–Child Interaction.* New York & London: Plenum Press.

Litowitz, B., & Litowitz, N. (1977). The influence of linguistic theory on psychoanalysis: A critical, historical survey. *International Review of Psycho-Analysis, 4*: 419–447.

Loden, S. (2003). The fate of the dream in contemporary psychoanalysis. *Journal of the American Psychoanalytic Association, 51*: 43–70.

López, B. (1988). Las invariantes del método en las diferentes teorías y prácticas. *Psicoanálisis, 10* (3).

López, D. (1982). "El modelo secuencial onírico como guía y evaluación de las fases progresivas de un análisis." Unpublished thesis, Instituto de Psicoanálisis.

López, D. (1986). Modelo secuencial onírico. Su utilización en psicoterapia psicoanalítica. *Cuadernos de Psicoanálisis, 19*: 99–105.

López, M. I., & León de López, N. (1992). Historia y orientación del tratamiento psicoanalítico de niños y adolescentes. In: *Manual de pscoanálisis de niños y adoelscentes.* Mexico City: Planeta.

Machado, A. (1969). *Antologia Poética.* Madrid: Salvat.

Mahoney, P. (1987). Towards a formalist approach to Freud's central dream. In: *Psychoanalysis and Discourse.* London & New York: Tavistock.

Maldavsky, D. (2001). Complejizaciones teórico-metodológicas en psicoanálisis. *Revista de Psicoanálisis (Número Especial Internacional, Psicoanálisis e Interdisciplina), 8.*

Maldavsky, D. (2003a). A contribution to the development of a psychoanalytical methodology for research into language: A systematic study of narration as an expression of sexuality. *International Journal of Psychoanalysis, 84*: 607–635.

Maldavsky, D. (2003b). La clínica y la investigación en psicoanálisis. El analista trabajando. *Revista de Psicoanálisis, 40* (4).

Mannoni, M. (1980). *La teoría como ficción.* Barcelona: Editorial Crítica S.A.

Mannoni, O. (1969). *Clefs pour l'Imaginaire ou l'Autre Scène.* Paris: Seuil. [Also published as: *La otra escena. Claves de lo imaginario.* Buenos Aires: Amorrortu Ed., 1973.]

Marcondes, D. (1926). "O simbolismo estetico na literatura. Ensaio d'uma orientacao para a critica literaria baseada nos conhecimientos fornecidos pela psycho-analyse." Unpublished manuscript.

Marty, P. (1984). Los sueños en los enfermos somáticos. *Pierre Marty y la psicosomática,* ed. M. T. de Calatroni. Buenos Aires: Amorrortu, 1998.

Marty, P., & M'Uzan, M. (1983). El "pensamiento operatorio". *Revista de Psicoanálisis, 40* (4): 711–721.

Marucco, N. C. (1978a). Momentos o neurosis transferencial? Reflexiones sobre la transferencia en la obra de Freud. *Revista de Psicoanálisis, 35* (1).

Marucco, N .C. (1978b). Narcisismo, escisión del yo y Edipo. Una introducción a manera de epílogo. *Revista de Psicoanálisis, 35* (2).

Marucco, N. C. (1979). Para la teoría de una resistencia final (RTN o "necesidad de enfermar"?). *Revista de Psicoanálisis, 36* (4).

Marucco, N. C. (1980). Introducción de (lo siniestro) en el yo. *Revista de Psicoanálisis, 37* (2).

Marucco, N. C. (1997). The Oedipus complex, castration and the fetish. *International Journal of Psychoanalysis, 78*: 351.

Marucco, N. C. (1998a). *Cura analítica y transferencia. De la represión a la desmentida.* Buenos Aires: Amorrortu Ed.

Marucco, N. C. (1998b). La identidad de Edipo. Acerca de la escisión del Yo, de la compulsión a la repetición y de la pulsión de muerte. In: *Cura analítica y transferencia. De la represión a la desmentida* (chap. 2). Buenos Aires: Amorrortu Ed.

Marucco, N. C. (1998c). La neurosis hoy: En las vías de acceso a las "zonas psíquicas" (Posfacio). (Conferencia Magistral pronunciada en el 32 Congreso Latinoamericano de Psicoanálisis, Cartagena, Colombia.) *La Revista Latinoamericana de Psicoanálisis.* [Also in: *Cura analítica y transferencia. De la represión a la desmentida.* Buenos Aires: Amorrortu Ed.]

Marucco, N. C. (2000). El placer en al realidad y en la fantasía. Acerca de la pulsionalidad de la fantasía. *Revista de Psicoanálisis, 57* (1).

Marucco, N. C. (2001). Algunas puntuaciones psicoanalíticas desde mi práctica clínica. *Revista Francesa de Psicoanálisis, 65* (Hors Serie "Courants de la psychanalyse contemporaine", ed. André Green).

Marucco, N. C. (2003a). Algunas puntuaciones psicoanalíticas. Formación psicoanalítica. Transmisión del psicoanálisis. *Revista de Psicoanálisis, 40* (2): 379–394.

Marucco, N. C. (2003b). El analizado de hoy y lo inconciente. *Revista de la Sociedad Psicoanálitica de Porto Alegre (Special 10th Anniversary Issue).*

Marucco, N. C. (2004). La posición del analista [el otro] y la clínica actual. In: L. G. Fiorini (Ed.), *El otro en la trama intersubjetiva.* Buenos Aires: APA Editorial–Lugar Ed.

Marucco, N. C., Korol, L., Marchionni, H. M., Rozitchner, E. M., & Vertzner de Marucco, A. (1995). La función analítica y (la presencia de) el analista. El papel de la singularidad real en la transferencia. *Revista de Psicoanálisis, 42* (3).

Matte Blanco, I. (1975). *The Unconscious as Infinite Sets. An Essay in Bi-logic.* London: Duckworth.

Matte Blanco, I. (1981). Reflecting with Bion. In: J. S. Grotstein (Ed.), *Do I Dare Disturb the Universe? A Memorial to Wilfred R. Bion.* Beverly Hills, CA: Caesura Press [revised edition London: Karnac, 1983].

Matte Blanco, I. (1988). *Thinking, Feeling and Being: Clinical Reflections on the Fundamental Antinomy of Human Beings and World.* London: Routledge.

Matte Blanco, I. (1989). Comments on "From Symmetry to Asymmetry" by Klaus Fink. *International Journal of Psychoanalysis, 70*: 491–498.

McDougall, J. (1990). *Plea for a Measure of Abnormality.* London: Free Association Books.

McLaughlin, J. (1991). Clinical and theoretical aspects of enactment. *Journal of the American Psychoanalytic Association, 39*: 595–614.

Meltzer, D. (1984). *Dream-Life.* Strath Tay: Clunie Press/Roland Harris Trust Library [London: Karnac].

Merleau-Ponty, M. (1942). *La structure du comportement.* Paris: Presses Universitaires de France. [Also published as: *The Structure of Behavior,* trans. A. L. Fisher. Boston, MA: Beacon Press, 1963.]

Merleau-Ponty, M. (1945). *Phénoménologie de la perception.* Paris: Gallimard.

Miller, J.-A. (1979). *Cinco conferencias caraqueñas sobre Lacan* [Five Caracas Lectures on Lacan]. Caracas: Ateneo de Caracas.

Minerbo, M. (1993). Some comments on Baranger's paper using Jacob's clinical examples. *International Journal of Psychoanalysis, 74* (6).

Mitchell, S. (2000). *Relationality: From Attachment to Intersubjectivity.* Hillsdale, NJ: Analytic Press.

Morin, E. (1977). *La méthode. La nature de la nature.* Paris: Le Seuil.

Morris, C. W. (1938). *Writings on the General Theory of Signs.* The Hague: Mouton, 1971.

M'Uzan, M. de (1995). *La boca del inconciente. Ensayos sobre la interpretación.* Buenos Aires: Amorrortu.

Nissim Momigliano, L., & Robutti, A. (1992). *Shared Experience: The Psychoanalytic Dialogue.* London: Karnac.

Nosek, L. (Ed.) (1994). *Álbum de família. Imagens, fontes e idéias da psicanálise em São Paulo.* São Paulo: Casa da Psicólogo.

Ogden, T. H. (1994a). The concept of interpretive action. *Psychoanalytic Quarterly, 63*: 219–245.

Ogden, T. H. (1994b). The analytical third: Working with intersubjective clinical facts. *International Journal of Psychoanalysis, 75* (1).

Ogden, T. H. (1996). Reconsidering three aspects of psychoanalytic technique. *International Journal of Psychoanalysis, 77*: 891–897.

Ogden, T. H. (1999). *Reverie and Interpretation.* London: Karnac.

Ornstein, P. H. (1987). On self-state dreams in the psychoanalytic process. In: A. Rothstein (Ed.), *The Interpretation of Dreams in Clinical Work* (pp. 87–104). New York: International Universities Press.

Panel (1992). Enactments in psychoanalysis. (M. Johan, reporter.) *Journal of the American Psychoanalytic Association, 40*: 827–841.

Pardo, M. L. (1996). *Derecho y Lingüística.* Buenos Aires: Nueva Visión.

Parres, R. (1962). *La psicologia del yo y el problema de la adaptacion.* Mexico: Pax-Mexico.

Pascal, B. (1669–70). Pensées [Thoughts]. *Pensamientos. Sobre la religión y otros asuntos* (3rd edition), trans. with Port-Royal additions conveniently distinguished by E. D'ors. Buenos Aires: Editorial Losada, 1964. [Also published as: *Thoughts.* New York: P. F. Collier, 1909–1917.]

Paz, R. (1994). Round table discussion: "Contratransferencia y clínica". *Revista de la Asociación Escuela Argentina de Psicoterapia para Graduados, 20*: 47–48.

Peña, S. (1991). Historia del psicoanálisis en el Perú. In: M. Lemlij (Ed.), *El múltiple interés del psicoanálisis—77 años después.* Lima: Peruvian Library of Psychoanalysis.

Perestrello, M. (1987). *História da Sociedade Brasileira de psicanálise do Rio de Janeiro—suas origens e fundação.* Rio de Janeiro: Imago Ed.

Pérez de Plá, E. (1994). Migración y asentamiento de las teorías psicoanalíticas en México. Reflexiones a partir del análisis de niños. In: *Psicoanálisis de niños y adolescentes en América Latina: Desarrollos y perspectivas, Vol. 1.* (Fondo Ed., Biblioteca Peruana de Psicoanálisis.) Lima: FEPAL.

Pichon Rivière, E. (1979). *Teoría del vínculo.* Buenos Aires: Nueva Visión.

Picollo, A. (1994). Funcionamiento psicótico y cambio en la escucha. In: *Interpretar, conocer, crear Diálogo desde la interdisciplina.* Montevideo: Trilce.

Pontalis, J.-B. (1965). *Après Freud*. Paris: René Julliard.

Pontalis, J.-B. (1977). *Entre le rêve et la douleur*. Paris: Gallimard. [Also published as: *Frontiers in Psychoanalysis: Between the Dream and Psychic Pain*, trans. C. Cullen & P. Cullen. New York: International Universities Press, 1981; and as: *Entre el sueño y el dolor*. Buenos Aires: Ed. Sudamericana, 1978.]

Porras, L. (1991). Analizando una forma particular de duelo. *Revista Uruguaya de Psicoanálisis, 72–73*: 187–202.

Prag, P. W. (2003). Stress, burnout, and social support. A review and call for research. *Air Medical Journal, 22* (5): 18–22.

Prigogine, I. (1996). *O fim das certezas. Tempo, caos e as leis da natureza*. São Paulo: Editora da UNESP.

Puget, J., Kaës, R., Amati, S., et al. (1991). *Violencia de estado y psicoanálisis*. Buenos Aires: Centro Editor de América Latina.

Puget, J., & Wender, L. (1982). Analista y paciente en mundos superpuestos. *Psicoanálisis, 4*: 503–536.

Racker, H. (1948). La neurosis de contratransferencia. (Presented to the Asociación Psicoanalítica Argentina in September 1948.) In: *Estudios sobre técnica psicoanalítica* (pp. 182–221). Buenos Aires: Ed. Paidós, 1977. [Also published as: A contribution to the problem of counter-transference. *International Journal of Psycho-Analysis, 34* (1953): 313-24; republished as: The countertransference neurosis, in: *Transference and Counter-Transference*. London: Hogarth, 1968; reprinted London: Karnac, 1982.]

Racker, H. (1953). Los significados y usos de la contratransferencia. (Paper presented to the Asociación Psicoanalítica Argentina, May 1953.) In: *Estudios sobre técnica psicoanalítica* (pp. 222–295). Buenos Aires: Ed. Paidós, 1977. [A contribution to the problem of psychopathological stratification, *International Journal of Psychoanalysis* 38: 223–239; republished as The meanings and uses of counter-transference in Racker, *Transference and Counter-Transference*. London: Hogarth, 1968; reprinted London: Karnac, 1982.]

Racker, H. (1954). Consideraciones sobre la teoría de la transferencia. In: *Estudios sobre la técnica psicoanalítica* (pp. 79–89). Buenos Aires: Paidós, 1960. [Considerations on the theory of transference, in: *Transference and Counter-Transference*. London: Hogarth, 1968; reprinted London: Karnac, 1982.]

Racker, H. (1956). Técnica analítica y el masoquismo inconciente en el analista. (Paper presented at 1st Congreso Psicoanalítico Latinoamericano, Buenos Aires, 1956.) In: *Estudios sobre técnica psicoanalítica* (pp. 296–305). Buenos Aires: Ed. Paidós. [Also published as: Psychoanalytic technique and the analyst's unconscious masochism. *Psychoanalytic Quarterly, 27* (1958): 555–562.]

Racker, H. (1958). Sobre técnica clásica y técnica actuales del psicoanálisis. (Official address to the 2nd Congreso Lationoamericano de Psicoanálisis, San Pablo, Brasil, 1958.) In: *Estudios Sobre Técnica Analítica* (pp. 41–110).

Bueños Aires: Ed. Paidós, 1977. [Classical and present techniques in psychoanalysis, in: *Transference and Counter-Transference.* London: Hogarth, 1968; reprinted London: Karnac, 1982.]

Racker, H. (1960). *Estudios sobre técnica psicoanalítica.* Buenos Aires: Paidós. [*Transference and Countertransference.* London: Hogarth, 1968; reprinted London: Karnac, 1982.]

Ramírez, S. (1959). *El mexicano. Psicología de sus motivaciones.* Mexico: Pax, 1968.

Rascovsky, A. (1960). *El psiquismo fetal.* Buenos Aires: Paidós.

Rascovsky, L. (1976). Un sueño de dos y dos sueños de uno. Compulsión, repetición y elaboración. *Revista de Psicoanálisis, 33* (1).

Read, H. (1943). *Education through Art.* London: Faber & Faber.

Recanati, F. (1995). The alleged priority of literal interpretation. *Cognitive Science, 19*: 207–232.

Renik, O. (1993). Analytic interaction: Conceptualizing technique in light of the analyst's irreducible subjectivity. *Psychoanalytic Quarterly, 62*: 553–571.

Renik, O. (1995). The ideal of the anonymous analyst and the problem of self-disclosure. *Psychoanalytic Quarterly, 64*: 466–495.

Renik, O. (1998). The analyst's subjectivity and the analyst's objectivity. *International Journal of Psychoanalysis, 79* (3).

Rey de Castro, Á. (1977). Freud and Honorio Delgado. Una aproximación psicoanalítica a la pre-historia del psicoanálisis peruano y sus secuelas. In: M. Lemlij (Ed.), *El múltiple interés del psicoanálisis—77 años después.* Lima: Peruvian Library of Psychoanalysis, 1991.

Rezende, A. M. (1992). O pensamento de Bion. Um universo em Expansão. *Revista Brasileira de Psicanálise, 26* (3): 273.

Rezende, A. M. (1994). *A metapsicanálise de Bion, além dos modelos.* Campinas: SP. Papirus Ed.

Rezende, A. M. (1995). *Wilfred Ruprecht Bion, uma psicanálise do pensamento.* Campinas: SP. Papirus Ed.

Rezende, A. M. (1999a). *A questão da verdade na investigação psicanalítica.* Campinas: SP. Papirus Ed.

Rezende, A. M. (1999b). *Ser e não-ser, sob o vértice de "O".* Taubaté: Cabral Editora-Universitária.

Rezende, A. M. (2000). *O paradoxo da psicanálise. Uma ciência pós-paradigmática.* São Paulo: Via Lettera Ed.

Rezende, A. M. (2001). *A psicanálise atual, na interface das novas ciências.* São Paulo: Via Lettera Ed.

Rezende, A. M. (2003). "Caesura", no limiar do quarto quarto. In: *Panorama.* São Paulo: SBPSP.

Ricoeur, P. (1965). *De l'interprétation essai sur Freud.* Paris: Éditions du Seuil.

Ricoeur, P. (1969). *Le conflit des interprétations. Essais d'herméneutique.* Paris: Éditions du Seuil.

Rodrigué, E. (1956). Notes on symbolism. *International Journal of Psychoanalysis, 37* (2/3): 147–158.

Rosenthal, L. (1945). El psicoanálisis en la Argentina hace 35 años. *Revista de Psicoanálisis, 3*: 202–213.

Rosolato, G. (1978). *La relación de desconocido.* Barcelona: Petrel.

Rosolato, G. (1981). Culpabilidad y sacrificio. In: *La relación de Desconocido.* Barcelona: Petrel.

Rozenbaum de Schvartzman, A. (2004). "Había una vez: El psicoanálisis de niños y adolescentes: Su historia y desarrollo en APA." Paper presented at the Asociación Psicoanalítica Argentina, 21 September.

Ruesch, J. (1957). *Disturbed Communication.* New York: W. W. Norton.

Safran, J., & Muran, C. (2000). *Negotiating the Therapeutic Alliance: A Relational Treatment Guide.* New York: Guilford Press.

Salles, M. (2002). Historia del psicoanálisis infantil en México. *Cuadernos de Psicoanálisis, México* (July–December).

Sánchez Medina, G. (1990). *Psicoanálisis ayer, hoy y mañana. La historia del psicoanálisis en Colombia.* Bogotá: Industrias Gráficas Gaviota.

Sandler, J. (1976). Countertransference and role-responsiveness. *International Review of Psycho-Analysis, 3*: 43–47.

Sandler, J., Dare, C., & Holder, A. (1992). *The Patient and the Analyst.* London: Karnac.

Santamaría, A. (1983). Los sueños contratransferenciales. El sueño Irma. *Cuadernos de Psicoanálisis, 16* (3/4): 103–115.

Santamaría, A. (1984). La enseñanza del psicoanálisis infantil en México. *Cuadernos de Psicoanálisis, México* (June).

Santamaría, A. (1990). Los sueños como fuente de creatividad. *Cuadernos de Psicoanálisis, 23*: 165–174.

Scott, C. (1948). Some embryological, neurological, psychiatric and psychoanalytic implications of the body scheme. *International Journal of Psychoanalysis, 29*: 141–155.

Scott, C. (1949). The body scheme in psychotherapy. *British Journal of Medical Psychology, 22*: 140–149.

Searle, J. (1969). *Speech Acts.* Cambridge: Cambridge University Press.

Searle, J. (1979). *Expression and Meaning.* Cambridge: Cambridge University Press.

Segal, H. (1957). Notes on symbol formation. *International Journal of Psychoanalysis, 38* (6): 391–397.

Segal, H. (1998). Interview. *VEJA magazine,* 22 April.

Silveira Araujo, M. (1988). Sociedade Psicanalítica de Porto Alegre. *Revista Brasilera de Psicanalise, 22* (1).

Sperber, D. (1994). Understanding verbal understanding. In: J. Khalfa (Ed.), *What Is Intelligence* (pp. 179–198). Cambridge: Cambridge University Press.

Sperber, D., & Wilson, D. (1986). *Relevance.* Cambridge, MA: Harvard University Press.

Sperber, D., & Wilson, D. (1995). *Relevance: Communication and Cognition* (2nd edition, pp. 266–278). Oxford: Blackwell.

Sperber, D., & Wilson, D. (2002). Pragmatics, modularity and mind-reading. *Mind and Language, 17*: 3–23.

Stagnaro, J. C., & Wintrebert, D. (1996). Entrevista. *Vértex*, 7 (26): 260–274.

Steiner, R. (2000). *Tradition, Change, Creativity: Repercussions in the New Diaspora on Aspects of British Psychoanalysis.* London: Karnac.

Stern, D. (1985). *The Interpersonal World of the Infant.* New York: Basic Books.

Stolorow, R., & Atwood, G. (1992). *Contexts of Being: The Intersubjective Foundations of Psychological Life.* Hillsdale, NJ: Analytic Press.

Strachey, J. (1934). The nature of the therapeutic action of psycho-analysis. *International Journal of Psychoanalysis, 15*: 127.

Suárez, J. (1993). A propósito del cincuentenario de nuestra Revista. *Revista de Psicoanálisis, 50* (2): 471–493.

Symington, N. (1983). The analyst's act of freedom as agent of therapeutic change. *International Review of Psycho-Analysis, 10*: 283–291.

Tamez, A. (1993). The transferences. In: M. Lemlij (Ed.), *Psychoanalysis in "Latinamerica"* (pp. 219–247). Lima: FEPAL-Perú.

Thomä, H., & Kächele, H. (1985). *Teoría y práctica del psicoanálisis, Vol. 1: Fundamentos.* Barcelona: Herder, 1989.

Treszezamsky, J. (1993). La trayectoria de Ángel Garma en la investigación psicoanalítica de los sueños. *Revista de Psicoanálisis, 50* (2): 479–493.

Ungar, V. (2001). Psicoanálisis y psicoterapia en el tratamiento de niños. Pensando desde la frontera. *Newsletter de la IPA, 10* (2): 25–26. [Also published as: Psychoanalysis and psychotherapy in the treatment of children. Thoughts from the frontier. *International Psychoanalytical Association Newsletter, 10* (2).]

Van Dijk, T. (1997). *Discourse as Structure and Process.* London: Sage.

Van Steenberghen, F. (1952). *Ontology.* New York: Joseph F. Wagner; London: B. Herder.

Vezetti, H. (1989). *Freud en Buenos Aires.* Buenos Aires: Paidós.

Vezetti, H. (1996). *Aventuras de Freud en el país de los argentinos. De José Ingenieros a Enrique Pichon Rivière.* Buenos Aires: Paidós.

Viderman, S. (1970). *La construction de l'espace analytique.* Paris: Denoël, Gallimard, 1982.

Viñar, M., & Viñar, M. (1993). *Fracturas de memoria. Crónicas para una memoria por venir.* Montevideo: Trilce.

Viñar, M., Viñar Ulriksen, M., & Bleger, L. (1989). Troubles psychologiques et psychiatriques induits par la torture. *Encycl. Med. Chir.* [Paris, Psychiatrie, 37889 A20, 5–1989.]

Vinocur-Fischbein, S. (1996). Psicoanálisis y lingüística. Contactos e intercambios. *Revista de Psicoanálisis (Lo femenino), 8* (2).

Vinocur-Fischbein, S. (1998). Subjetividad y discurso hacia el final del milenio. Los vasallajes del yo en el fin del milenio. *Revista de Psicoanálisis, 55* (4).

Vinocur-Fischbein, S. (2000). El poder de las palabras: La interpretación.

(Paper presented at the 23rd Encuentro de Discusión & 18th Symposium of the Asociación Escuela Argentina de Psicoterapia para Graduados, Buenos Aires, 5–7 October.) In: *Poder y Ética, su implicancia clínica.* Buenos Aires: AEAPG, Ed.

Vinocur-Fischbein, S. (2003). Algunas reflexiones sobre el lugar del lenguaje y la expresión de los afectos. In: *El triángulo de la comunicación: Cuerpo, afecto, lenguaje.* Lima: Judith Cachay.

Vinocur-Fischbein, S. (2004). "Actividad onírica y proceso analítico. Una reflexión semiótica sobre la teoría de los sueños de W. Baranger." [Oneiric activity and the analytic process. A semiotic perspective on Willy Baranger's theory of dreams]. Unpublished manuscript.

Vygotsky, L. S. (1984). *A formação social da mente.* São Paulo: Martins Fontes.

Vygotsky, L. S. (1989). *Pensamento e linguagem.* São Paulo: Martins Fontes.

Waugh, W. F. (1912). Aplicación de las teorías de Freud. *La Semana Médica* (Buenos Aires, 5 December). [Also in: *Internationale Zeitschrift für Psychoanalyse, 1* (1913, No. 198).]

Wender, L., Torres, D., & Vidal, I. (1995). Argentina. In: P. Kutter (Ed.), *Psychoanalysis International: A Guide to Psychoanalysis throughout the World.* Stuttgart: Frommann-Holzboog.

Whiting, C. (1980). Notas para la historia del psicoanálisis en Chile. *Revista Chilena de Psicoanálisis, 2* (1): 19–26.

Widlöcher, D. (1996). *Les nouvelles cartes de la psychanalyse.* Paris: Ed. Odile Jacob.

Widlöcher, D., & Miller, J.-A. (2003). El porvenir del psicoanálisis. (B. Granger, coord.) *Revista de Psicoanálisis, 60* (4): 1051–1070.

Wilson, D. (2000). Metarepresentation in linguistic communication. In: D. Sperber (Ed.), *Metarepresentations.* Oxford: Oxford University Press.

Wilson, D. (2003). New directions for research on pragmatics and modularity. *UCL Working Papers in Linguistics, 15*: 105–127.

Winnicott, D. (1949). Hate in the countertransference. *International Journal of Psycho-Analysis, 30*: 69–75. In: *Collected Papers: Through Paediatrics to Psycho-Analysis.* London: Tavistock, 1958 [Reprinted as *Through Paediatrics to Psycho-Analysis.* London: Hogarth Press & The Institute of Psycho-Analysis, 1975; reprinted London: Karnac, 1992.]

Winnicott, D. (1954). Metapsychological and clinical aspects of regression within the psycho-analytical set-up. In: *Collected Papers: Through Paediatrics to Psycho-Analysis.* London: Tavistock, 1958 [Reprinted as *Through Paediatrics to Psycho-Analysis.* London: Hogarth Press & The Institute of Psycho-Analysis, 1975; reprinted London: Karnac, 1992.]

Winnicott, D. (1958). *Collected Papers: Through Paediatrics to Psycho-Analysis.* London: Tavistock. [Reprinted as *Through Paediatrics to Psycho-Analysis.* London: Hogarth Press & The Institute of Psycho-Analysis, 1975; reprinted London: Karnac, 1992.]

Winnicott, D. W. (1960a). Counter-transference. In: *The Maturational Pro-*

cesses and the Facilitating Environment: Studies in the Theory of Emotional Development. London: Hogarth Press & The Institute of Psycho-Analysis, 1975 [reprinted London: Karnac, 1992].

Winnicott, D. W. (1960b). The theory of the parent–infant relationship. In: *The Maturational Processes and the Facilitating Environment.* London: Karnac, 1990.

Winnicott, D. W. (1963). Fear of breakdown. In: C. Winnicott, R. Shepherd, & M. Davis (Eds.), *Psycho-Analytic Explorations.* New York: Karnac, 1989; Cambridge, MA: Harvard University Press, 1989.

Winnicott. D. W. (1971). *Playing and Reality.* London: Tavistock.

Winnicott, D. W. (1986). *Home Is Where We Start From,* ed. C. Winnicott, R. Shepherd, & M. Davis. London: Penguin.

Winograd, B. (1985). Criterios de curación según Liberman. Criterios de curación y objetivos terapéuticos en psicoanálisis. *Revista de la AEAPG, Buenos Aires, 11.*

Winograd, B. (1999). "Los aportes rioplatenses y la clínica psicoanalítica." Unpublished manuscript.

Wittgenstein, L. (1953). *Philosophical Investigations.* Oxford: Blackwell, 1978.

Yutaka Sagawa, R. (1994). A história da Sociedade Brasileira de Psicanálise de São Paulo. In: L. Nosek (Ed.), *Álbum de família. Imagens, fontes e idéias da psicanálise em São Paulo.* São Paulo: Casa da Psicólogo.

Zac de Goldstein, R. (1974). El pensamiento psicoanalítico pionero de Ángel Garma. *Revista de Psicoanálisis, 31* (4): 843–879.

Zizek, S. (1989). *The Sublime Object of Ideology.* London: Verso.

Zuckerfeld, R. (2000). Inconscientes y tercera tópica: Articulaciones teórico-clínicas. *Revista de la SAP, 3.*

Zysman, S. (2004). "Theories as Objects (An Enquiry into Minds and Theories)." Paper presented at the 43rd IPA Congress, New Orleans.

INDEX

For Product Safety Concerns and Information please contact our EU
representative GPSR@taylorandfrancis.com
Taylor & Francis Verlag GmbH, Kaufingerstraße 24, 80331 München, Germany

www.ingramcontent.com/pod-product-compliance
Ingram Content Group UK Ltd.
Pitfield, Milton Keynes, MK11 3LW, UK
UKHW021512250926
475702UK00043B/227
9780952390565